LEVINAS, THE FRANKFURT SCHOOL AND PSYCHOANALYSIS

LEVINAS, THE FRANKFURT SCHOOL AND PSYCHOANALYSIS

C. Fred Alford

WESLEYAN UNIVERSITY PRESS
Middletown, Connecticut

To Elly, again and again

Published by Wesleyan University Press, Middletown, CT, 06459
www.wesleyan.edu/wespress

First US edition 2002

ISBN 0-8195-6602-0 (hardback)
     0-8195-6603-9 (paperback)

Cataloging-in-publication Data for this book is available from the Library of Congress

Typeset by YHT Ltd, London
Printed and bound in Great Britain by Biddles Ltd, Guildford and King's Lynn

Contents

Preface

I wrote the first draft of this book without a lot of contact with either critics or followers of Levinas. When it finally saw the light, several early readers of the manuscript found its tone unremittingly critical. That surprised me, as I find so much to admire in Levinas. I've softened the tone, but a problem remains. One can admire someone with whom one disagrees. That's easy. But can one admire someone whom one thinks has it fundamentally wrong? The answer, in this case, is still yes.

What is it to be fascinated and deeply affected by someone whom one thinks has it quite wrong? Surely a part of me must think Levinas is right, or hope he is. I have tried to give that part of me its due. One effect of writing is that one learns what one thinks. Another effect, not always intended, is to erect a memorial for everything one rejects in the silences between the words, as though the silence that surrounds words takes as its form the opposite of what they say. With Levinas, at least, I have no objection to this unintended memorial, one appropriately characterized by its non-being.

Though this book draws heavily upon psychoanalysis, it is not a psychoanalytic interpretation of Levinas, or anything else. It is an argument about what it is to "be human among humans," as Ismene puts it to her sister, Antigone. Object relations theory in psychoanalysis is, I believe, a fine teaching of what it is to be human among humans, and that is why I turn to it, not because I want to perform the exercise of applying one teaching to another.

The Frankfurt School of Critical Theory is the third major player in this book, after Levinas and psychoanalysis, but it too is not treated as a school or position with which I would have Levinas contend. Rather, it represents another way of thinking about human relations, a way that shares Levinas' chief concern, that humans not impose themselves and their schemes on others. But, while the Frankfurt School shares Levinas' concerns, it does not share his conclusions. The same goes for D. W. Winnicott, and the novelist and philosopher Iris Murdoch, both of whom I try to bring to the table with Levinas, so that they might have a conversation. The political philosopher Hannah Arendt and the Greek tragic playwrights are important latecomers to this conversation, not appearing until the last chapters.

What a motley crew, the reader might respond, and he or she would be right. But disparate partners often generate the most interesting conversations. In the end this is the great lack in Levinas. For all his brilliant evocation of what we owe the other, there is little room for conversation. There is, in other words, something lonely about Levinas' world: his philosophical world, that is. From stories about him, as well as published encounters, one has the impression that he was thoroughly engaged. Certainly I felt that way while writing this book.

I have been fortunate in finding critics who, while often quite disagreeing with my conclusions, have taken the trouble to say why. As a result we have had a conversation. Among these critics are Jeffrey Bloechl, Aryeh Botwinick, Tony Molino, and Ed Wingenbach.

Sean Eudaily helped me with "in the groove," and Victor Wolfenstein shared the lyrics of "Colours" with me.

American Imago published an earlier version of my encounter between Levinas and Winnicott.

1

Someone Rings Your Doorbell

Abstract and evocative, writing in what can only be described as the language of prophecy, Emmanuel Levinas has become everything to everyone. We pretend we get it, writing in much the same style, so as to say whatever we wanted to say in the first place. The Levinas Effect it has been called, the ability of Levinas' texts to say anything the reader wants to hear, so that Levinas becomes a deconstructionist, theologian, proto-feminist, or even the reconciler of postmodern ethics and rabbinic Judaism (Davis, 1996, p. 140). Even a Levinas-inspired squatters' rights group exists. Those who disagree with Levinas often criticize him from within the framework of his project, sharing his assumptions while trying to make Levinas more Levinassian.[1]

Homogenizing Levinas does him no favor. His obituary in *The New York Times* (December 27, 1995) portrays him as a kind old man who developed an ethical theory that put others first. Levinas did no such thing. He defined the subject as persecuted hostage to the other in such a way that they can have no real relationship except what Levinas calls substitution: I suffer for your sins. Much of value is gained in this formulation, and much is lost. Better to count the gains and losses than to pretend that we the readers don't have to make any choices, or choose any values, when we praise Levinas.

Levinas divides the world in such a way that ethics no longer has anything to do with ordinary human attachments, what he calls transfers of sentiment. Sometimes Levinas sounds like Kant (1959) on "pathological love," by which Kant means a love that prefers some over others ("Substitution," p. 91). But Kant didn't write twenty-five pages on the phenomenology of the nude woman. Levinas did (T&I, pp. 254–80). A passion is present in Levinas that has nothing to do with Kant. A more apt comparison is between Levinas and Socrates of Plato's *Symposium*, a dialogue to which Levinas frequently refers (T&I, pp. 53, 254, 292). Aristophanes has it wrong, says Levinas. Humans don't really seek their other halves in order to be whole. If they seem to, it is because they are really seeking mastery over the other, even when they call it love. True love seeks infinity. "The true Desire is that which the

Desired does not satisfy, but hollows it" ("Philosophy & the Infinite," p. 114).[2]

A number of critics have commented on Levinas' interpretation of the *Symposium*, wondering, as I do, how close Levinas really comes to Plato.[3] What can another book, my own, add? Not just about Levinas and Plato, but about Levinas' project as a whole. Must not any book on a well-worn topic (and by now Levinas is that, at least in certain intellectual circles) justify itself?

Most books on Levinas are critical interpretations. Accepting the premises of his project, they try to show where Levinas goes too far, or where he becomes involved in self-contradiction. What proves so terribly difficult is approaching Levinas from outside his project. One reason is because Levinas weaves a world so comprehensive, fascinating, and hard to understand that one begins to feel that any other standpoint is incommensurable with it, as though one were a denizen of a distant planet. One sees how difficult it is to gain a little distance on Levinas (with distance comes perspective) when one observes how many who write about Levinas adopt his language, as though to understand Levinas means being able to write in the style of Levinas. Once one does this all is lost. The trick is to bring a perspective to bear on Levinas, persisting in it through all the twists and turns of his project. This does not mean that Levinas' language must be avoided at all costs (certainly I don't), only that sounding too much *like* Levinas makes thinking *about* Levinas more difficult.

My perspective is that of psychoanalysis, though putting it this way may make my view sound narrower than it is. By psychoanalysis I mean British object relations theory, particularly as it is exemplified in the work of D. W. Winnicott. In this tradition, psychoanalysis has more to do with relationships than it does with drives or instincts. Called object relations theory in deference to Freud, who wrote about the object of a drive, it might be more accurate to call object relations theory simply relationship theory, particularly as it is practiced by Winnicott.[4]

Every novelist who ever lived has written about relationships. What makes the approach of object relations theory psychoanalytic is the belief that our relationships to real others correspond with mental images of them, images that are created in interaction with our fears, hates and desires.

> The term 'object relations theory,' in its broadest sense, refers to ... the potentially confounding observation that people live simultaneously in an external and an internal world, and that the

relationship between the two ranges from the most fluid inter-
mingling to the most rigid separation. (Greenberg and Mitchell,
1983, pp. 11–12)

This is not an observation unique to psychoanalysts, though the man of
letters generally puts it more elegantly. Chateaubriand (1827), quoted by
Greenberg and Mitchell) puts it this way: "Every man carries within
himself a world made up of all that he has seen and loved; and it is to this
world that he returns, incessantly, though he may pass through, and seem
to inhabit, a world quite foreign to it."

One expects that a psychoanalytic approach would pay more attention
to the dynamic unconscious, the way in which our mind transforms new
relationships into old ones (transference), others into parts of ourselves
(introjection), and parts of ourselves into others (projection). But there is
no fundamental difference between a psychoanalytic approach and the
approach of any novelist, philosopher, or essayist sensitive to the com-
plexities of human relationships. For this reason I turn in Chapter 3 to the
novelist and philosopher Iris Murdoch, and the philosopher Theodor
Adorno. About aspects of Levinas' project they say as much, and more, as
any psychoanalytic account. Rather than interpreting their projects in
psychoanalytic terms and then applying them to Levinas, I allow Murdoch
and Adorno to speak for themselves in their own language. Or rather, I do
this as much as any interpreter can.

My psychoanalytic interpretation of Levinas is not, I hope, that of a
man with a template: here is my psychoanalytic concept, there is Levinas'
concept that I will reinterpret psychoanalytically, showing how he misunderstands his own project. For me, psychoanalysis is an account of
human relatedness and unrelatedness, the way in which we need others,
both the reality of others, and our fantasies of others. Sometimes these
fantasies get in the way of our relatedness; sometimes they enrich it,
allowing us access to the inner worlds of others and ourselves unavailable
in the wide-awake everyday attitude toward life. It is the peculiar way in
which Levinas writes about human relations that I analyze, drawing upon
psychoanalysis as a way of thinking about the complexity of human
relations.

If psychoanalysis is an account of the dynamic unconscious, is it fair to
apply it to Levinas, for whom the unconscious is not a central theme? Or is
it? Tina Chanter (1998, pp. 15–16) puts it this way. "Levinas' philosophy
is infused with the drama of psychoanalysis: the language of trauma,
obsession, insomnia, anxiety, boredom, compassion, pain, compensation,

tragedy, horror, death, weariness, refusal, evasion, fatigue, suffering, effort, condemnation, withdrawal." Still, Chanter continues, we should not conclude that Levinas is talking about the same thing as psychoanalysis. True enough, but while Levinas is not talking about the same thing as psychoanalysis, they share the same concern with experiences beyond (wouldn't it be more accurate to say beneath?) words, experiences that nonetheless press to be put into words.

Levinas praises and damns psychoanalysis in the same breath. Levinas praises psychoanalysis for helping destroy the I, the *cogito* upon which Descartes rested self-certainty. "The reflection of the cogito can no longer arise to ensure the certainty of what I am ... Psychoanalysis casts a fundamental suspicion on the most unimpeachable testimony of self-consciousness" ("I & Totality," p. 24). Looking deep into myself, I find symbols referring to symbols referring to symbols in an infinite regression of desire. Trouble is, the desire is always the same, to found myself in myself.

Levinas believes in the power of the unconscious. He just does not respect it. The unconscious "rehearses the game played out in consciousness, namely the search for meaning and truth as the search for the self" ("Substitution," p. 83). Not the unconscious, but the beyond consciousness, is at stake, what Levinas calls "the hither side of consciousness." If psychoanalysis could develop some new fables to further that voyage it might be more helpful. Biblical fables might be more availing in this regard than the Greek ones favored by psychoanalysis, suggests Levinas, as they are more likely to turn us toward the infinite ("I & Totality," p. 34; "Hegel & Jews," p. 238).

In an interview that took place in 1982, Levinas says he is not a Freudian because Freud assumed that *Agape* is but another version of eros, and that cannot be ("Philosophy, Justice & Love," p. 113). It turns out that this is the fundamental difference between them. If Freud is right, Levinas is wrong, and vice versa. Much of this manuscript looks to eros and its relatives as an alternative to the subjection of the self to the other that Levinas writes about. Strange as it may sound, one of eros' relatives is pity, the topic of the last chapter.

ETHICS AND NATURE

Consider how Levinas opens *Totality and Infinity*, asking whether Hobbes' war of all against all is a permanent state of being. Yes, is his answer. The state of war is a permanent state of being, which is why we must seek non-being. The radical egoism of humans shows that no natural or rational solution is possible. No one would naturally give up his place in the sun. Ethics depends upon escaping nature. "Ethics is, therefore, *against nature* because it forbids the murderousness of my natural will to put my own existence first" ("Dialogue with Levinas," p. 24, author's emphasis). All that is ethical about humans stems from our transcendence of nature.

> It is through the condition of being a hostage [to the other] that there can be pity, compassion, pardon, and proximity in the world—even the little there is, even the simple "after you sir." All the transfers of sentiment (*transferts du sentiment*) which theorists of original war and egoism use to explain the birth of generosity (it isn't clear, however, that there was war at the beginning: before wars there were altars) could not take root in the ego were it not, in its entire being, or rather its entire nonbeing, subjected not to a category, as in the case of matter, but to an unlimited accusative, that is to say, persecution, self, hostage, already substituted for others. ("Substitution," p. 91)

Elsewhere Levinas refers to the biology of human fraternity, marked by a "Cain-like coldness," which sees the world in terms of freedom or contract (*Of God*, p. 71). Transfers of sentiment and the biology of human fraternity are not the same concept, but they mark the ends of the same continuum, the continuum of human relatedness according to Levinas. Either humans care for each other for the same reason they cry at a sentimental movie, to have a cheap thrill, or they cooperate on the basis of self-interest, in order to further their freedom or increase their income.

Consider carefully what Levinas is saying. When we treat others decently it is not because we recognize them as fellow humans, but because we see in them the face of infinity that we are called upon to serve, though that puts it too weakly. Not service but self-mortification comes closer to the mark. Levinas' is a rare and radical teaching. I think Levinas is mistaken, but I will not be able to prove it. What matters is recognizing how far Levinas has removed himself from even the seemingly most trivial claims of humanism, such as that humans are occasionally generous because they recognize in others a fellow humanity. Levinas removes himself for a noble purpose: to protect the other from the self. I argue that there are other, more humanly related ways to serve Levinas' noble purpose.

It will not do here to get into a debate about the meaning of humanism. Suffice to say that while Levinas is a critic of humanism, it is on the grounds that humanism has not been humanistic enough. Instead of abandoning humanism we should create a new humanism, a humanism of the other human, a humanism that puts the other person first ("Transcendence & Height," p. 14; *Humanisme*, pp. 11–16). It is this that I question. Humanism is not about whether I put myself or the other first. Humanism is about relationships among humans.[5] Because humanism is not very popular these days (postmoderns write about the arrogance of humanism, and they are not all wrong), it has been easy for readers of Levinas not to struggle with this aspect of his teaching, in which every human relationship is subjected to the standards of infinity.

I pursue this argument by creating encounters between Levinas and authors who have thought about ways of relating to others that share Levinas' concerns, but not his conclusions. Not all are psychoanalysts. All, however, think like a good psychoanalyst, by which I mean no more than that they understand how subtle and complex human relations really are, how much other people are a part of ourselves. Our lives are woven together, and it is important to know this, lest we treat others as parts of ourselves, what Levinas calls totalization. Disentangling the threads that bind us is a subtle and difficult task, so much so that the dichotomous categories favored by Levinas, such as other and same, are not likely to be very helpful. "You are like me in some ways, different in others, but precisely when I thought you were most like me you revealed yourself to be most different. And that which I thought we never shared, now I see we do. But I wonder how I shall see it tomorrow." Any adequate account of human relations must be at least this complex.

Against totality, the tendency to reduce the other to the same, a version of me, the authors I draw upon, above all D. W. Winnicott, Iris Murdoch, and Theodor Adorno, all posit particularity, a loving knowledge of the reality of the other person. To be sure, there are differences. "What breaks the drive of consciousness to totality is . . . an encounter with a concrete other person," says Murdoch (Antonaccio, 2000, pp. 181, 223). Winnicott, on the other hand, stresses not the concrete reality of the other, but relationships that involve paradox and play, closeness and distance at the same time. Adorno probably falls somewhere in between. But Winnicott, Murdoch, and Adorno share a basic assumption: particularity overcomes totality. Not Levinas, for whom not particularity but infinity is the answer to the hegemony of universals. Why Levinas chooses infinity, and the costs, above all the cost in human relatedness, are the topic of my essay.

Creating encounters between Levinas and authors whose works he did not know ignores a real encounter, the encounter that made Levinas famous, introducing him to the world of postmodernism: the meeting between Levinas and Jacques Derrida, an encounter that culminated in Derrida's eulogizing Levinas. Sounding surprisingly humanistic, Derrida (1978) argues that the other Levinas keeps talking about is not really an absolute other, but simply other than me. How could it be otherwise, how could I know the other except in contrast to me? I have no universal perspective. Levinas takes Derrida's criticism to heart, and in *Otherwise than Being* and elsewhere writes less about the other, and more about the position and meaning of the subject in relationship to the other, thus mitigating Derrida's objection that to write about the other is to define the other.

Those who write about Levinas can be categorized in terms of those who do and don't believe a gulf divides *Totality and Infinity*, an earlier work, from *Otherwise than Being*. I believe that a gulf divides them, and that the later work is not better but worse for meeting Derrida's objection.[6] *Otherwise than Being* abandons Levinas' tortured but fascinating struggle with human erotic relatedness, in which I caress the other and touch infinity at the same time. His account doesn't always make perfect sense, it requires that the feminine be essentialized as the other, but in *Totality and Infinity* Levinas struggles with (or rather at) the limits of human relatedness. *Otherwise than Being* introduces categories such as "saying" that sound related, but they're not. Saying has nothing to do with conversation, and everything to do with my silent exposure to the other. Levinas avoids "totalizing" the other by avoiding contact with the other. It is not necessarily progress.

LETTER FROM A FRIEND

Before continuing with my argument, which has already invoked a number of impressive names with whom I will have Levinas contend, it may be helpful to quote a letter from a friend, one who has studied Levinas, but who would not be insulted if I said he is not an expert on Levinas. My friend is a well-educated, thoughtful man who has found some inspiration in Levinas. Like Levinas, he is Jewish, and while I don't think that is terribly important in this context, the reader will have to judge that for him or her self. This is what he said. These are a mix of his words and mine, but they are all his thoughts.

Dear Fred, you say Levinas misunderstands the connection between human relatedness and infinity. As orthodox Jew and Talmudic scholar, he knew only too well that to serve and love G-d is to serve and love others in the real world. Care for the widow, orphan, and the stranger are Hebraic values that personify compassion and social justice. In other words, wouldn't Levinas argue with you that human relatedness is the condition of the experience of the infinite? I don't think you understand the paradox. By depersonalizing the other, so to speak, that is by making our responsibility to the other an impersonal obligation and divine command, we deepen, broaden, and strengthen the capacity to give purer love, love for non-narcissistic reasons. If you see it this way, you will see the connection between Levinas, the Jewish tradition, and the teachings of Buddha and Jesus as well. Levinas' teaching is not so different from the Great Tradition that seems to encompass most believers. I can't deny that Levinas is sometimes abstract, but his purpose is to write about the religious impulse in a non-mythic way, religion absent the supreme Being, that old father figure. But his teaching is religious in the sense that the path to G-d is through service to men and women. That in any case is how I, and some of my more religious friends, see Levinas.

Any serious encounter with Levinas must, I think, address my friend's concerns. Levinas is playing in two contests at once: religious and philosophical. To think that one has rebutted Levinas by citing the self-contradictory way Levinas writes about the other is to have missed half the point. Levinas inspires because he brings the spiritual impulse to philosophy, bestowing upon modern (even post-modern) men and women a non-mythological version of the religious spirit, one that does not depend upon a supreme being.

Let me tell you how I answered my friend. Only it is no answer, but a promise that, if I am successful, requires an essay to redeem.

Dear Friend, I don't know if a religion of the supreme non-being makes sense. If it does, and it may, then it must be a religion of the fellow human, not the other human, as Levinas would have it. To talk of a religion of the supreme non-being is to talk of awe before the mysteries of the universe and death, of wonder at a world in which I wasn't, am for a little while, and then will never be again. And all that I cherish is equally transitory. That's the real, human, meaning of infinity.

Awe before this reality is good. It should inspire humans to be modest and humble, creating by contrast a human community that provides warmth and comfort in the face of an infinity that apparently cares nothing for humans. This is the one thing humans can do for each other in that short space between infinities. It might sometimes seem as though this is what Levinas is writing about. I don't think it is. Levinas doesn't just "depersonalize" the other, as you put it. He "infinitizes" the other, rendering the other not just more but less than human. To write of the other as though he were my death, as Levinas does, is no longer a human teaching, even if Levinas welcomes this death.

Would [your wife and children] like it if you became their hostage (how Levinas characterizes his ideal), abandoning yourself utterly for and to them? I don't think so. They want to share you, including your self-assertion on your behalf, as well as theirs. They want, in other words, to create and share a human world with you. I think this human world takes on added value in the face of the infinite. Not because it shares in the infinite, but by contrast.

Levinas is too much in love with the infinite, too eager for escape from the horror of being. I haven't stressed this in my response to you because you did not to me. Instead, you stressed his continuity with "traditional" religious values. I think everything changes once one abandons this "traditional" religion for infinity. Infinity isn't God. Trying to get infinity to do the work of God means, I think, turning others into gods, instead of fellow humans.

Not until the last chapter, where I turn to Greek tragedy as an account of how humans might live in the face of infinity, will I explicitly return to my friend's challenge and my response. But my essay is not long, and I ask my readers to keep these issues in mind. They are the frame within which the more technical issues only make sense. From time to time, my essay may read as though it were a response to my friend (at least I hope it does). That is intentional, an attempt not to get too caught up in the esoteric language of Levinas', or anyone else's, philosophy.

Levinas is not, in the end, best seen as a problem in philosophy, but as a problem in life. Franz Rosenzweig (1985), to whom Levinas so frequently refers he does not bother to cite him, says much the same thing (T&I, p. 28). The questions with which both are concerned are finally not metaphysical, but empirical: how we live and experience life in this world. From time to time I will compare Franz Rosenzweig with Levinas. More traditional (in precisely the sense the term is used above) than Levinas, Rosenzweig does not imagine that infinity might be another name for God. If he were to use infinity as synonym for God, Infinity for Rosenzweig could only be a proper noun, designating a supreme being, not a supreme non-being.

CAN A CHRISTIAN REALLY UNDERSTAND LEVINAS' PHILOSOPHY?

Levinas is not just a philosopher. He is also a Talmudic scholar. Only in Chapter 3 do I take up this aspect of his work, and then only briefly. Levinas insists that his philosophy does not depend on his religious vision, and that is probably correct. But it remains possible that his philosophy can only be completely understood by someone who shares his religious tradition. Many Christians have taken up Levinas' work as inspiration without explicitly worrying about the distance and difference between them. As Levinas has taught us, this should lead us to suspect that a difference is being suppressed.

I have looked long and hard for that difference. Not just any difference, but a difference in experiencing and understanding religion, a difference in religious sensibility between Christian and Jew, as Hilary Putnam (1999, p. 4) puts it. Two differences suggest themselves. First, a conception of God as infinitely other, the supreme non-being, is easier for a Jew to make sense of than a Christian, because Christians tend to personify God more. Jesus Christ is the supreme example. The trouble with this theory is that there is lots of personification in the Pentateuch:

- Even to talk about God as being merciful or just is a personification, for these are human terms drawn from human experience.
- God strolls in the cool of the evening in the Garden of Eden, talking with Adam (Genesis 3:8–10).
- Moses, Aaron, and others sit down to eat dinner with God, though there isn't much conversation (Exodus 24:9–11).
- Moses sees God's back while hiding in the cleft of a rock (Exodus 33: 18–23).
- God tells Moses that he will descend in the form of a cloud, so that the people can hear Him (Exodus 19:9).

Personification is not the same as incarnation, but they are not entirely different either. In dozens of places in the Pentateuch, God comes close, not always taking human form, but a form in which humans can experience Him directly. Not that it isn't dangerous. To see God face to face for the most part still means death, but it would be mistaken to conclude that the Hebrew God is distant and remote in a way the Christian God is not. On the contrary, Jews bring God close and push Him away much as Christians do, always trying–but never succeeding–in finding the right distance. That is the theme of the Pentateuch.

Consider the experience of Franz Rosenzweig. As a young man he thought he must convert to Christianity in order to feel close to God. "He thought that a true experience of faith calls for the mediator, Jesus." Planning to convert, Rosenzweig attended Day of Atonement services in 1931 for what he thought was the last time, only to have what he called a direct experience of God. "In this moment man is as close to God ... as it is ever accorded to him to be." Shortly after Rosenzweig abandoned plans to convert to Christianity, saying that one does not have to convert to reach the Father (another personification) because He was already with and in him (Glatzer, 1999, p. xii). Rosenzweig had a common religious experience of communion with God, one shared by millions of Christians and Jews, among others. Of course, individual Christians and Jews will differ enormously in their experience of God's closeness (Porpora, 2001). My argument is only that the differences among Jews and Christians are likely as great as between them.

If the Jewish religious sensibility does not differ fundamentally from that of Christians regarding the closeness of God, perhaps the difference is more subtle. Perhaps Christians experience the love of God in more personal terms, terms more redolent of sensuality. Certainly the Eucharist is a sensual experience, the Word made flesh. If this were so, then it might be more difficult for a Christian to grasp Levinas' insistence on separating eros and ethics, a separation I shall frequently question.

This distinction does not seem to work any better than the first. Yahweh loves his people in the most dramatic and personal way, choosing them for no particular virtue of theirs, only that he loves them. "You shall be my treasured possession of all peoples" (Exodus 19:4–6). One can easily imagine a loving mother saying that to her child. In Hosea (3:1), God loves his people as passionately as a man ever loved a woman. "The Lord said to me, go again and love a woman loved by another man, an adulteress, and love her as I, the Lord, love the Israelites, although they resort to other gods." One wants to say that the love of Yahweh is less sensuous than the love of Jesus Christ, but not even that seems to be true.

Luce Irigaray (1991, pp. 116–17) distinguishes between "the God who makes his presence known in the law from the one who gives himself through his presence, as nourishment, including nourishment of the senses," by which she means erotic enjoyment. Contrast the Song of Solomon with the Pentateuch, she suggests. Hers is an important distinction, just not one that has much to do with the difference between Christian or Jew, as anyone familiar with the letters of St Paul must know.

"There is not a single thing in a great spirituality that would be absent from another great spirituality." That great theorist of difference and otherness, Emmanuel Levinas, said that (Of God, 93). To be sure, there are both differences and similarities between Judaism and Christianity, enough differences so that the "Judeo-Christian tradition" often functions as *glissade*. Nevertheless, these differences do not seem to touch on what makes Levinas' philosophy so intriguing and problematic, his fascination with infinity. Along the way, I wonder if there are other ways to "love your neighbor," ways that avoid totalizing your neighbor while still maintaining a human and humane affinity between you and your neighbor. Indeed, this is the theme of my essay.

IF LEVINAS IS WRONG, IS POSTMODERN ETHICS WRONG?

If Levinas is wrong in the way I say he is, what difference does it make for all who have turned to him, above all postmoderns and deconstructionists? What difference does it make for postmodern ethics? Though I do not answer this question directly in my essay, an answer is implicit. I state this answer here in something close to propositional form. The reader can draw his or her own conclusions about what to do about it.

What many postmoderns have done is what Levinas invites us to do, but which is not quite intellectually straightforward: treat difference and the other as though they possess an ethical nimbus, without delving into what engenders this nimbus, a belief in God. Structurally, the situation is identical with that of relativism and tolerance. Relativism implies tolerance, but it also implies intolerance. Relativism implies anything at all. If all beliefs are equal, then I may as well suppress some, all, or none. Similarly, if the other is totally different from me, why should I not conclude that this makes his or her welfare irrelevant to me, a happening on a distant planet? The answer, of course, is that the face of the other carries the trace of God. It is for this reason that Levinas introduces

Illeity (*illéité*), a neologism formed on the Latin or French for he. Illeity is God.

Levinas' tendency to separate his theological and philosophical writings contributes to the tendency of some postmoderns to write as if one could carry over into the philosophy the nimbus of the theological while writing as if one had nothing to do with the other, as though one could get the nimbus without its source.

Though one hesitates to name names, the best example of this tendency (best because most egregious, and because it is the most thoughtful, systematic and intelligent) is Simon Critchley's *The Ethics of Deconstruction: Derrida and Levinas* (1999). Levinas' ethics, says Critchley, puts the self into question, so that the self can have access to otherness (ibid., pp. 4–5). This statement about Levinas, which is true, is used to argue that the work of Derrida rests upon an "unconditional categorical imperative of affirmation," one that produces a reading that commands respect for the other (ibid., p. 41). Ignore, if you will, the move from people to texts, a move which itself deserves scrutiny, but not here. Critchley is drawing upon the ethical nimbus of the other in Levinas, a nimbus engendered by the other's status as stand-in for the infinity that is God, to turn respect for difference into a categorical imperative. As though Levinas could transform Derrida into a postmodern Kant![7]

There is a related misreading of Levinas that would achieve much the same end by a less circuitous route. It is by far the more popular misreading. It is, roughly, the misreading that I finally adopt in the last chapter. The difference is that I do not attribute it to Levinas.

The misreading runs something like this. When we open ourselves to the experience of the radiant human face, we open ourselves to an experience that combines sympathy for humanity with an awe that reminds us of the awe humans feel in the presence of the holy. Faced with an experience that combines human relatedness with sacred awe, we find we cannot kill or harm the other. Examples of those who pursue this misreading are Susan Handelman (1991, pp. 208–17) and Steen Halling (1975).

In fact, there is enough evidence for this reading in Levinas that it would be more accurate to call it a partial and incomplete reading rather than a misreading. Nevertheless, for reasons that will be explained in the course of this essay, Levinas cannot in the end bear this reading, as it implies too much mutuality on the one hand, too much a vision of man made in God's image on the other. Levinas would explode the myth of mutuality, and with it the myth of a supreme being, one capable of being characterized by any image at all, let alone a human one. It is to this explosion that I now turn, an explosion that can be characterized in an experience of answering the ringing at the door.

SOMEONE RINGS YOUR DOORBELL

Imagine that someone rings your doorbell and disturbs your work. As you walk to the door you are distracted, still thinking about your latest project. It takes you a moment to recognize your neighbor at the door, the one who lives upstairs. As soon as you recognize his face you invite him in. You talk for a while. He tells you his problem; you tell him what you might do to help him. You share some pleasant conversation, and soon enough your neighbor leaves. What you originally experienced as an interruption you now experience as a pleasant interlude, in which some understanding has passed between you and your neighbor. Or so it seems to you.[8]

Instead of immediately returning to your work, or allowing the memory of a pleasant interlude to linger, Levinas asks that you try to recapture the shock of the other's intrusion, the moment when you were first confronted with the other person's face, but before you recognized him. What did you experience in this fraction of a second? You experienced, says Levinas, an encounter with the other in all his or her immediacy, but with none of his or her particularity. The face (*visage*, but occasionally *face*), says Levinas, is naked and vulnerable, common to all humans and absolutely unique at the same time. Confronted with the face of the other, I may be tempted to kill the other in order to overcome his or her terrible otherness. But, even that is impossible. I can murder the other person, perhaps, but not his or her otherness. "This temptation to murder and this impossibility of murder constitute the very vision of the face," says Levinas ("Ethics & Spirit," p. 8).

You can, it is apparent, fight against your experience of the other. Murder would be the ultimate option. You cannot, however, protect your ego from the shocking, shattering experience of the other. Far better to open yourself to the irruption of the other: not just into your life, but into the order of your world. Just for a moment did you not feel that a door had been opened into another world, not just into the hallway of your apartment building, but into infinity?

One could hardly characterize such an experience as pleasant, but perhaps it was a relief. The world of your apartment, your desk, and your work is fulfilling, but limited. You soak up the morning sunlight that pours in through the big windows, and at night the sparkling lights of the city make it seem as if you live in an enchanted world, ready to meet your needs. The women who come and go through your life have this same quality.

If one were going to characterize your life prior to the encounter at the door, it would come closest to a story told by Jean Jacques Rousseau. Not Rousseau's "noble savage," but his story about the earliest stages of civilization that follow, when men and women live together in families and towns, "maintaining a golden mean between the indolence of the primitive state and the petulant activity of our vanity" (Rousseau, 1964, pp. 150–1). An epigraph that introduces Levinas' *Otherwise than Being* is from Pascal: " 'That is my place in the sun.' That is how the usurpation of the whole world began." It sounds like Rousseau talking about the advent of private property, only for Levinas it is not property, but the individual's belief that he owns himself that spoils things.

Strikingly similar to Levinas is Rousseau's emphasis on the narcissism of this earliest stage of civilization, in which men and women use each other without acknowledging their dependence, their need for others.[9] It is not just property, but mutual dependence, that spoils this idyllic state. Or as Levinas puts it, "in enjoyment I am absolutely for myself. Egoist without reference to the Other, I am . . . outside of all communication and all refusal to communicate" (T&I, p. 134). Levinas puts it this way because he wants awareness of separateness without awareness of difference, for that would imply a totality that encompasses you and the other through which you can know both. For Levinas, you encounter others in your world, having intercourse with them, but they remain part of the wallpaper of your life, present but unnoticed.

Though you live a satisfying existence in your apartment, something is missing from your life, and your encounter with the face at the door reminds you of what it is: the rest of the world, one that extends to infinity. When you heard the doorbell ring it could have been anyone, a world of infinite possibilities at your door. Or at least so you might have imagined for a moment. For a moment the order of your world was exposed to the disorder of infinite possibility.[10] Your neighbor could have been anyone, needing anything, asking everything.

Levinas' work is a reflection upon this moment of infinite possibility, though it is I, and not Levinas, who locates this moment in time, and it is I who makes it a reflection. Levinas would call it an imperative, the experience a command to serve the other. For Levinas it is an experience that comes from somewhere beyond "scientific" time, which is why one cannot say that it occurs prior to becoming an adult, a responsible human being, or whatever (E&I, p. 27). It is prior to everything. One experience follows the other only because that is how I have to tell it, step by step, as story time is linear. In reality you were always already in thrall to the other; you just didn't know it yet. It is the encounter with the other at the door that reminds you of what you already knew, although that puts it too much like Plato's anamnesis. Levinas understands the encounter in terms closer to the medieval *nunc stans*, an encounter beyond time. The result is not so much to lift you out of nature as to expose you to the heavens above. Levinas calls it an experience of exteriority.

How might you respond to this experience of the infinite? You feel shocked, maybe a little scared, but mostly you feel gratitude for being released from your little world of pleasures and worries. It is a defeat of your self-satisfied little world that is ultimately a victory, as you now belong to another. You feel small and insignificant, but not devalued, because your life now has a purpose, to serve the other. It is almost as if you were called to devote your life to a god.

Prior to your exposure to the other you existed in your own little world, like the apartment in which you were working before the doorbell rang. Others existed, they met your needs, but they were part of the background. One might say the same thing about your self. It is only with your exposure to the other that you come to be. Not, however, by means of what Hegel called the dialectic of mutual recognition, in which you define yourself through struggle with another. Dialectic requires dialogue, contact, even conflict, and across the infinite space that separates you from the other there can be little human contact. Levinas calls it a "relation without relation." An encounter takes place, but it is "without relation," as the other remains absolutely other (T&I, p. 80).

The face of my neighbor at my door renders me guilty as one who has done less than he could. (Here I must change grammatical subjects, for I may only talk about my guilt, not yours, according to Levinas.) I can never do enough, because doing enough would require that I know the other's needs as I know my own, and it is precisely this reduction of the other to the same that Levinas would avoid. The best I can do is devote myself to serving the one whose true need must forever elude me. I can never get it right, which is why I must devote myself to trying. Once I am exposed to the other, I can never return to my desk and forget about the other, no matter how much I might want to. The other has intruded itself between me and myself. Responsibility is persecuted subjectivity, the only way in which subjectivity may be known, as the prosecution of the narcissism of the I. "The word I means to be answerable for everything and for everyone," says Levinas ("Substitution," p. 90).

Levinas calls this experience of the other counter-violence, occasionally using the term non-allergic violence (OB, p. 15).[11] John Llewelyn puts it this way.

Peace is the traumatic violence of my being hostage to the Other, called to . . . expiate for him or her. It is because Levinas can find no hint of this peaceful violence in Heidegger's thinking of being and letting be that he judges it to be a letting be of totalitarian violence and war. (1995, p. 177)

In good violence, "the other persecutes me right up to my death" (ibid., p. 199). The alternative to this good violence, says another commentator, is to have contempt for the different and infinite, and so participate in the usurpation of the world (Peperzak, 1997, p. 11).

Are these really the only choices, to be persecuted by the other unto death, or to usurp the world? Has not Levinas cleaved the ethical world in two, leaving no place for human relationships of sympathy and empathy? For make no mistake, sympathy and empathy, what Levinas derides as "transfers of sentiment" (*transferts du sentiment*), play no role in his account of human ethics. Ethics is not a human connection, but a human separation, a relation without relation, as Levinas calls it. Good violence is what separates us, turning us from partners in a strained human relationship, the dialectic of master and slave as Hegel put it, into lord and bondsman, who participate in no dialectic (that is, dialogue) at all. About this Levinas is insistent. This is what a relation without relation means.

The question we have to answer is whether this experience of the subject is really good violence? Mine is not a logical question, as in "isn't good violence an oxymoron, a logical contradiction?" Rather, mine is a practical question: is good violence necessary so that humans not be contemptuous of each other, so that they do not usurp the world? It is hard to imagine that it is. This is, in any case, the topic of my essay.

What about the effect of good violence on the other? That question has already been answered by Derrida (1978) in "Violence and Metaphysics," so I do not have to repeat his argument here, but only the conclusion. Levinas' refusal to see the other as an alter ego risks becoming itself a type of violence to the other. Because he insists on seeing the other person as strictly other, not an other person, just other, Levinas risks not seeing the other as a fellow human. "To refuse to see in it [the Other] an ego in this sense is, within the ethical order, the very gesture of all violence" (Derrida, 1978, p. 125). Francis Jacques goes further, suggesting that to render the other person absolutely other has the ironic effect of leaving me as the only human in the world (Jacques, 1991, pp. 129–52; Bernasconi, 2000, pp. 80–1). Paul Ricoeur (1992, pp. 335–6) makes a similar argument in *Oneself as Another*.

Not just a sappy humanism, but any ethical approach to human beings, requires that we recognize them as fellow humans, similar and different at the same time. That, after all, is who the stranger is. As Derrida (1978, p. 127) puts it: "the other, then would not be what he is (my fellow man as foreigner) if he were not alter ego."

One can put this same point in a slightly different way. Levinas insists that the ethical relation with the other is not just a modification of intentionality, but a reversal of intentionality, akin to the experience of God that Descartes writes about in his third Metaphysical Meditation (1641), God thinking himself in me and so breaking me open. What we must ask is whether turning the other person into a God in order to grant him or her the power to break me open, denies the humanity of the other person, who after all is not God. Is this denial not itself a type of violence, and not necessarily the good kind?

Levinas would, of course, disagree. Good violence does not turn the other into a god (except perhaps in the particular sense discussed below). On the contrary, good violence is the condition of the only humanism that deserves the name, the humanism that knows that it is the other human who comes first, defining me as the other's hostage. I am able to be (that is, to experience my own subjectivity) only as a hostage to the other. The subject comes into existence only through its exposure to the other, which is what Levinas means when he defines subjectivity as the other in the same. I am responsible to the other because my existence as individuated, self-conscious subject depends entirely on my relationship to the other. Before that I was not much different from a contented cow, but one that drank up the milk of the world.

Levinas is not making a psychological claim about human development. He is making what can only be called a transcendental phenomenological claim: this is what our primordial encounter with the world must be like if we are to have the experiences we do, experiences that run the gamut from narcissism to awe of the sheer otherness of the other. Put this way, there actually is not so much difference between the phenomenological and the psychological. In "On Selfhood and the Development of Ego Structures in Infancy," Henry Elkin (1972) turns to the empirical work of Rene Spitz, arguing that there is a primordial stage of development, emerging at about six months of age, in which the individual is in communion with the other, while not yet fully recognizing the otherness of the other. It is this experience, argues Elkin, that is the foundation of religion. Elkin is, of course, not the only psychoanalyst to make this argument. Freud (1961, p. 11) made a similar suggestion about an experience "of something limitless, unbounded—as it were, 'oceanic.'"

More recent psychological research into human development does not unambiguously support Elkin's claim. In *The Interpersonal World of the Infant: A View from Psychoanalysis and Developmental Psychology*, Daniel Stern (1985) reviews a number of studies of cognitive and emotional development, concluding that at no time is the infant so cognitively and emotionally undeveloped that it experiences itself as fused with mother and world. Rather, this notion is an elaborate secondary construction.

Stern has been criticized for segueing too readily from empirical discoveries about cognitive development to their emotional significance. Nevertheless, we should not simply assume that the infant and young child is fused with its mother-world. Nor should we assume that this fusion is what Levinas is talking about. On the contrary, Levinas' position actually falls somewhere between Elkin and Stern, though it would be more accurate to say that it falls outside the continuum between them. For Levinas, the other is in me while remaining an alien presence, an uncomfortable but welcome intrusion, as it releases me from my little world. Here is a category of experience not so readily woven into the more familiar accounts of developmental psychology. How well this experience fits with what Winnicott calls transitional experience, an experience of another that is neither me nor not me, is the topic of the next chapter. The fit is far from perfect, the other more akin to an alien intruder than a transitional object.

What is Levinas trying to say with this story about answering the doorbell? It will take an essay to explain, but it may help to anticipate where I think Levinas is going. If God is absolutely other, and the other person is absolutely other, then they are functionally equivalent, so to speak. To encounter the other is the same as encountering God, for if both are absolutely other, how different can they be? Absolutely other is absolutely other. Trouble is, to make this equation work Levinas must strip the experience of the other person (but not the other person) of its human resonance. This is precisely what he does. It is the human cost of doing so that I object to, but at least now we can see why he would pay the price, and what he gets in return: the trace of God in this world. Some might think the price is worth it, and it would be hard to say they are wrong.

There is, however, another way to think about this story, and another way to think about the absolutely other. Imagine that Death rang your doorbell. For Levinas, there's not much difference between death and the other person at your door, "as though the approach of death remained one of the modalities of the relationship with the Other" (T&I, p. 75). If it is the absolute otherness of the other that counts, then death will serve as well as another person. Commenting on Levinas' claim that "the other is in no way another myself, participating with me in a common existence," Richard Cohen says:

> Although Levinas is explicitly discussing the encounter with the alterity of death, this sentence and the ones following it conjure up the encounter with the alterity of the other person. What is common to death and social life is an encounter with radical alterity ... the encounter with the alterity of death is like nothing so much as the encounter with the alterity of the other person. (T&O, p. 75, fn. 52)

Sartre (1956, pp. 221–3) said the same thing, that the other is the death of me. But Sartre did not welcome this death as Levinas does. While Sartre said the same thing, he did not mean the same thing. For Sartre, the other is the death of me because his or her reality restricts my infinite possibilities. For Levinas, the other is the death of me because the other is so radically different from me as to be tantamount to the radical difference that is death. Think twice about a theory that sees the other person as so different and distant as to be synonymous with my death.

Think twice, but do not reject the theory out of hand. Instead, ask if there is not some way to realize Levinas' ambition, a relationship that stands in respectful awe of the sheer otherness of the other, while at the same time recognizing a human connection with this other person. Are these as contradictory as all that? Must awe belong to the ethical, human sympathy to the ontology of everyday life, a distinction that makes more sense in theory than in practice? Not until the end of the second chapter will I have constructed the argument to reject this distinction, but the reader will know by now that this is the direction the argument is heading.

A RELATION WITHOUT RELATION

Students of Levinas are quick to note the "relation without relation" that marks the encounter with the other at the door. "Even to describe the relationship with the Other as a relationship implies a totalizing perspective," says Davis (1996, p. 45). An encounter takes place, but it is "without relation," as the other remains absolutely other. I serve the other, but I am not attached to the other, in the sense of needing or desiring the other. Though Levinas uses the term "proximity" to characterize the relationship to the other, proximity is as much about distance as closeness.

Equally important, but less remarked upon, is the encounter with the other in the pre-doorbell state, before his or her otherness is recognized. Levinas describes the pre-doorbell state in terms of "living from" (*vivre de*). "We live from 'good soup,' air, light, spectacles, work, ideas sleep ... These are not objects of representation. We live from them" (T&I, p. 110). We need others in the sense of needing to consume them as we consume soup, but we don't need them for themselves. In some ways it sounds like Eden, "a utopia in which the 'I' recollects itself in dwelling at home with itself" (T&I, p. 156).[12] What it is not is a place of human relationships. Nor is the pre-doorbell state a place of inhuman relationships. The term "relation without relation" that Levinas uses to characterize the encounter with the other applies here too. I use others, but I don't know them as other. After my encounter with the other, I know the other only as other. Never were we intimate. For Levinas, we move directly from babies to saints.

Attachment as need for others, the desire for particular others, the desire for one's other half in order to feel whole, the desire that Aristophanes talks about in Plato's *Symposium*, is absent in the encounter with the other, which is not surprising. It is absent in the Edenic but empty state before the encounter with the other as well. Two reasons are generally given for this absence. The first has already been suggested. Relatedness and need define self and other in terms of their need for each other, and thus risk falling into totalization. The second reason is that a self who needed the other too much could never serve the other.

One way to think about the absence of attachment in Levinas is in terms of Enlightenment psychology, the psychology of egoism, the psychology of Freud, who wrote about object of an instinct, in which one seeks others to satisfy a drive, not for purposes of relationship. Though Levinas opposes this way of thinking, his own thought is defined by this opposition. As it often is with great thinkers (and probably lesser thinkers as well), they are imprisoned by what they oppose, the prison of standing another thinker on his feet. If the human problem were not egoism, if the problem were not "that is my place in the sun," then the solution would look different too. What if the human problem were really our terrible dependence on others? Not "I want my place in the sun," but "I need you in order to be me." If this were the human problem, we might even treat others worse.

In defining human nature as the enemy of ethics, Levinas writes in the grand tradition of Enlightenment philosophers such as Kant. Only instead of reason that can give itself universal laws, Levinas rests ethics on an encounter with the infinitely other. Still, humans must be prepared by their own nature for such an encounter. Whereas Kant found this natural basis in what he called good will, Levinas finds the natural basis in a surprising place: man and woman's natural narcissism, which guarantees that humans will not need each other. When we finally do encounter the other, it shall not be on the basis of a terrible, clinging, appropriating desire. Because humans do not really need others, we shall be free to serve them. The real enemy of the other is not egoism, but clinging, dependent need that cannot let the other be. The real enemy of the other is one's need for the other.

Another way to think about the absence of attachment is in terms of the tendency to read Levinas as a postmodern. We are accustomed by now to thinking that the postmodern problem is to preserve diversity and difference, and that almost any relationship must spoil it. As Iris Marion Young (1990, p. 303) says, "this metaphysics consists in a desire to think things together in a unity, to formulate a representation of a whole, a totality." By "this metaphysics" she refers not to philosophy, but to community, as though the desire of people to feel close to one another was automatically and inevitably an attempt to "totalize" them. Often it is; sometimes it is not. When we write about attachment in the language of metaphysics, we forget what it is to think about the richness of actual human attachments. As Levinas divides the participants in relationships into egoists and hostages, so he divides concepts into totality and infinity

In metaphysics, the tendency is to think in terms of abstract opposites, such as other and same. This tendency is encouraged by the use of an abstract language: not "me" and "other people," but "Same," and "Other," as though we were no longer talking about humans but some entity more profound than you and me. It is an entity that only has two values, like an off–on switch: me and not me. If, however, we remember that we are talking about humans and their relationships, then the possible combinations are almost endless, as many permutations as there are different human relationships. Or rather, as many permutations as there are relationships times minutes of the day, for the combinations change constantly. These are experiences that can be put into words only if we make distinctions more delicate than other and same. This is not to deny that we live in a web of words referring to words, the world as wall-to-wall text as Edward Said puts it. It is to say only that our words may point to experiences that are beyond words. How well our words point depends on the subtlety of our terms.

Levinas refers to this aspect of language (that it refers to itself, and yet somehow points beyond itself) with his distinction between saying and said. Saying (*le Dire*) is the unspoken, unwritten dimension of the said. The said (*le Dit*) is the text, my words, what I say. Saying is my exposure to the other, in which I wordlessly assert the irreducible premise of any utterance, any communication: "here I am, naked and exposed to you." It is this aspect of Levinas' work that many deconstructionists have become so intrigued with, as it seems to justify what is sometimes called reading against the grain. But notice what saying is not: conversation. In saying I expose myself to the other, but I do not talk with the other. Saying is not a dialogue (OB, pp. 153–62).[13]

I am asking the reader to think about experiences with others that involve dialogue, experiences that involve give and take, experiences of exchange between sovereign selves. Out of such experiences the same sometimes becomes a little more like the other, and vice versa. Sometimes same and other even like their exchange, each enriched by the other. Think about experiences with others that are more subtle, complex, and paradoxical than other and same, experiences such as "like me, but different at the same time." Experiences like these are the stuff of human relations.

The infinite distance between self and other posited by Levinas is not necessary to protect the other. Other people are not that fragile. Sometimes they like a little contact, even a little friction. A human distance is enough. Does anyone really want his partner to become his hostage, the term used by Levinas to characterize the subject's relationship to the other? Don't we really want mutuality? Sharing? The relationship most respectful of the other, suggests D. W. Winnicott, is play. In play we encounter the other while granting him or her the freedom to create him or her self. Wouldn't the other rather have someone to play with than a hostage? Wouldn't you?

A follower of Levinas might respond that I am confusing realms, the ontological with the ethical. When he talks about ethics, Levinas is talking about a relationship with the infinitely other, the profoundly distant and different. When he talks about ontology, Levinas is talking about our everyday relationships with other people, relationships that run the gamut from erotic relationships to the institutions of law and justice. I fail to observe the distinction, the Levinassian might argue. Indeed, Levinas himself posits an intermediate realm, midway between the narcissism of Eden and the encounter with the other. In this realm people vainly try to salve the solitude of their suffering through work, friendship, and eros; failing this they seek power over others (T&O, pp. 58–77). It is in this intermediate realm that most of what we call human history takes place.

Criticism that I confuse Levinas' discussion of this intermediate (what Levinas and his followers call ontological) realm with his ethics is relevant, but for two reasons not decisive. First, Levinas often writes about ethical relationships as though they were real relationships with real people. The rhetorical, almost magical, power of his texts stems from this strategy. One moment the other is a person, the next a mirror whose face is infinity. Alphonso Lingis, translator of *Totality and Infinity*, says that with the author's permission he capitalizes the word "Other" (*autrui*, in contrast to *autre*) when the word refers to another person, the "personal Other, the you" (T&I, p. 24). Most of the appearances of the term are capitalized. One might still argue that when he talks about the infinitely other, Levinas is referring to an aspect of our relationship with real others (that is, not every aspect), and that would be true. What is not true is that Levinas is talking about some Other more august and transcendent than real other people. That would miss the point Levinas is trying to make, that we know the infinite only in and through other people.

Derrida (1978, pp. 151–2) argues that Levinas' account of the encounter with the other is an "empiricism," by which Derrida means that Levinas is offering a concrete description of experience, not a transcendental account of how reality is constituted. Robert Bernasconi (2000, p. 84) demurs, arguing that "much of the language of *Totality and Infinity* seems to explicitly evoke a transcendental reading." Jill Robbins (1999, p. xiv) splits the difference, preferring the term "quasi-transcendental," concluding that "the status of the ethical 'event' that Levinas describes is precarious." About the precarious status of the encounter with the other, Robbins is correct, though terms such as "quasi-transcendental" do not seem very helpful. A decision must be made, not on behalf of Levinas, but for the sake of reading him, lest we take him insufficiently seriously, assuming that Levinas is talking about something quasi-transcendental when what we really mean is that his claims do not seem to fit our ordinary experiences of human relations.

I cannot see any other way to read Levinas but as one who is concerned with real experiences. Not only is such an interpretation attentive to the origins of Levinas' project in phenomenology, but it requires us to see his radical encounter with the world as an experience that can be right or wrong: or rather, a more or less accurate and complete account of how humans encounter the world. If we do not do that, how can we take Levinas seriously? Needless to say, one can interpret Levinas in a realistic fashion and still appreciate that his goal is transcendence. More precisely put, his goal is to describe an experience between transcendence and immanence (T&I, p. 52). Not quasi-transcendental, which presumably refers to this in between experience, but transcendental realism is the best term to describe Levinas' project: an archaeology of the experiences through which humans encounter their world. Simon Critchley (1996) puts it this way, and he seems just right:

> For me, what remains essential to Levinas's writing (and his extraordinary style of writing should be noted here: strange, elliptical, rhapsodic, sensual) is not its contribution to arcane debates in moral philosophy, but rather its powerful descriptions of the night, insomnia, fatigue, effort, jouissance, sensibility, the feminine, Eros, death, fecundity, paternity, dwelling, and of course the relation to the other. To my mind ... Levinas is concerned with trying to excavate the pre-theoretical layers of our intentional comportment towards the world, an archaeology of the pre-reflective constitution of existence.

If one assumes that Levinas is writing about real experiences, than Derrida's objection is profound. Drawing upon the Stranger in Plato's *Sophist* (254c), Derrida argues that the category of other is always relative to some other. Other always means "other than." Thinking he is privileging the other, Levinas is unavoidably defining the other in terms of the same, for he can do no other. No one can, so it is better to know it and say it. The fact that in earlier works Levinas defined woman as the passive, receptive counterpart of man only reinforces Derrida's argument (T&O, pp. 84–90; T&I, p. 258). Levinas would have been better off, concludes Derrida, if he had not been so overwhelmingly critical of Husserl's concept of the alter ego, the other as another ego, rather than simply other. To see the other person as strictly other comes close to an act of violence, as argued above.

Derrida might have followed Plato's Stranger one step further, where the Stranger argues that categories like other and same not only imply each other, but must be understood as mutually elaborating each other if we are not to fall silent. Says the Stranger, "this isolation of everything from everything else means a complete abolition of all discourse, for any discourse we can have owes its existence to the weaving together of forms" (260a).[14] In this and the chapters that follow I will be doing some weaving of my own, suggesting that self and other are woven together in relationships that need not be completely unraveled in order to protect and foster the other, or even the same.

To be sure, Levinas does not suggest that we live our lives in distant awe of the other. Our relationships are equivocal compounds of ethics and ontology, as the distinction between infinity and empiricism has come to be known in Levinas studies. Particularly in his discussion of the erotics of the tender caress, Levinas recognizes the way in which otherness and closeness are woven together. "The tender designates a *way*, the way of remaining in the *no man's land* between being and not-yet-being" (E&I, p. 259, author's emphasis). While Levinas calls the equivocal a no man's land, we might equally as well call it a woven land, the place where all and nothing meet, mingle, and change each other. We might, in other words, talk about the equivocal as a realm between losing and fusing, connections that recognize separation, and separations that recognize connection.

How does this work in practice, the practice of human life? Norman O. Brown puts it this way in *Love's Body*.

The existence of the "let's pretend" boundary [between people] does not prevent the continuance of the real traffic across it . . . There is a continual unconscious wandering of other personalities into ourselves: Every person, then, is many persons; a multitude made into one person." (1966, pp. 146–7)[15]

Imagine that *this* is the state of nature, the pre-doorbell state. Where we start from makes all the difference in the world. For Levinas, we start as thinking stones, "an *I think* as substantial as a stone or, like a heart of stone" (*Of God*, p. 71). Because we start as stones, the problem is to crack us open, so that otherness might enter. Levinas is, as he tells us, fond of "atomic metaphors," such as the nucleus of the I (*moi*) blown apart from its ego (*Moi*) by an encounter with the other (*Of God*, p. 72).

We only need to be blown up when we are closed to begin with. Put more academically, we only need to remember an immemorial experience of rupture if the problem is cloture. If we start from the condition described by Norman O. Brown, then the problem is to sort through the pieces of a self woven of many selves. When we do this, it becomes clear that nothing is pure. Once we admit that all our relations (indeed, all our selves) are compounds all the time, then the pursuit of purity becomes the pursuit of pure nothingness.

"To hear a God not contaminated by Being is a human possibility," says Levinas (OB, p. xlviii). Perhaps it is, but consider the purification of the self necessary, the elimination of every human particularity. The most straightforward reading of this statement is that humans contaminate the non-being of God with their being, but this seems unlikely. Until, that is, one recognizes that Levinas is implicitly contrasting his approach with that of Heidegger, his former teacher, who seeks "to bring Being out of the oblivion in which it is said to have fallen" (OB, p. xlviii). Since it is not God, but Heidegger, who is contaminated with being, then it must be humans who are to be purified, so that they are enough like the non-being of God to hear Him. Of course, living humans cannot really be purified of being, and Levinas does not imagine that they can. He does imagine that humans can transcend their nature, devoting themselves to the infinitely other, and so becoming the servant of Non-Being. In contrast, my approach is to consider a range of impure, equivocal relationships (that is, relations with relation), marked by the mixing, and even the confusion of self and other, in order to see how much these relations have to offer *to* Levinas: that is, to one who is properly in awe of the other person.

Levinas tells a story intended to illustrate in a practical way what it is to be obsessed with the other. Shortly after lecturing in Louvain, Levinas was taken to a student house called a pedagogy. There he found himself surrounded by South American students, almost all priests. Obsessed with the situation of the masses in South America, what they called the supreme trial of humanity, the priests asked Levinas to give them a practical example of the Same preoccupied with the Other "to the point of undergoing a fissioning of itself?" Levinas' answer, of course, was that it was they. "Here, in this group of students, of intellectuals who might very well have been occupied with their internal perfection and who nevertheless had no other subjects of conversation than the crisis of the Latin American masses. Were they not hostages?" (*Of God*, p. 81).

Unconcerned with their "internal perfection," the students achieved a type of sainthood for Levinas because they had achieved an external perfection, expressed as their hostage-like devotion to the abstract other, the Latin American masses. My point is not to cast suspicion on the motives of these noble men, only to point out that Levinas' criticism of the ideal of internal perfection does not mean that he has abandoned the ideal of perfection, which I regard as synonymous with purity. On the contrary, Levinas idealizes a type of external perfection, in which one abandons one's ego in order to dedicate oneself to an abstract other. But what if the priests' psyches came closer to that described by Norman O. Brown, already filled with selves representing masses, selves representing elites, and other selves besides? Then a single act of purifying fission would not be what was needed. Needed instead would be a conversation among the selves, leading to an eventual ordering of better and worse selves, one in which elite does not mean better. For all his discussion of "saying," Levinas has little place for that discussion in his bipolar world, divided into self and other.

To be sure, Levinas has a point. No matter how similar I am to another person in sociological terms, no matter how much others wander in and out of me, there is a sense in which I am completely and utterly different from you by virtue of being a separate person. Says Levinas, "it is not a question of a difference that is due to the absence or presence of a common trait; it is a question of an initial difference that is entirely self-referential. That is the I ... What is unique in each man—and this is ultimately a banality—is that he is" ("Transcendence & Height," pp. 28–9). Does this formulation not rescue a limited sense of absolute difference between me and another person? Yes, but this difference is hardly enough to support the type of experience Levinas refers to in his story about answering the doorbell. That I am I, and he is he, does not make me responsible for him. Another type of experience, or at least another dimension of this experience, is needed.

Levinas has increasingly emphasized another experience of the absolutely different, in which the emphasis is not on the otherness of the other, but the way in which otherness shatters my categories of being, interposing itself between me and my ego. In other words, Levinas has increasingly emphasized not the other *per se*, but my experience of the other, focusing on the shattering of my interiority, which opens me to the world. Here the categories of infinity and otherness have the quality of the experience of God that Descartes wrote about, in which the idea of God exceeds me. Rather than thinking God, it would be more accurate to say that God thinks himself in me. Similarly, to encounter the other is to have an experience that exceeds me, breaking me open. The other becomes me, what Levinas calls substitution ("Substitution").

Substitution means that "the other is in me and in the midst of my very identification" (OB, p. 125). Levinas radically rethinks identity, what it means to be a self in the world. What it means is that the other is already in me, standing between me and my ego. "The psyche in the soul is the Other in me, a malady of identity" (OB, p. 69). All my struggles to ground and found myself are doomed attempts to obliterate the other who seems to stand between me and becoming myself. These attempts are doomed because the other has insinuated him or her self so deeply that I cannot eradicate the other without obliterating myself. Substitution is fusion without attachment, a binding, self-defining connection to the other in the absence of a relationship with the other, a relation without relation.

Substitution is not a moral choice. On the contrary, substitution is not just pre-moral, but pre-conscious. Substitution stems from the primordial experience of the other, an experience that precedes my relationship to myself. "The relationship with the non-ego precedes any relationship of the ego with itself" (OB, p. 118). This does not mean that I am not a separate being, with my own ego. On the contrary, Levinas insists on my separateness. If I were not separate, I could not substitute myself for the other. I would in some way already be the other. Substitution defies the distinction between separate and fused. The other is already in me, closer to me than I am to myself, but the other is not me. The other is my saving grace, an alien presence that allows me to open myself to the world, a foreign body that wedges itself between me and my ego, and so allows me to escape my narcissistic soul by devoting myself to the other in me (*l'autre dans le même*) (OB, p. 111).

Who or what is this other? The question can no longer be avoided. Sometimes the other sounds like another person, his or her presence in me the reason I am infinitely obligated. Taken hostage by the other, I so identify with my calling as hostage that I become a hostage-being. In psychological terms, I have introjected the other into my ego, so that I identify with the other person in me. Freud (1959, pp. 35–42) said we do this when we fall in love, and when we mourn. But this is not really what Levinas is talking about, even if it would help explain the obligation inherent in such a relationship. It would be more accurate to say that Levinas is talking about the opposite, as though I introjected nothing, or rather nothingness. Levinas frequently refers to Descartes' account of the decentering experience of the infinite in me when trying to explain this experience.

My perception of the infinite, that is God, is in some way prior to my perception of the finite, that is myself. For how could I understand that I doubted or desired—that is, lacked something—and that I was not wholly perfect, unless there were in me some idea of a more perfect being which enabled me to recognize my own defects by comparison. (Descartes, *Meditations*, 1988, p. 31)

A simple but not simplistic way to think about the other in Levinas' work is as the trace of a Cartesian God, one who disrupts me in the same way Descartes' God does. When Levinas says the trace of God is given in the face of the other this is what he means: the other disrupts me as God does ("Trace," p. 359). If this is so, then deconstructionists who have turned to Levinas for ethical inspiration have missed a beat. Derrida and others find an ethical sanction for deconstruction in Levinas' questioning of the self in the name of the other. Deconstructing the claims of the autonomous self to knowledge, freedom, and even being becomes an ethical act. But only if the other is more valuable than the self. Otherwise there is nothing to choose between self and other, and no reason to choose one over the other. For Levinas the choice is clear, the other a trace of God, even if it is a God who shatters an old order without founding a new. Leave even this God behind, and there is little to choose between self and other. In other words, one needs *illeity*, Levinas' pseudonym for God, to transform a traumatic relationship with the infinitely other into an ethical one, as Michael Newman (2000, p. 91) has seen.

The separation of the self from itself, so that the self becomes other to itself as a result of its exposure to the infinitely other, is hardly a conventional religious experience. Saul on the road to Damascus is a misleading parallel. Not rebirth but "pre-death" comes closer to the mark, as I am shattered by an experience of otherness so profound it seems like I no longer exist. Levinas calls this experience "dead time" (*le temps mort*), where one lives between being and nothingness (Keenan, 1999, p. 8). In colloquial French, "le temps mort" refers to what we would call down time, or wasted time in English. For Levinas it sometimes seems to refer to the interruption in infinity that is my life. Or rather, to the million little deaths that interrupt my life every day.

The expression "in one's skin" is not a metaphor ... it refers to a recurrence in the dead time or the *meanwhile* which separates inspiration and expiration, the diastole and systole of the heart beating dully against the walls of one's skin. (OB, p. 109)

In this "meanwhile" I become infinity a hundred thousand times a day, assuring me that my time on this earth is not wasted in mere being.

For Levinas "meanwhile" is liberating, a promise of things to come, escape from the burden of being. But what happens to other people in all this? The simple answer (the all too simple answer, but I will spend the rest of this essay qualifying it) is that my obligations to other people chain me to this world, and so prevent me from joining infinity until it is my time. It is the need of the other that keeps me in this world. My subjection to another guarantees that he or she will stand over me, weighing me down, keeping me from floating off into infinity. Socrates (*Symposium* 211c) taught that with the other I could climb the ladder of love hand in hand to the stars. Levinas hopes that the other will weigh me down, lest I rush away up the ladder too soon. The other is not only the trace of God, but the gravity that pulls me back to earth. The other person is not only the avatar of infinity, but the alternative.

Infinities

Much of the hypnotic effect of Levinas' prose stems from the delicate way he segues from one sense of the term "infinity" to another. In this and the chapters that follow I shall try to keep the different senses straight when it seems helpful to do so. For now I shall just list the different senses of the term infinity that are implied, even by their absence, in the doorbell story.

The first sense of infinity is timelessness, in the sense of going on forever, as if I could just keep counting forever, 1, 2, 3 ... Only occasionally does Levinas use the term "infinity" in this sense.

The second sense of infinity is timelessness in the sense of the medieval *nunc stans*, eternity as a place outside of time. The shattering experience of the other about which Levinas writes is located (if that is the right word) under this sense of infinity. The question I will ask is not how Levinas knows this, but from where he knows it. Where must he presume to stand in order to know this? Must he not presume to stand *sub specie infinitas*?

The third sense of infinity is difference, as in an infinity of difference between you and me. This is the "practical" version of infinity, so to speak, how it manifests itself in our ontological world. The other is so different from me that we cannot be compared. I am identical with myself, not other than you. Levinas frequently implies this sense of the term when writing about the other person. Conversely, to write of the other person as an alter ego would deny this sense of the term. The other would be alter, but we would still have ego in common. For Levinas we quite literally have nothing in common. I argue that Levinas cannot render the other person absolutely other without consequences that not just we, but he, would find unacceptable, such as the suppression of the other's humanity.

The fourth sense of infinity is an intrusion of otherness so shocking and complete it tears me from my ego. "The epiphany of the other, which is the concrete form of the infinite" (Peperzak, 1993, p. 182). Here infinity refers not just to otherness, but a shattering experience of non-being, as though someone ripped open the vault of the heavens to reveal nothing. The other exceeds my idea, and explodes my world (T&I, pp. 50–1). I ask whether this awesome experience, powerful as it is, is tantamount to infinity. Is this not stretching the term to the breaking point?

The fifth sense of infinity is generative power, a profusion of endless possibilities. This sense of the term is related to the first sense, as here there is no sequence, just endless, proliferating possibilities. It is in this sense that Theodor Adorno uses diversity as synonym for infinity. "If delicately understood, philosophy would itself be infinite. Its substance would lie in the *diversity* of objects that impinge upon it" (Adorno, 1973, p. 13). Only one sense of this use is possibly present in Levinas, that of infinite obligations to the other, who may ask anything and everything, needing more than I could ever give. Even here, the sense of profusion is not strong, the need of the other coming closer to the first sense of infinity, an endless succession of needs. One wants to find traces of infinity as profusion in Levinas' discussion of fecundity, seemingly similar to generative power. There is a hint of this sense there, but Levinas devotes most of his discussion of fecundity to characterizing a realm between transcendence and sensuality, not the same thing (T&I, pp. 267–9).

The sixth sense of infinity is non-being, a synonym for death. This use of the term infinity appears in Levinas' account of the experience of the infinitely other (the third sense of infinity), which is said to be the death of me, by which Levinas means that the other shatters my ego and its paltry projects. The next chapter argues that this shattering experience is good violence only if another has his or her arms around me as it happens. Only within the framework of human relationships is my death not simply violent.

The seventh sense of infinity is God, what Levinas sometimes calls *illeity*. Illeity might best be translated as he-ness, or Him, or God, but it is a God come closer to an abyss than a ground. For Levinas, the infinity of God has little to do with His infinite mercy, justice, wisdom or power. God is infinite in His otherness, the supreme non-being. Abraham

Heschel writes that for the religious man, "it is as if things stood with their backs to him, their faces turned to God." For Levinas, one wants to say that God stands with his back to man, so that we might see His face in the other. Only that would not be correct. For Levinas, even God's back is too close, an image of being and relatedness closer to myth than poetry.

Levinas rarely defines what he means by the term infinity (*infini*). When he does, the definition is likely to be rhetorical, as when he asks whether infinity is originally a noun or an adverb. Is infinity "something," or is it simply the "how" of otherness, the infinitely other? Levinas answers that the infinite is where these distinctions disappear (*Of God*, p. 94). If this is so, then one can see how the infinite otherness of the other person would segue into the infinite otherness that is God, as otherness is not a state so much as a contrast: absolutely other than me.

Though conceptual clarification is important, it is not an end in itself. The question I want to ask, the question that requires the different senses of infinity be held separate, is to what kind of human experience does infinity refer? Is not all human experience relative, in between, one thing measured against another? (This insight is the basis of Derrida's observation that other must mean other than me.) One might respond, as Levinas does, that the experience of infinity is not an experience so much as a shattering of experience. What does not seem correct is Levinas' assumption that only infinity can shatter me. Even ordinary experiences with other people can splinter my ego.

Levinas began as a phenomenologist, and in many ways this remains the strength of his project—the way in which he continues to locate philosophical concepts in experiences of desire, fear, insomnia, and all the rest. One of the most important human experiences to which infinity refers is the experience of losing the continuity of going-on-being, as Winnicott puts it. One way we lose this continuity is by standing alone too close to death. This is the topic of Chapter 2.

LEVINAS EFFECTS AND PSYCHOANALYSIS

In the chapters that follow I do not refute the Levinas effect. He could be all the things that his readers have found him to be, a proto-feminist deconstructionist theologian who reconciles postmodern ethics and rabbinic Judaism. I suspect a loss of intellectual rigor in those who find all this in Levinas, but one might argue that the intellectual imagination to discover it there is at least as valuable. What I argue is that Levinas cannot place others at an infinite distance from oneself while continuing to value human relations. This is true even when one appreciates that Levinas is not writing about others *per se*, but about an experience of others, a dimension of one's total experience of others. Positing absolute otherness as the leading principle of God, and ethics, has consequences not just for theology but for human relations.

My only theological argument is no argument at all, just the occasional counter-example of Rosenzweig, another great critic of totality. Like Levinas, Rosenzweig finds in Hegel all that is bad and totalizing in Western philosophy. Unlike Levinas, Rosenzweig (1985, pp. 23–4) defines God as the non-Nought, and "in front of us there lies as goal an Aught: the reality of God." God is the negation of nothing, which means something. God remains infinite in the sense of being beyond all definition. Here is yet another sense of infinity, related but not identical to the third sense. But the infinity of God does not render Him beyond being. God, says Rosenzweig, is another being, as solitary as man, "each of them a solitary self" (1985, p. 84). The task is to bring these two solitary selves closer. For that we need to learn the speech-thinking of God's language. For Levinas, on the other hand, being itself is always suspect, even when the being in question is the supreme being.

Not the theological but the human consequences of infinity are my chief concern. Here I have an argument, and the clearest way to crystallize its gravamen is to disagree with an important critic. Writing for *Radical Philosophy*, Simon Critchley (1996) says that the usual summary of Levinas' project as transforming ethics into first philosophy fails to capture the richness of his project. What's special about Levinas is his focus on the individual in front of me. "For Levinas, the relation to the other takes place in the concrete situation of speech or discourse ... where I focus on the particular individual in front of me and forgo the mediation of the universal."

It's just not true. Levinas forgoes the mediation of the universal not by focusing on the individual, but by transforming (or should I just say "mixing") every particular experience into an encounter with absolute otherness. Is not infinity (in the third sense) the greatest mediator of them all, letting me get just close enough to see the other's face, but not close enough to know the color of his or her eyes, as Levinas puts it? (E&I, p. 85). To be sure, one is inclined to think that it is infinity that needs mediating, lest we be overcome with otherness. But perhaps the other person needs mediating too, lest we become confused at this being before us, one who is like us in some respects, unlike us in others, and often we are not even sure which is which. By transforming the encounter with another human being into an encounter with absolute otherness, Levinas renders this human encounter simpler than it really is. Or rather, Levinas' remarkably subtle and complex understanding of human relations, often called his phenomenology, is not always well connected with his ethics, particularly in his later works. Making the connection explicit requires, I believe, that we rethink Levinas' ethics, but not perhaps as much as Levinas sometimes seems to fear. Nature, in other words, is not necessarily the enemy of the ethical.

2

Levinas, Winnicott, and "There Is"

Like many great thinkers, Levinas has created a world so comprehensive that the only choice seems to live in it, or leave it for another, a land so different they share not even a lingua franca. But all lands have things in common. One is motherhood, a leading trope in Levinas, one of the ways in which he characterizes what he means by our infinite responsibility to the other.[1] The psychoanalyst D. W. Winnicott has also written about motherhood, though it might be more accurate to say that Winnicott writes about mother- and baby-hood, for he always said he'd never seen a baby without a mother (Winnicott, 1975a). I hope that the lingua franca of motherhood will provide a common language, or at least a patois, by which denizens of different lands might communicate.

Winnicott's land is Athens, the land of emerging individuality and creativity, where the self-conscious psyche (the Greek term we translate as both soul and self) first emerged. Levinas' land is Jerusalem, the land of prophecy, faith, and worship of a being so infinitely other that it is beyond being. Yet, philosophers and prophets have spoken to each other before.

Does it matter that Winnicott is a psychoanalyst? Does that make the land from which he speaks even more distant and obscure? Not necessarily. Several Levinassians have found psychoanalysis a useful medium by which to think about Levinas, and it is not hard to see why.[2] Much of Levinas' work is an attempt to put words to the ineffable, feelings and experiences not so much beyond as beneath words. In this he shares much with psychoanalysis. Still, we must be careful about bringing psychoanalysis to bear on Levinas, so that we do not combine incommensurables. Most important is to pick the right psychoanalyst.

Because they differ so sharply on eros, Freud is not the right psychoanalyst to compare with Levinas. Unless, that is, one is content to end up with incommensurables. Nevertheless, it will be helpful to lay out the differences between Freud and Levinas before turning to Winnicott.

EROS, AGAPE, SUBLIMATION

Recall Levinas' claim that he is not a Freudian because Freud assumed that agape is but another version of eros, and that cannot be. Agape is brotherly and sisterly love, sometimes called charity. It is the term used in Christ's new commandment to "love your neighbor" (Mark 12:31; Matthew 22:39; Luke 10:27; Romans 13:9; Galatians 5:14; James 2:8). It is, of course, not the term used in the Old Testament commandment to "love your neighbor as yourself" (Leviticus 19:18).[3] There the Hebrew term for love is *ahab* (aw-hab). Interestingly, *ahab* comes much closer to eros than agape, as *ahab* covers the entire spectrum of love, from love of family and sexual love, to the human appetites for food, drink, sleep, and wisdom, and finally to the love of God.

The problem with eros for Levinas is not just that it is about desire, which is presumably always to some degree selfish. The problem is that in the Platonic tradition eros is deficient, lacking, always seeking to fill itself up with others (*Symposium* 175c–e), or to merge with them (*Symposium* 189c–193d). The parents of Eros, says Socrates, are *Penia* and *Poros*, Poverty and Contrivance (*Symposium*, 203b–e). Poor and weatherbeaten, Eros is always scheming to get what he lacks. Levinas knows this story well, which is why he rejects this account of eros (T&I, pp. 254–5).

Freud agrees with Socrates, but not without qualification. For Freud (1915), eros originates not in the need of others but in narcissism. Only later is eros extended to others. But this "later" is everything. Enormously plastic, eros is readily sublimated, by which Freud means that it becomes subject to the ego. The result is that eros may motivate the highest cultural achievements, from writing a symphony to building a university to caring for the poor. Something similar happens in Socrates' account, in which it is finally Eros that leads us up the ladder of love to the experience of the ideas (*Symposium*, 211a–212e).

Whether there is much difference between Freud's and Socrates' account of the sublimation of eros has been debated. Boas sees virtually no difference between the views of Plato and Freud.

> The libido, as a term for generalized desire ... by reintegrating humanity and its strivings into the natural world ... has revived in a new form the kernel of Diotimas' speech in the *Symposium* ... Since love in the *Symposium* is found not only in sexual attraction but also in scientific research and philosophic meditation, there is only a verbal difference between the two philosophies. (1967, p. 94)

Cornford (1950, pp. 71, 78), on the other hand, argues that, for Plato, the self-moving energy of the soul resides in the highest, not the lowest, part of man. Freud does not accept this distinction, characterizing eros not so much in terms of its locus as its function.

> As for the "stretching" of the concept of sexuality . . . anyone who looks down with contempt upon psychoanalysis from a superior vantage point should remember how closely the enlarged sexuality of psychoanalysis coincides with the Eros of the divine Plato. (Freud, 1962, Preface to 4th edition)

One wants to say that the Freudian concept of sublimation shows Levinas to be overly concerned with the province of eros, where it comes from. Not where it comes from, but what eros is capable of doing should be our concern. To focus excessively on love's origins is to demand a purity that is almost inhuman. But while one wants to say this, it is not quite so simple, largely because the Freudian concept of sublimation is less than crystal clear.

Freud was never able to distinguish sublimation from repression in terms of his energetic model. Paul Ricoeur (1970, pp. 484, 317) puts it well when he states that the concept of sublimation is both "fundamental and episodic" in Freud's thought. The disproportion between the psychological transformations of desire, which are limited, and the vast variety of forms which sublimation can assume, implies that the process cannot be adequately accounted for by "the economics of desire." In other words, we know the experience of eros. We think we know that activities vastly removed from eros, such as playing a concerto, seem somehow to be expressions of eros, but we do not know what the transformation process looks like. In particular, we do not know exactly how or where eros loses its selfishness, subjecting itself to the standards of ideal form, such as the form of the concerto.

I will not be able to solve the problem of sublimation, only to call attention to it. From Plato to Freud, the highest achievements of humankind have been seen as connected to the most primitive desires. For neither does this connection spoil the highest achievement. For Levinas it does.

Consider reparation, as the psychoanalyst Melanie Klein calls it. Originating in eros (for Klein, there is only love and hate), reparation reflects the desire to make amends for the harm we have done to others. Not just with our hate, but with our selfish need that Klein conceptualizes in terms of a primitive greed that would scoop out the substance of the other, caring nothing for the integrity of the other. This, presumably, is what babies would do. Soon enough, however, as early perhaps as the first year of life, the young child comes to feel remorse and regret, a concern for the integrity of the other. "Feelings of love and gratitude arise directly and spontaneously in the baby in response to the love and care of his mother," says Klein (1964, p. 65). Not merely an aim-inhibited expression of libido, love expresses genuine care and concern for the other. The result is "a profound urge to make sacrifices," to make others happy out of genuine concern for the other qua other. For Klein, reparation is how we overcome our terrible feelings of depression and despair, originating in the often unconscious knowledge that we really did want to take all the other had to give and more, that once we were ruthless in our greed and desire. One who knew Klein well said that her studies on reparation are "perhaps the most essential aspect of Melanie Klein's work" (Riviere, 1952, p. 60).

One can see an affinity between Klein and Levinas, in so far as they both recognize the ruthless selfishness of primitive love. The difference is that Klein sees the selfishness of love as curing itself, transmuting itself into a genuine love and concern for the other, what she calls reparation. It is from the selfish love of the other that we learn to love the other unselfishly. I do not know that Klein is correct, and that Levinas is mistaken. No one has adequately explained the transformations of eros. Sublimation is more a definition than an explanation. What I believe I know is that Levinas is too insistent on the separation of eros and agape, as though they could never be related lest eros contaminate agape. What I believe I know is that nothing human is pure, that our unselfish love for others is not, and need not, be held utterly separate from our selfish love. Love's knowledge is the recognition that to possess the object of one's desire is to lose it. It is on the basis of this pathetic insight that we become moral. In other words, morality is not unnatural, even as it carries us beyond mere nature.

Levinas associates eros with the aura of Shakespeare's witches, "an order in which seriousness is totally lacking . . . an irresponsible animality" (T&I, pp. 263–4). Responsibility for the other (which *is* seriousness) depends upon an experience of the other that not only lifts us out of nature, but out of the realm contaminated by being (OB, p. xlviii). In fact, it's not quite this simple. Even in *Totality and Infinity*, where Levinas writes about eros as stuck in the order of animality, he still considers the possibility that the erotic experience of the female other might transport us past the other to infinity. Here his argument is almost identical to that of Socrates in *The Symposium*. Tina Chanter (1991, p. 133) disagrees, setting the disappearance of eros earlier in Levinas' project: "Eros and the feminine are predominant in 1947 (in *Le temps et l'autre* and *Existence and Existents*), whereas *Totality and Infinity* (1961) seems to privilege the ethical relationship." In any case, it would not be incorrect to state that there are moments earlier in Levinas' project where he plays with the conjunction of eros and ethics, and hence necessarily with the possibility that eros might become ethical.[4] Nevertheless, the splitting, dichotomizing tendencies in his project win out in the end, which means that ethics can take nothing from nature.

When technical issues in the history of psychoanalysis, such as sublimation, illuminate a larger issue, such as the nature of love, I will raise them. Nevertheless, this is not how I plan to invoke psychoanalysis. For all its positing of mechanism and structure, psychoanalysis is an account of what it is to be human in a world of humans. What psychoanalysis adds is that there are humans within us as well as with out. "There is a continual unconscious wandering of other personalities into ourselves," is how Norman O. Brown (1966) puts it. "Be human among humans" says Ismene to Antigone in a modern version of the play.[5] Antigone has fallen in love with death, and her sister Ismene would bring her back to the human world. That is my perspective. Of course, anyone can have a perspective. The trick will be to bring it to bear on Levinas in a sympathetic way, one that does not criticize him for not being someone else, or for not being psychoanalytically inclined. Not Levinas' failure to be psychoanalytically inclined, but his assumption that ethics must forever stand in opposition to nature, is what I question. Psychoanalysis is a vehicle to raise this question.

WINNICOTT, LEVINAS, INFINITY

How can one relate to another without imposing oneself on the other, without doing violence to the other's awesome otherness? This is the chief concern of both Winnicott and Levinas. It is what they share with each other that neither shares with Freud. I say it is Levinas' concern as well because a relation without relation is still a relation. The only question is what kind.

Both Winnicott and Levinas make the dyad central. Others count, but unlike Freud, for whom it is the Oedipal triangle that structures psychic reality, it is the intimate but unsymmetrical relationship between two people that makes a world for both Winnicott and Levinas. This distinguishes both from Martin Buber, for whom the relative symmetry of the I–thou relationship is pivotal.

Like Levinas, Winnicott upholds the infinite distance between self and other. The distance between self and other in Winnicott is properly called infinite (in the third sense listed in Chapter 1) because Winnicott holds that the true self is silent, never to be known; to know the true self is to destroy it (1965b). Unlike Levinas, Winnicott makes this distance part of the relationship itself, the relationship he calls holding. The result is that gratitude, what Winnicott calls concern, results not in hostage-being, but a separation that is still a connection, a transitional space. We cannot, it seems, do without oxymorons. The trick is to pick the right ones.

In turning to Winnicott, I am turning to a theorist who defines violence much as Levinas does—imposing oneself on another self, so as to make the other like me. Totalization Levinas calls it, bringing everyone and everything under my categories. The difference is that Winnicott does not create a metaphysical (that is, beyond the physical laws of this world) boundary between self and other in order to contain the violence of totalization, finding instead other more human limits, limits that originate in the ordinary relationship of mother and child.

A deeper connection between Levinas and Winnicott is present to my mind, although I cannot prove it. I can only suggest it to the reader. Much of what Levinas says about the original experience of the other may be read as an account of an original experience of mother, the original other. Not the first experience of mother, but the first experience of conscious awareness of mother as a distinctly separate human being whose radiance brings light and meaning to a world darkened by her absence.

Consider Levinas' emphasis on the height of the other, the radiant face of the other, my lowness compared to the other's highness: are these not adult ways of talking about a young child's experience of mother stepping in to raise him or her from loneliness ("Transcendence and Height")? Are not gratitude and awe the emotions we felt: gratitude at the presence of salvation in the world, and awe that it exists outside, no longer my possession, but become my frightening, wonderful god? Not for a moment do I wish to reduce the experience of the infinitely other to a psychological moment, only to suggest that the experience of the mother as separate being is an enormous developmental step, perhaps the single most important step we will ever take. Upon this step rests the ability to know others as others. To suggest that what Levinas says about the experience of the infinitely other recalls this step only honors its importance.

The ordinary devoted mother, as Winnicott calls her, is with her child so that her child can be alone. Because mother is attuned to her child and its needs, the child need not be constantly attuned to her. Her child is free to be, which includes being free to imagine that he or she is omnipotent. "I am hungry, and lo milk appears." This is what the child imagines when mother is in tune.

This will be a frequent experience if the mother is in tune with her child, frequent enough in any case so that the child need not confront his or her own terrible dependence for a while. The result is the birth of creativity, in which the infant believes in his capacity to create a reality that corresponds to his or her needs.

> The baby says (wordlessly of course): "I just feel like ... ," and just then the mother comes along and turns the baby over, or she comes with the feeding apparatus and the baby becomes able to finish the sentence: " ... a turn over, a breast, nipple, milk, etc. etc." We have to say that the baby created the breast, but could not have done so had not the mother come along with the breast just at that moment. The communication to the baby is "Come at the world creatively, create the world; it is only what you create that has meaning for you." Next comes: "the world is in your control." From the initial *experience of omnipotence* the baby is able to begin to experience frustration, and even to arrive one day at the other extreme from omnipotence, having a sense of being a mere speck in the universe ... Is it not from *being God* that human beings arrive at the humility proper to human individuality? (Winnicott 1987, pp. 100–1, his emphasis)

If this does not happen, if the mother does not foster this feeling of creative control, the young child will be on the way toward developing a false, compliant self, ready to act in whatever way can convince another to meet its needs. The child will, in other words, be made prematurely aware of the sheer otherness of the world, which cares nothing for the child. Compliance is the opposite of creativity, and compliance reigns when the child is convinced that it must adapt and conform to the intrusions of a mother who does not share the child's world.

While the model is mothering, Winnicott makes much the same point about friendship. It too is based upon the capacity to be alone while in the presence of another. In friendship, the attunement is mutual, but the principle is the same, each friend responsive to the other while taking care not to intrude upon each other's sacred space, which Winnicott imagines as residing in an untouchable part of the self, unknowable even to the subject, but evident in such moments as the spontaneous gesture (Winnicott 1965a, p. 33).

The problem between friends, the human problem par excellence, is to stay related without being penetrated, to remain connected without being compromised. Just being left alone won't help. To be left alone is to have to care for oneself constantly, which means never being free to just be. Being alone with another is the only answer, what Winnicott calls holding (1986).

Does Winnicott's account of holding not sound like responsibility for the other that Levinas writes about, a responsibility that Levinas characterizes as "the evocation of maternity" (OB, p. 104)? "As mother, I bear the other within me, without fusing together" (Peperzak 1993, p. 223). Holding is care without encroachment. Consider too Winnicott's insight that we must have once believed ourselves to be gods to know our own smallness. Does this not help explain how we move from the narcissism of the pre-doorbell state to the encounter with the other?

MATERNITY

In fact, Winnicott's holding and Levinas' evocation of maternity are more different than first appears. Consider the different but closely related ways in which Levinas uses the term "maternity" as a way of talking about responsibility for the other.

- Maternity is passivity, existing totally for the other, being totally open toward the needs of the other, even—or especially—when this involves my suffering for the other (OB, p. 71).
- Maternity means to become insubstantial, devoting one's substance to the other, as though every bite the pregnant woman ate went to her baby.
- Maternity means to become responsible for the persecutions one has undergone, much as an ideal mother might smile softly at her child's tantrum ("Mommy, I hate you!") knowing that this is what mothers are supposed to do. Or as Levinas puts it, "Maternity, which is a bearing par excellence, bears even responsibility for the persecuting by the persecutor" (OB, p. 75).
- Maternity is substitution, carrying the other in me, and so putting the other first, existing only for the other, as though the other became me.

"Maternity," says Levinas, "is the very gestation of the other in the same, of the other in the same that would be the psyche itself" ("True Disclosure," p. 102).

- Maternity means to be obsessed with the other, akin to what Winnicott calls the primary maternal preoccupation, the mother's obsession with her baby for the first few months of life, the world reduced to baby and me.

Are Levinas and Winnicott not talking about the same thing? No. Winnicott is talking about a type of symbiosis, a mutual attunement between mother and child. In this attunement the mother does most of the work. She, and not the baby, must search the different channels in order to feel where her baby is. A simple example: is baby crying because she is cold, hungry, lonely, wet, bored, bloated? But if mother does most of the work, the goal remains a type of rhythmic participation in each other's company. Levinas, as we will see, is deeply distrustful of rhythm and participation, regarding each as pagan pleasures. Of course, Levinas is not talking about mothers and babies, but that is where our experiences of rhythm and participation begin. For Levinas, it is also where they should end.

One sees the difference between Winnicott and Levinas most clearly when considering Levinas' insistence that the maternal is not natural, but pre-natural. "Rather than a nature, earlier than nature ... this maternity ... is older than every past present" (OB, p. 75). Levinas must say this, lest maternity as an image of responsibility for the other be seen as little more than a "transfer of sentiment." Were maternity, with its mutuality, attunement, participation, and rhythm (just imagine mother cooing to her baby) to become a paradigm for ethics, then everything Levinas says would be wrong. Ethics would be in some sense natural. Sensuousness would become if not a ground, at least a resting place for ethics, providing a type of ethical guidance. Levinas must denature maternity in order to make it safe for ethics. Maternity is only a metaphor.

Different as they are, Levinas is not totally out of tune with Winnicott. Certainly the violence that Levinas writes about sounds like the violence of the intrusive mother, the mother who is out of tune with the child. Is it too strong to call this violence? Not for Levinas, and not for a host of post-moderns, for whom even writing is a violent act, fixing a shimmering subjectivity forever. Levinas puts it this way on the first page of *Totality and Infinity*:

Violence does not consist so much in injuring and annihilating persons as in interrupting their continuity, making them play roles in which they no longer recognize themselves, making them betray not only commitments but their own substance, making them carry out actions that will destroy every possibility for action (T&I, p. 21).

No concept was more important to Winnicott than the interrupted continuity to which Levinas refers. Winnicott was preoccupied with gaps and spaces: the gaps and spaces in the experience of the self that arise from a lack of attunement with mother and others, as though one's self had disappeared along with mother, a gap in going-on-being. The continuity of being stems from the infant's subjective experience of being merged with mother, a merger so perfect it feels little different from autonomy, what Winnicott means when he refers to the experience of the infant as god, in perfect tune with the world. The experience comes close to that of the pre-doorbell state of "living from" that Levinas writes of, in which I drink up the goodness of the world without ever knowing how much I depend upon others.

The result, for both Winnicott and Levinas, is a self-confidence that runs deep, so deep that I don't have to worry about holding myself together. I can let myself go, knowing, feeling, that someone will be there to pick up the pieces. Winnicott (1989a) calls this letting go a transitional experience, in which I am connected to the one who holds me and separate at the same time. Conversely, the greatest burden of being is always having to hold myself together. When I must do that, I lose the vitality of living, as I must be forever attuned to others and their reaction to me, lest I find myself left with nobody but myself to hold me. Dedicated to the reactions of others, I can never just be.

Levinas emphasizes the autonomy of the pre-doorbell state in order to imagine a person self-confident and free enough to serve others without needing them, and so dragging them into one's indigent little world. Winnicott puts this ideal a little differently. Not an individual autonomous enough not to need others, but a person who has needed others without having been constantly reminded of this fact: here is the source of freedom.

Lest this sound a little abstract, let me put it in the plainest possible terms. Winnicott is talking about attunement, the sense one has of being in emotional contact with a separate human being.[6] It is through attunement that one is able to recognize another's moods and feelings and respond appropriately, which does not mean identically. Play is the paradigm of attunement, in which mother coos as baby smiles, or one friend smiles sympathetically at another's chagrin. In play we respond to each other in creative ways, the response neither forced nor programmed, but spontaneous. The partners are in emotional contact, but they are not feeling the same thing; they are feeling each other. Attunement is emotional rhythm.

Attunement is the way the "transfer of sentiment" really works. It's not as though I pick up a feeling and give it to you, as though feelings were things. Rather, my feelings evoke comparable, but not identical, reactions in you, as when I feel sad when you cry. Attunement is the language of human relatedness. There is no attunement in Levinas. Or if there is, it is the attunement of the hostage, infinitely sensitive to the other, but always in the spirit of perfect service. Does not the hostage, dedicated to the reaction of the master, epitomize what causes us to lose the feeling of going-on-being? Only for Levinas this is good, or at least not unambiguously bad. *Temps mort*, the interrupted continuity of being, the space between breathing in and breathing out, is also the promise of infinity, that one day I will no longer be prisoner in my own skin.

ATTUNEMENT AND PARTICIPATION

Attunement is a subtle combination of otherness and identification, and no such dialectic emerges in Levinas. On the contrary, Levinas spurns rhythm, so similar to attunement, for by rhythm Levinas refers not just to musical harmony, but harmony of almost any kind (T&I, p. 78). Levinas rejects rhythm and harmony because they suggest a mystical participation between people; boundaries are blurred, and people get carried away with each other. Rhythm and harmony represent a type of non-Platonic participation, a term Levinas takes from the ethnologist Lucien Lévy-Bruhl, to refer to a way of thinking that is indifferent to the laws of contradiction.

Platonic participation is entirely different, says Levinas. "Mystical participation is completely different from the Platonic participation in a genus; in it the identity of the terms is lost ... The participation of one term in another does not consist in sharing an attribute; one term *is the other*" ("There is," pp. 32–3). Platonic participation respects boundaries.[7] Not rhythm and play, but discord and dissonance are Levinas' goods, for these are what it takes to shake me out of my self-satisfied little world. The human soul, says Levinas, is "naturally Christian," by which he means it longs to participate in salvation and myth (*Proper Names*, p. 67). But natural is generally the opposite of good in Levinas' work. Substitution does not play with boundaries. Substitution is the reversal of boundaries, a much clearer phenomenon. In substitution I become the other's hostage. What could be clearer than that, the usual hierarchy totally reversed, its members once again perfectly distinct? Levinas would grant almost nothing to Dionysus, so that Apollo is always ready to serve.

Participation, which Levinas derides, sounds something like the substitution that Levinas praises, but the similarity is deceiving. Under the influence of rhythm and harmony, I might experience myself as self and other at the same time. I might have what Winnicott calls a transitional experience, one that invites the blurring of boundaries. "In rhythm there is no longer a oneself, but rather a sort of passage from oneself to anonymity ... Consciousness, paralyzed in its freedom, plays, totally absorbed in the playing" ("Reality & Shadow," pp. 132–3). Play "is one of the most negatively charged terms in his work," says Robbins (1999, p. 86) about Levinas, and now we see why. In play we flirt with boundaries. Substitution is not play. Play, like the participation of which it is an instance, mimics transcendence, becoming a type of false transcendence in which I lose myself somewhere in myself, as though my unconscious were the other whom I am bound to serve. As though it hardly mattered which was which. Nothing could be more unethical for Levinas than this.

Levinas is right to be concerned. In writing about reparation, Melanie Klein (1964) ventures that we may make reparation for the harm done to others by creating something beautiful, such as a work of art. This, as Richard Wollheim (1984, pp. 216–8) argues, is the great moral flaw in Klein, her tendency to confuse the impulse with the act, as though the desire to make reparation were more important than its subject. For instance, Klein suggests that white settlers make reparation for the destruction of native populations by repopulating the land with their own people. As though it matters more that I have the satisfaction of making reparation than that the one who was harmed be made whole (in so far as this is possible). Perhaps this is a tendency inherent in any psychoanalytic account of ethics, as Wollheim suggests. If so, then Levinas is an important corrective, reminding us not just that ethics is first of all about the reality of others, but that precisely *because* we often feel good about helping others we risk confusing self-satisfaction with ethics.

Winnicott and Levinas agree upon a central point: the terrible danger of intruding upon the otherness of the other, and the violence that so often masquerades as love or concern, but is really an attempt to subordinate the other to oneself. This is the leading theme of each. The difference is that Winnicott believes that a human relationship can combine both attachment and separation in a single act, staying in tune with the needs of the other so the other can risk being alone—that is, risk being. A relation with relation (that is, with rhythm, but without intrusion) is Winnicott's ideal. In that seemingly most natural of institutions, motherhood, Winnicott finds the paradigm of this relationship, but it is only the paradigm, Winnicott finding it everywhere friends meet. Even when they are alone, they are alone together (1965a, pp. 33–4).

Winnicott is the theorist of play. Play likes surprises. Play is the realm of the authentic gesture that surprises the self even more than other. Play is a spontaneous expression of self in a world of others. For Levinas that is the problem. "We name this calling into question of my spontaneity by the presence of the Other ethics" (T&I, p. 43). Compare this statement with Winnicott's claim that the spontaneous gesture is the trace of the authentic self. For Levinas the authentic self is not so much an illusion as valueless, because it is not just private, but locked in itself, a little narcissistic economy, unable to know the good that others reflect.

It is no valid criticism of Levinas to argue that he does not recognize or appreciate what Winnicott calls the true self. Of course he doesn't. That's the point, the difference between Athens (even the Athens of Plato, which aims toward the good), and Jerusalem. For Levinas, the true self is the self that devotes itself to the trace of the infinitely other in the other. Freedom is the freedom of giving oneself over totally to the infinitely other, not so unlike the passivity of drinking in the milk of the world that characterizes the narcissistic economy. "In this most passive passivity, the *Self* is freed from every [particular] Other and from itself" ("Substitution," p. 90). This, it seems, is the goal.

Winnicott would understand. For Winnicott, freedom is the freedom to fall into chaos, but only because one is held by another. Unfreedom means always having to hold oneself in check in order to keep the pieces from falling apart. Though Winnicott posits a true self, it is not a stable core, but a place of creative chaos (1965b). The difference with Levinas is that for Winnicott the freedom to be chaotic stems from real attachments to particular others.

Only this puts the difference a little too sharply, or at least too irrevocably. What if we thought about Levinas' amazingly difficult and confusing discussion of the other as a way of trying to preserve the other's status as transitional object? By transitional object Winnicott (1984) means an object that is neither me nor not me, but both and neither. The teddy bear or favorite blanket is often the child's first transitional object, but transitional objects are not just for children. Culture is the transitional object *par excellence*. Culture makes no sense if it is not part of me. But if it were only in me culture would be no more than an illusion. The power of the transitional object disappears, continues Winnicott, when we ask what it really is: self or other, created or discovered? The only way to preserve its magical power is not to ask. Most parents know this intuitively. Busy making distinctions, philosophers do not always know this.

One way to read Levinas' texts (particularly *Otherwise than Being*, the most obscure) is as veils of contradiction, designed to prevent us from gaining enough clarity to ask whether the other is outside or inside, human being or trace of the infinite, by in effect saying both at once, and neither. The mark of the other is that it is the infinite difference to which we are fused, because the other is already in me, more me than me. Doesn't that sound like a transitional object?

Levinas' texts keep us off balance, saying one thing, then its opposite, and so preventing us from asking which the other really is. About Levinas' literary style, Davis (1996, p. 121) says: "the text hovers on the edge of nonsense . . . Similes are adopted but simultaneously undercut . . . Levinas's text strains to describe something that it characterizes as lying beyond any experiential or cognitive measure." One might, of course, see Levinas as trying as hard as he can to say the ineffable, as when he writes of "the passation of the past," or the "futurition of the future" ("Other, Utopia, & Justice," p. 232). One might just as well see Levinas as trying to keep us off balance, so we won't (and perhaps so he won't) succeed in saying it.

Putting it this way stresses the covert continuity between Levinas and Winnicott. The continuity is real, originating in the way both attend to others as though they were sacred trusts. But it would be too easy to end on this note, as so many who have written about Levinas have done, rendering him compatible with virtually any anti-Enlightenment thinker who owes no great debt to Nietzsche, as well as some who do, such as Derrida. Winnicott has an affinity with anti-Enlightenment thinkers in so far as he holds that feeling real, rather than self-knowledge, is the goal of therapy (1975b). In this regard his vision of truth is aesthetic, putting him at greater distance than one might suppose from Freud, whose motto is that of the Greek Enlightenment: *gnothi sauton* (know thyself).

To be sure, Levinas recognizes that human attachments occur. But in the end, love and affection fall outside his categories into an impure netherworld of equivocal encounters. This is why, I believe, he has the lover's caress seeking not another person, but nothingness—that is, infinity. "A movement unto the invisible" he calls the caress (T&I, p. 258). Not even Plato goes that far in purifying erotic love of its earthly taint. For Plato, the best lover seeks a partner with whom he (for Plato it is always a he) can become better. Together the lovers will come closer to infinity than either would alone (*Phaedrus* 255b–257c; Nussbaum, 1986, pp. 200–3). For Levinas we are most alone when we caress another.

INFINITY IS NOT TRANSITIONAL SPACE

It is easy to miss the alliance between infinity and human unrelatedness in Levinas, because the language Levinas uses for the experience of infinity is the language of human relationships. Susan Handelman (1991, p. 210) writes of the face as though it were the introduction of particularity in Levinas' work. "The face connotes the distinctive mark of the individual human personality, unique to each person." Nothing could be further from the truth; the face is the obliteration of particularity in Levinas' work. "Transcendence is only possible when the Other (*Autrui*) is not initially the fellow human being or the neighbor; but when it is the very distant, when it is ... an abstraction" ("Transcendence and Height," p. 27).[8] Or rather, the face is an attempt by Levinas to have it both ways, otherness without the burdensome particularity of unique others.

Earlier we saw why the other must remain abstract. Particularity mediates, reminding us of the uniqueness of the other, which buffers or mediates the experience of absolute otherness. Levinas would remove this buffer, so that the experience of the absolutely other shatters me. This requires that the other be shorn of his or her qualities, becoming not even another person, just other. Only when the other is abstract in the third sense of infinity listed in Chapter 1, absolutely other, can the other generate the experience that is the fourth sense of infinity listed there, the experience of the absolutely other that shatters my ego and opens me to infinity, including the infinity that is God, the seventh sense of infinity. Somewhere in this way of thinking the reality of other people seems likely to get lost.

"Saying," which takes the place of "the face" in Levinas' later work, is a similar story. Saying does, however, emphasize another aspect of this experience of the other. Being exposed to the infinitely other means being exposed to oneself as oneself. To know the infinitely other is, at exactly the same time, to confront one's separate being. "One must show in Saying, qua approach, the very de-posing or de-situating of the subject, which nonetheless remains an irreplaceable uniqueness, and is thus the subjectivity of the subject" (OB, pp. 47–8).

Once again Levinas and Winnicott make common cause, if not with each other, then at least against those moderns who would assert the subject's sovereignty, as well as against those postmoderns who would argue that the subject does not exist. The subject exists, but not in isolation, only in relationship to others. The difference with Winnicott is that for Levinas this relationship is so terribly abstract that it is no comfort, at least not to the subject. Levinas, though, is not looking for comfort. He is looking for exit. My infinite responsibility to the infinitely other allows me to participate, in as much as humans are able to participate, in transcendence, understood as leaving the burden of my being behind as I devote myself to others.

Winnicott understands something of the burden of being. "I suggest that this I AM moment is a raw moment; the new individual feels infinitely exposed. Only if someone has her arms around the infant at this time can the I AM moment be endured, or rather, perhaps risked" (Winnicott 1965c, 148). Could it be that Winnicott is right not just about infants, but about all of us throughout our lives, though of course the holding may become more symbolic? Could it be that only if someone has his or her arms around us when we are exposed to the infinite (in the third, possibly fourth, and definitely sixth senses listed in Chapter 1) can we stand in awe of otherness? Could it be that becoming the other's hostage is a way to escape the exposure of "I AM"? Better to be held in another's arms than by the chains that make me hostage, but better to be held as hostage than not to be held at all. To be held hostage is still being held.

If Winnicott is correct, then Levinas has misunderstood something important about the connection between human relatedness and our experience of the infinite. Human relatedness and the experience of infinity are not two parallel experiences that become equivocal, mixed. Relatedness is rather the standpoint from which we may know infinity, such as the death of one who means the world to me. Relatedness connects us to these experiences of unrelatedness, and so lets us know them. Relatedness is not the alternative to infinity, but the medium through which we know it, as those who we love and care about, the ones who have held their arms around us, pass into the endless night. In the absence of experiences such as these, experiences of loss and longing, infinity would lack human meaning. Infinity would be merely abstract, inhuman.

Levinas writes of totality *or* infinity; the former is the enemy of the latter. Holding *and* infinity would come closer to the mark. We know infinity best in the company of others, as Plato reminds us in the *Phaedrus*. That too is the point of the ladder of love. We climb it holding on to each other, hand in hand. And when we reach the top, do we see infinity, or only each other? Let us take a page from Winnicott's book and pretend I did not ask that question.

The temptation is to say that Winnicott and Levinas share at least one thing, the recognition that the I is not sovereign, but depends upon the recognition of others. But not even that is true. For Levinas, the other is not the one who recognizes me. The other is the one who interrogates me, questioning my right to exist. Exist how? As a self-sufficient monad who would drink up the milk of the world and not even know his or her need. It is Levinas who posits a state of primary narcissistic unrelatedness, and in this respect, at least, comes closer to Freud (1914) than Winnicott. Levinas does this, I believe, because it is not selfishness but need of others that is most threatening to the search for infinity, because need binds us to the beings of this world.

USE OF AN OBJECT AND THE MORALITY OF RUTHLESSNESS

Toward the end of his career, Winnicott (1989b) turned his attention from transitional relations and relationships to what he called "the use of an object."[9] Transitional relations are marked by mutual fantasy, based on the reluctance of both parties to ask who's who and what's what. The use of an object is marked by the ruthless exploitation of the other, the greedy consumption of everything the other has to offer and more.[10] That sounds bad. Winnicott thinks it is good, for it is through this process that the reality of the external world is created. "It is the destructive drive that creates the quality of externality. This is central in the structure of my argument," says Winnicott (1989b, p. 226). If, that is, the object resists destruction. The result is not just the recognition of an objective reality outside the self, but frequently joy at a world outside myself. Only through the unsuccessful attempt to destroy objective reality do we come to recognize a reality separate and distinct from the self.

Winnicott treats the ruthless use of an object as a type of communication, frequently inventing little dialogues (mock Punch-and-Judy dialogues, Adam Phillips calls them) to illustrate the relationship:

The subject says to the object: "I destroyed you," and the object is there to receive the communication. From now on the subject says: "Hullo object!" "I destroyed you." "I love you. You have value for me because of your survival of my destruction of you. While I am loving you I am all the time destroying you in (unconscious) *fantasy*." (1989b, p. 222)

Consider, Winnicott continues, a man who buys a beautiful painting. He cares for and protects the painting in order to destroy it in unconscious fantasy over and over again. If he didn't, he couldn't really relate to the painting; it would never be an independent source of enjoyment, one that "can feed back other-than-me substance" (1989b, p. 227). Of course, were his painting to be destroyed by a vandal, that would be entirely different. It would be the difference between fantasy and reality. It would not, however, be a difference in the strength of the destructive impulses, only in the ability to sublimate them creatively (ibid., p. 232). Maturity is about destroying the object in fantasy so that one can use it in reality. "The price has to be paid [for the reality of the external world] in acceptance of the ongoing destruction in unconscious fantasy" (ibid., p. 223).

Winnicott's idea is stranger than first appears. For Freud, one would destroy the object because it is beyond one's omnipotent control, because its independent reality frustrates the will. This is the way of thinking that Levinas assumes in his critique of totality: we reduce the other to the same out of rage at its separateness, its existence beyond the realm of my control. ("Idealism as rage" at a world too different to be dominated, is how Adorno puts it.) Winnicott is saying the opposite. It is the destructive impulse that creates the quality of externality, and it is this externality that makes the object available for satisfaction. With the term "creates" Winnicott means something like Kant's synthetic a priori: destructiveness allows us to discover in nature what our minds allow to be there, the real separateness of the object.

Nor is Winnicott's use of the object similar to Klein's view. For Winnicott, "Klein's concept of the depressive position now seemed more like a protection-racket, a sophisticated version of being nice to mother" (Phillips, 1988, p. 132). Not the act of reparation, but the mother's continued survival in the face of her child's attacks, is what makes not just a separate reality, but a valued one. The object survives on its own, and the child is overjoyed. Now the child has someone to use, which brings pleasure to both mother and child. People want to be used. It is a deep source of satisfaction. "For most people the ultimate compliment is to be found and used" (1987, p. 103). Using and being used by other people is one of the ways people get close to each other, almost as though one could reach out and take what one needs from inside the other person. It sounds destructive, invasive, and it is, but only if we cannot distinguish between reality and fantasy must it hurt the other.

If Winnicott is correct, then Levinas' distant approach to the other, a relation without relation, must actually make it more difficult to know, or rather feel, the separateness of the other. If it is only through a ruthless encounter with the other that we become convinced of the other's separateness, then the absence of this encounter must make it seem as if the other is not only incredibly vulnerable (as one has not had the experience of the other successfully resisting one's attempts to destroy it) but not quite separate. Or rather, the separateness of the other must itself seem so terribly tenuous, to be guarded and guaranteed by the stringent self-control that marks hostage-being, or saying. If one has not bumped up against the other and felt its resistance, then one will be terribly careful about even touching the other. The other's otherness will continue to be recognized, but somewhere there will always be a doubt, if not about the other's otherness, then about the other's ability to resist intrusion. This seems to characterize Levinas' attitude toward the other, so fragile and vulnerable because one has never bumped up against it and felt its resistance.

In response one might argue that this ruthless encounter with the other finds its place in Levinas in his account of the pre-doorbell state, as I have called it. But that is not right either. The pre-doorbell state is one of narcissistic unawareness of the other's difference. At its best this state comes close to what Winnicott calls a transitional state, in which one does not question differences too closely. In this state one does not yet fully know or recognize the otherness of the other. That takes an encounter marked by the ruthless use of the object, and it is this that Levinas seems to have no place for. Earlier I argued that for Levinas we move directly from babies to saints. It would be more accurate to state that we move from narcissists to moralists, so anxious that we will totalize others that we can barely let ourselves know the other qua other. This is what a relation without relation means. If we used the other more (use, not abuse), we might learn that the objective reality of the other is not quite so fragile as Levinas imagines.

Not so fragile as Levinas imagines, but still fragile. Though Winnicott is not just talking about mothers and babies, that remains his model, and we are all fortunate that babies cannot destroy everything they get their hands and mouths on. Adults can, and while Winnicott draws a sharp distinction between destruction in reality and in fantasy, it is not enough. As Levinas reminds us, the other *is* naked and vulnerable, and what is needed is a morality of ruthlessness, if I can put it that way.

Not the same as reparative morality, not even as elaborated by Wollheim, a morality of ruthlessness would know that we unavoidably engage the world in ways that use and even exploit it, taking from it what we need to survive, and learning in the process the reality of the other. Consider the difference between consensual sex and exploitative sex; both use the other, but only one respects the other while using him or her. Or consider the difference between corporate agriculture and organic farming. Or between hunting and fishing for food (or catch-and-release fishing) and the slaughter of animals. Or between strip mining and mining that protects and reclaims the land. The list goes on, the point being that the use of the object is bound up with what it is to be human in the world. Man's metabolism with nature, as Marx called it, is not confined to inhuman nature. We eat and breathe each other. What's needed is an ethic of limits and responsibility.

Levinas is helpful here, but not as helpful as he might be because there are really no limits for Levinas. If I owe you everything, if I'm responsible for your sins, if there is nothing I dare withhold, then it actually becomes more difficult to think about limits, above all the limits that circumscribe the necessary ruthlessness of life. Infinity is not a limit. Levinas' political theory, with its introduction of the third (*le tiers*), addresses this issue, as discussed in Chapter 4. But it does not address it in the spirit considered here, a morality of the inherent exploitation that is life. If Winnicott is correct, life is inherently exploitative not just because we use others to survive, but because in using others we discover they are real. Exploitation is the price of knowledge of the reality of others. Absent this knowledge, Levinas must work twice as hard to protect others, which is why he posits such a terrible distance between humans.

To all this the reader might respond that I am doing psychology, while Levinas is doing philosophy. In other words, Levinas is not concerned with the developmental experiences that lead to knowledge of others, but only with how we should approach them. There would be some truth to such a response, though it is the great virtue of Levinas that he refuses to practice this distinction, as Critchley argues in the passage quoted toward the end of Chapter 1. Nevertheless, my point in turning to Winnicott's account of the use of an object is not to say that he has it just right, but to compare two attitudes toward the world, attitudes as much philosophical as psychological.

The first attitude, which is shared by Levinas and Theodor Adorno, is marked by fear and trembling before the ego. Enraged at a world that forever remains beyond the grasp of its omnipotence, the ego would incorporate everyone and everything. To protect the world, distance must be created between ego and other, even at the cost of loneliness and alienation, lest ego devour the world. One might argue that this too sounds like what Winnicott is talking about, the ruthless use of the object. It is, but Winnicott assumes a certain *naïveté* on behalf of the subject. There is no anger in the destruction of the object, Winnicott assures us (1989b, pp. 245–6). Rather, the attitude is more akin to the naïve greed of the infant. There is an innocence about original sin, as the sinner does not yet know he or she is sinning. This aspect of the use of an object comes close to the attitude of the pre-doorbell state in Levinas, though one wonders whether Winnicott is too dedicated to the denial of sadistic motives, the pleasure in destruction.

The second attitude says that the reality of the other is made real for the subject through its greedy encounter with the other. Though others are fragile, they are not quite so fragile as Levinas and Adorno imagine, and so are often able to resist intrusion and destruction. When they do, joy happens: the subject feels in his or her bones the separate reality of the other, and so can engage and use the other in a responsible manner. This does not, *pace* Winnicott, happen automatically. It must become the subject of ethics, but it is an ethics that starts from an assumption that engagement and use are not necessarily exploitation of the object, and are often enjoyable for subject and object alike. One might argue that the difference here is strictly one of tone, and perhaps it is, but it is a difference in tone that makes all the difference in the world as to how one ethically situates oneself in the world.

Referring to Rainer Maria Rilke's *Raum* and *Welt*, Winnicott (1989b, p. 240) says,

Raum is an infinite space in which the individual can operate without passing through the risky experience of destruction and survival of the object; Welt is by contrast the world in so far as it has, by survival, become objectified by the individual, and to be used."[11]

We need both Raum and Welt. Levinas brilliantly deploys Raum in order to defend Welt, but one sometimes misses an encounter with Welt. Could Welt sometimes miss us in return? Could this mutual missing be the source of "there is?"

"THERE IS"

If a good philosopher is, as Iris Murdoch (1970b, p. 72) suggests, one who tells us about what he is most afraid, then Levinas is a great philosopher. Levinas is not just concerned about reducing the other to the same. Levinas is afraid that love for the being of another will trap the human in being. In one respect Levinas is absolutely right, of course, which is why Winnicott reflects one aspect of Levinas' project so brilliantly, but only one aspect.

Levinas is most afraid of what he calls "there is" (*il y a*). The temptation to treat "there is" as a psychological phenomenon is almost irresistible, though Levinas asks us to resist the temptation. Consider how Levinas evokes the experience of "there is."

> My reflection on this subject starts with childhood memories. One sleeps alone, the adults continue life; the child feels the silence of his bedroom as "rumbling." It is something resembling what one hears when one puts an empty shell close to the ear, as if the emptiness were full, as if the silence were a noise ... *Existence and Existents* tries to describe this horrible thing, and moreover describes it as horror and panic. (E&I, p. 48)

Though the idea of "there is" occurred to Levinas for the first time while he was in the stalag (Levinas was imprisoned in a camp for French officers during World War II), the experience evidently began in his childhood, during those long nights in which he could not fall asleep.

Should we resist the temptation to treat "there is" as a psychological phenomenon? Yes, we should resist the temptation to reduce "there is" to a psychological problem of Levinas, or of anyone else. But, no, we should not resist the temptation to see the experience of "there is" as a subjective experience, albeit one in which it is subjectivity itself that has fled. If "there is" is not a subjective experience of the loss of subjectivity, what else could it be?

Levinas insists that he is not writing of a psychological experience. "It is not a matter of 'states of the soul,' but of an end of objectivizing consciousness, a psychological inversion" (E&I, p. 50). "There is" is not a psychological phenomenon because all that makes an experience psychological, that is subjectively knowable, is overwhelmed with the dread of mere existence, mere being. The dread of existence is an end to objectivizing consciousness because consciousness has become objectified, a thing, like all the other things of the world. I becomes it. Not because another treats me as an it. Then at least I have something to fight for my subjectivity. But because I am absorbed into the it; or rather the it engulfs me.

Experiences of depersonalization and derealization, as psychoanalysts call them, would come close to what Levinas is talking about, even as these terms lack ontological weight (Moore and Fine 1990, p. 52). For Levinas the "there is" is not a dissociative defense against anxiety, but its source—the terrible burden of being, an "existing that occurs without us, without a subject, an existence without existence" (T&O, pp. 45–6). "Might one then infer that the *il y a* mimes the transcendence it occludes?" asks Edith Wyschogrod (2000, p. xiii). Yes. A reverse transcendence, "there is" displaces the emptiness left by the fugitive ego with the incessant murmur of being, an emptiness that would otherwise prepare us for the liberation of nothingness. The linguistic relationship between "there is" (*il y a*) and illeity (*illéité*), Levinas' pseudonym for God, supports this interpretation of *il y a* as the inversion of infinity.

Søren Kierkegaard writes that we dread "the presentiment of something that is nothing" (1957, p. 38). We dread nothingness, our own non-being, not just our death and dissolution, but the gaps in going-on-being about which Winnicott writes. Levinas is writing about an experience that is in important ways the opposite, the presentiment of nothing that is something, the absence of everything that returns as a presence that threatens to drown me in being (T&O, p. 46). Under the horizon of "there is," I become some thing.

"There is" is being without nothingness," says Levinas (T&O, p. 50). The experience of nothingness takes a self. So does Kierkegaard's dread, in which subjectivity itself is in danger. "There is" is prior to the experience of subjective emptiness and threatened dissolution, though exactly what Levinas means by "prior" is puzzling. Ontologically rather than historically prior is the way Levinas puts it, a formulation that will be examined shortly. Here it is best to linger with Levinas' phenomenology of "there is:"

One confronts this dread of being in experiences such as insomnia. In insomnia one can and one cannot say that there is an "I" which cannot manage to fall asleep. The impossibility of escaping wake-fulness is something "objective," independent of my initiative. This impersonality absorbs my consciousness; consciousness is depers-onalized. I do not stay awake: "it" stays awake ... In the maddening "experience" of the "there is," one has the impression of a total impossibility of escaping it, of "stopping the music." (E&I, p. 49)

The roar one hears when putting an empty shell to one's ear is another example of the same experience, says Levinas. It is almost as if one were hearing the echo of the horror of finding oneself being in the world. Not "being alone" in the world, just being—that is the true horror. "Being is evil (*mal*) not because it is finite but because it is without limits" (T&O, p. 51). Being just goes on and on, or so it seems when in the grip of "there is." "A night in a hotel room where, behind the partition, 'it does not stop stirring'; 'one does not know what they are doing next door.' This is something very close to the 'there is'" (E&I, p. 50). Would it be too simple to suggest that Levinas is talking about feeling unbearably lonely?

John Llewelyn (1995, p. 9) opens his book, *Emmanuel Levinas: The Genealogy of Ethics*, with these lines. "With hindsight it can be seen that the essay *On Evasion* published in 1935 announces the issue with which all Levinas' philosophical writings will be preoccupied: the issue of the issue from ontology."[12] By the issue of the issue from ontology Llewelyn means, of course, exit or outlet from the "brutal truth that there is being, *il y a de l'être*" (ibid., p. 11). Llewelyn titles the first chapter of his book "onto-logical claustrophobia," and the last chapter "ethical agoraphobia."[13] It is between these poles that Levinas' work lives. The last chapter of *Otherwise than Being* is titled simply "Outside."

We live our lives between claustrophobia and agoraphobia, between being crushed or dropped as Winnicott might put it, and Wilfred Bion (1984) did. What is problematic in Levinas is not the poles, but that there is so little time spent in the middle. The reason is evidently much to do with the sheer horror of the experience of "there is," but it is a horror made worse by the tendency to equate logical and psycho-logical experi-ence. I parse a statement of Levinas to make this point. It is from *De l'évasion*, which is best translated as *On Escape*. Not, insists Levinas, in the sense of escape from a bad lot in life, but from life itself:

1. "Existence is an absolute that affirms itself without referring itself to anything other. It is identity." From this experience of existence there can be no relatedness with others, for the self defines itself as itself, as in "A is A."

2. But man is of course not just a logical equation of identity. "His identity with himself loses the character of a logical or tautological form:

it takes on ... a dramatic form." Man confronts the drama of his life, which means that he is both audience and actor.

3. The drama man acts and observes suffering. "In the identity of the ego (*moi*), the identity of being reveals its nature as enchainment because it appears in the form of suffering."

4. This suffering "is an invitation to escape." We long to escape our suffering selves.

5. "So escape is the need to go out of itself, that is to say, to break the most radical, most irremissible enchainment, the fact that the ego is itself." (ibid., p. 73)

Does the conclusion not stem from the first premise? If man were not an identity unto himself (A = A), then the alternative would not be escape from being. The alternative would be relatedness, something like the relatedness that Winnicott writes about, a relatedness into which we are born. In fact, Levinas' position is more complicated. Being is identical with itself, and being is already outside itself, already longing for an exit, as though it were observing its own suffering from a distant star.

What human being is not for Levinas is one who is involved in conversation. In saying I expose myself to you, coming out from behind the little fortress of the said. But, never do we have a conversation, in which I allow you to enter me, knowing, fearing and hoping that you may change me forever. And you allow me to do the same. The term "conversation" comes from the Latin for convert, meaning to transform. In conversation, we open ourselves to being transformed by another. Is this not another way (the human way) to escape the entropy of "there is"? Is this not the conscious version of the unconscious wandering of other personalities into ourselves that Norman O. Brown writes of? In the case of conversation we invite them to visit.

De l'évasion, suggests Llewelyn (1995, p. 13), is not just an essay about escape. It is in some way a dramatic performance of what escape looks like. Others, including myself in the preceding section, have made this claim about Levinas. His obscure and prophetic formulations must be intended to keep the reader off balance, so that he or she can never be at home in the text. There is a place for this, of course, but it is well to remember that the first other is the reader, with whom one tries to have a conversation. We respect readers not just by keeping them off balance, but by trying to share experiences with them.

We never do, of course, not really. No one ever shares another's experience, and the distance between words and experiences is infinite (in something like the third sense of the term listed in Chapter 1). We can, however, try to evoke similar experiences in others, or else what is poetry for? In what follows I shall try to evoke experiences that resemble the dread of "there is," but whose origins more clearly refer to unrelatedness than identity. Or rather, I shall try to evoke experiences in which unrelatedness becomes identity. If this is the origin of "there is," then relatedness, rather than escape, becomes a solution.

"There is" stands closer to Winnicott's dread of "I AM" than first appears. The first experience that shows the connection is Thomas Ogden's account of losing the sensuous frame and form of experience. The second is Sartre's nausea.

Ogden, a psychoanalyst, tells the story of how he inadvertently destroyed the sensuous frame of experience. Sitting around after dinner one night, it suddenly occurred to Ogden how strange it was to call this thing in his lap a napkin, the conjunction of the terms "nap" and "kin."

> I repeated the two sounds over and over until I began to get the very frightening feeling that these sounds had no connection at all with this thing I was looking at. I could not get the sounds to naturally "mean" the thing they had meant only minutes before. The link was broken, and, to my horror, could not be mended simply by an act of will. I imagined that I could, if I chose to, destroy the power of any and all words to "mean" something if I thought about them one at a time in this way. (Ogden, 1989, p. 39)

Ogden tells this story to illustrate a type of anxiety he calls autistic-contiguous, in which the sensory floor of experience is lost. It is, he argues, the most primitive and primordial anxiety, the one that comes before all the rest. Ordinarily we think about primitive anxiety as the self becoming unglued, an experience associated with feelings of fragmentation and boundlessness. Levinas is writing about an experience that is in some ways the opposite, an experience of condensed being, as though one were a dark star sucking in all the matter in the universe.

It will not do to push the experience of "there is" into Ogden's framework, at least not yet, but it is worth noting the similarity. In both, the meaning of experience is lost because the capacity to feel a sensuous connection between self and experienced world is lost. In place of sensuous experience there is merely the experience of being: being absent the experience of being because no boundary or mediation between me and being remains. Not "I am being," but "being," is all that exists. In Sartre's language, I become like the objects of consciousness, the in-itself (*être-en-soi*).

Levinas said he first tried to deal with this horrifying experience (he means deal with it philosophically, but it is the beauty of Levinas that emotional experiences, insomnia, and philosophy often become one) by strategies that reconnect being to the world. "One refastens being to the existent" is how Levinas puts it, by which he means that one finds "an exit toward the world in knowledge." Trapped in the solitude of one's being, one tries to rejoin the larger world of being through knowledge of beings, that is, knowledge. It was not, says Levinas, a satisfactory solution. Every connection to a larger world felt like he was becoming more deeply enmeshed in the stickiness of mere being (E&I, pp. 51–2).

The resemblance to Roquentin's nausea in Sartre's novel of the same name is striking, especially when one considers that Levinas published *De l'évasion* three years before Sartre's *Nausea*. Roquentin is nauseated by the sheer thingyness of the Chestnut tree, or a glass of beer. The world becomes a swooning abundance of brute matter devoid of meaning. "To exist is simply to be there" says Roquentin, as his consciousness is inescapably drawn into the viscous, sticky world of things (Sartre, 1949, p. 179). Joining this world isn't the solution; it is the problem. Or as Levinas puts it, "it is not a matter of escaping from solitude, but rather of escaping *from being*" (E&I, p. 59, author's emphasis).

For Sartre (1956, pp. 221–3), the other is the death of me.[14] Levinas would agree. The difference is that for Levinas this is good. My death is my salvation, the death of my ego that opens me to infinity. Here finally is an exit from being, says Levinas, in an explicit reference to Sartre. Just answer the doorbell and it's there, relief from the horror of "condemnation to perpetual reality, to existence with 'no exits'" (Levinas, "There is," p. 34).

One can see the connection here between "there is" and what Levinas writes about as totalization, his philosophical *idée maîtresse*. Totalization means to bring everything under the horizon of the humanly knowable, as Western philosophy since Plato has done according to Levinas. Or as Roquentin puts it, "in vain I tried to count the Chestnut trees ... to compare their height with the height of the plane trees" (Sartre, 1949, p. 174). Roquentin tries, in other words, to subdue reality with the categories of his mind. Or consider Kant, for whom the basic categories that I discover in nature (the synthetic a priori) are really projections of human reason, the way the world must be, given humans as they are. For Levinas,

all Western thought is Kantian in this sense, an attempt to find the other
in the same (T&O, pp. 65–6).

We must reformulate the fundamental anxiety, as the phenomenologist
Alfred Schutz called it. This anxiety is not non-being. It is not fragmentation anxiety, or even Kierkegaard's dread. The fundamental anxiety
is not death. Hamlet, says Levinas, recoils not just against "not to be," but
also "to be," for he knows that mere being is already death ("There is," p.
33). The fundamental anxiety is mere being, being with no exit, being unto
eternity, being trapped in being. One would think that this would make
suicide an important option, a way out. Levinas does not agree. When one
is in the state of "there is," suicide is no option. Suicide is no option
because suicide assumes a tortured subjectivity rebelling against the pain
of an absurd existence. In the absence of subjectivity, not even suicide is
meaningful. Sunk deep in the experience of "there is," the real horror is
that not death but that life seems forever. The real horror is "the fact that
it is impossible to die" (T&O, pp. 50–1).

"There is" is inverted participation

Up until his rejection of the possibility of suicide, the reader believes that
Levinas' phenomenology of "there is," no matter how puzzling, is concerned with a real experience of actual humans. Now it is apparent that
"there is" is an abstraction, a perspective outside of lived human
experience. For individual humans do die (even if life does not, which is
evidently what Levinas means when he says it is impossible to die), and it
is hard to imagine an individual existence sunk so deeply in "there is" that
it cannot even contemplate suicide. Probably such existences occur. Perhaps the profoundly retarded or brain injured fall into this category,
existences in which it is meaningful to say that subjectivity has fled. But
these are exceptions. The rule is that suffering humans contemplate their
own demise, sometimes with relief. Xerxes, watching his Persian army
cross the Hellespont to invade Greece, pities the shortness of man's life,
that so many will soon die. No, King, responds Artabanus, his uncle,
"weep rather for this, that brief as life is there never yet was or will be a
man who does not wish more than once to die rather than to live"
(Herodotus, *Histories*, 7.46).

In fact, Levinas tells us that "there is" is an abstraction. We live as
though we were thrown into the midst of life, surrounded by others with
whom we are in constant contact. This is our history as humans. But it is

possible to stand back from the experience of life and imagine isolated existences, the experience that gives rise to "there is." "Let us imagine all things, being and persons, returning to nothingness. What remains after this imaginary destruction of everything is not something, but the fact that there is [il y a]" (T&O, p. 46).[15]

I'm disappointed. I thought the experience of "there is" was a description of experience, capturing feelings so profound yet subtle that only the finest novelists, such as Sartre and Maurice Blanchot, have been able to capture them. About absence, Blanchot (1995, p. 29) says it may return as an overwhelming presence, as though the absence of human relatedness were experienced not as nothing, but as the presence of some thing, as though I had become that thing.[16] I have to stretch myself to make sense of this experience, but when I think about how missing someone so bad can become a terrible weight, as though I were burdened by their absence, it makes sense. Now I find that the experience of "there is" is a phenomenological reduction, the abstraction of the philosopher who stands back not in order to better see life as it is lived, but to describe the essence of things, stripped of their inessential substance.

In fact, "there is" is both, philosophical abstraction and lived experience. One can hardly read Levinas' account of insomnia and not believe that "there is" captures a real horror of being. That Levinas began to write about this experience while a prisoner in the stalag is likely more than ironic. It was an act of imagination. Not an imagination that stripped away the inessential substance of things, but an imagination that grasped the emotional reality of the experience, what art and artists are for. Not only does Levinas frequently refer to artists such as Blanchot, Rimbaud, Huysmans, Zola, de Maupassant, Racine, and Shakespeare, when trying to explain the almost ineffable "there is," but his own evocations of "there is" are among his most artistic or literary passages ("There is," pp. 32–4). This, though, is not quite what it seems. The imagination of art, even his own, is no unalloyed virtue for Levinas.

One might be tempted to think of art and "there is" as opposites: art is concerned with the soaring imagination, "there is" with reification, as though imagination were trapped in being. In fact, both art and "there is" are instances of what Lévy-Bruhl calls participation, in which says Levinas, "the identity of the terms is lost. They are divested of what constituted their very substantivity ... The private existence of each term ... loses this private character and returns to an undifferentiated background ... We recognize here the *there is*" ("There is," p. 32).

One sees this particularly in Levinas' fascination with Shakespeare. As

Robbins (1999, p. 96) puts it, "it is in Shakespearean tragedy ... that Levinas finds the inability to escape from being, from anonymous existence, the nocturnal horror of the return of presence in negation, the return of phantasms, shadows, and ghosts."

If Levinas draws upon some of the richest literary imaginations in the world (including his own) to explain and explore "there is," then "there is" is hardly a brutal one-dimensional experience, like being reduced to a block of being. "There is" is instead an act of inverted participation. Rather than feeling enhanced by my participation in the cosmos, a type of religious experience that Freud (1961, p. 11) called oceanic, I feel threatened, as though I risked becoming as thingish as the things around me, what Sartre calls nausea. Nausea is participation in the realm of things. Nausea is inverse participation, in which things participate in me before I can participate in them.

Since Levinas is no fan of participation, regarding it as an act of ethical irresponsibility, one wonders whether Levinas brings "there is," understood as an act of inverse participation, on himself. Does the horrifying centrality of "there is" in Levinas' experience have something to do with his way of approaching the world, a way that denies satisfying experiences of participation? Is the inverse participation of "there is" the revenge of non-participation, or just its failed substitute?

Recall Ogden's account of losing the sensuous frame and form of experience, in which he could not connect the thing called napkin with the word that represents it. He calls this experience autistic-contiguous. Autistic refers to the experience of being closed up within oneself, similar to what Levinas calls "there is." Contiguous refers to proximity, contact between surfaces that is more than contact, but a shared boundary. Contiguous refers to an experience akin to participation. In his experience with the napkin, Ogden lost the balance, as though he were unable to emerge from himself to make contact with the intersubjective symbolic world. The result was dread and terror, in which not just words but being loses its meaning.

While autistic-contiguous experience may be dreadful, it is also the source of life and aliveness. Imagine, says Ogden (1989, pp. 30–46), an experience like that of two skins touching, except that instead of one skin touching the other the experience is of two surfaces whose contact creates one reality, shared skin. Imagine sitting in your chair and feeling neither the chair nor the pressure on your buttocks, but simply "impression," a feeling with no inside, no outside, and no locus. That is autistic-contiguous experience. Doesn't it sound like what Levinas calls being? Not

"I am being," just "being," with no distinction between me and the experience, so that I am lost to the experience.

Autistic-contiguous experience is a realm of meaning and immediacy beyond, or beneath words. It is the realm of bodily experience so immediate and so real that the distinction between bodily and symbolic experience is transcended, though perhaps undermined would be a better term. The paradigm of autistic-contiguous experience is the mother–infant bond, the infant unaware of where its surface ends and mother's begins, aware only of a boundary that is not so much a boundary as an experience, an experience of the other that is at once an experience of itself, an "impression," a shape without a frame because it is without location. If we did not have autistic-contiguous experience to draw upon all the rest of our lives, there would be something hollow and missing in life, a world of symbols whose connection to felt meaning would be obscure. Autistic-contiguous experience is the source of (or rather, is another way of describing) that feeling Winnicott calls going–on–being. Autistic-contiguous experience is rhythmic participation in the world. Autistic-contiguous experience is what I was referring to, at the end of the section on Winnicott, when I wondered if the source of "there is" might lie in the world (*Welt*) missing our participation in it.

Most religious experiences, the experiences that Freud called oceanic, experiences that are called transcendent, experiences that share a fuzzy boundary between you, me and infinity: all have their origin in autistic-contiguous experience. Autistic-contiguous experience is the source of what Lévy-Bruhl calls participation. Autistic-contiguous experience is woven experience, as Plato's Stranger (*Sophist*, 260a) calls it, inside and outside braided together a thousand times, so we no longer know which is which, as though we wove a Möbius strip with our lives. Or as Levinas puts it, in the experience of the infinite "one is ousted from his interiority as an ego and a 'being with two inner sides' " (*Of God*, p. 73).

Who is this being with two innersides? Those hermaphrodites who Zeus sliced in two according to Aristophanes' account in Plato's *Symposium*, suddenly confronted with an inside become an outside. Is not Levinas' philosophy a version of Zeus', cleaving humankind in two, separating the halves utterly, so that they will never have that source of autistic-contiguous satisfaction again? If so, then "there is" must be humankind's revenge, misdirected against itself. In choosing feeling real over truth as the highest value, Winnicott recognizes the mortal danger of this revenge to every human project.

If "there is" is autistic-contiguous experience tilted too far in the direction of the autistic dimension, then one must wonder whether Levinas' rejection of participation, experiences tilted in the direction of contiguity, does not help to bring on "there is."[17] Is not "there is" an experience of life bereft of the satisfactions of participation? If this argument is correct, then Levinas has made a mistake, imagining that the cure of "there is" is an exit from being, rather than a reconnection with the meaning of being, above all one's own lived experience of being, contiguous satisfaction, what Winnicott calls feeling real. Otherwise expressed, Levinas imagines that infinity is somewhere beyond being, rather than in, under, around, and through being. Infinity means unbounded. That does not have to mean the distant universe. Infinity is as close as the autistic-contiguous position, concerned with experiences beyond being— that is without a locus in being, like the impression that is neither buttocks nor chair that Ogden writes about, just impression. What a funny place to find infinity.

Consider how Bernet (2000) characterizes what Levinas calls proximity, the experience of the other. Bernet starts from Lacan's characterization of my body as "a bag of skin" (*sac de peau*).

> My skin is thus no ordinary bag, but a twisted surface where the inside is an outside, in the manner of a Moebius strip ... This appeal [of the other] pierces my skin in a way that I am turned inside out, depriving my interiority of its protective skin ... When skins are pierced on both sides and when fronts are overrun, it clearly makes no sense to continue to consider the encounter between two people as a matter of two opposites meeting ... This is why Levinas instead speaks of the Other's "proximity" to me, making clear at once that this does not mean a "fusion" between him and me. This proximity does away with distance and protection, with opposition and confrontation, but not with difference and separation. It leads to a mode of encounter that is necessarily traumatic because it is immediate, that is, without mediation of any sort. (ibid., pp. 47–52)

It is not just Bernet who evokes the language of skinship to characterize the encounter with the other. Levinas writes about proximity in similar terms, such as "a caress surprising itself to be a palpitation." Proximity is "the immediacy of a skin and a face, a skin which is always a modification of a face, a face that is weighted down with skin" (OB, pp. 82–5). "Weighted down" because the face is not just the human face, but the all too fleshy mirror of infinity. Earlier, in *De l'évasion*, Levinas wrote of a *"mal dans sa peau,"* a sickness of being inside one's skin.

The experience of proximity about which Levinas writes is another dimension of autistic-contiguous experience. Instead of leading to dread of mere being, this dimension of autistic-contiguous experiences connects meaning and being, telling me the meaning of my life: to serve the other, which means to be inspired by an experience of otherness that runs through me, becomes me, is me.

Infinity, it appears, cuts both ways. Understood as an experience of otherness and separation, even from myself, infinity may open me up to a world beyond myself. One might even call this opening up a type of participation. Too much otherness and separation, however, and I find it hard to breathe. The infinity that promises an exit from "there is" by creating gaps in my going on being instead creates such a void that I must devote myself to holding myself together at the cost of feeling alive. The gap between breathing in and out becomes terrifying, and I must hold myself together in order to keep the increasingly frequent gaps in being from overtaking the meaning of my life (OB, p. 109). I succeed, life goes on, but in devoting myself to holding myself together I lose the animating connection between psyche and soma, the vitality of the autistic-contiguous position. The result is "there is," mere being.

Levinas does not see it this way. For Levinas (and this is his leading dichotomy in an opus built on dichotomies), infinity is the opposite of "there is." Infinity breaks me open, and so saves me from suffocating in my own bag of skin. But consider the twofold way in which Levinas writes about insomnia. When writing about "there is," Levinas writes of insomnia as the senseless buzzing of being, consciousness without subjectivity (E&I, p. 49). But he also writes about insomnia as a type of "ecstasy" that is utterly open to otherness because it neither knows nor categorizes, but just is, waiting for nothing (*Of God*, pp. 58–9). In fact, insomnia is both, on the border between heaven and hell, the two dimensions of autistic-contiguous experience.

Which way we go depends on who is in bed with us, and whether they reach over and touch us in their sleep. I make this last statement in the spirit of Norman O. Brown, referring not just to real bed mates, but to all who have ever touched our souls. They remain in us, helping to shield us from infinity, even as their absence reveals (or rather is) infinity to us, the only infinity we can ever truly know, the non-being of those who have been being. Levinas suggests that infinity is a middle-ground between the philosophy of transcendence and a philosophy of immanence, a "beyond-within" (*au-delà-dans*) that he is trying to claim. Infinity could be this middle ground if it were conceived as known through experiences of death and loss, experiences that humans best encounter with their arms around each other. But this is not how Levinas writes about infinity.[18]

Wyschogrod is not mistaken to see "there is" as an inversion of infinity, though that is not quite right either. Not an inversion of infinity, but too much infinity too close, too much inhuman otherness too close to the center of my existence: this is the source of "there is." "There is" is infinity too large and too close to endure. "Beauty is nothing but the beginning of terror that we are still just able to bear," says Rainer Maria Rilke.[19] As the experience of infinity is akin to the experience of the sublime, we may say much the same about infinity. Only at a distance is infinity *deinos*, that marvelous Greek term that means both wonderful and terrible. Like death, which is its avatar, too much infinity too close is hell.

"There is" is an experience of infinity in the absence of someone with his or her arms around us, as Winnicott puts it. We ordinarily think about experiences like this as experiences of dissolution and panic, the self falling apart. In some ways that would be better. "There is" is the defense against dissolution and panic become a way of life, a way of being, the psyche holding itself so rigidly there is no room left for life. If this is so, then Levinas is not all wrong in thinking that the solution is exit. He is not all wrong, because exit involves giving oneself over to the terror, rather than mortifying one's being against it. This is, I believe, what Blanchot (1995, p. 41) means when he says that the danger is that the disaster will acquire meaning instead of body. To feel the body of the disaster—the disaster of being—is to feel alive, not deadened, by the wonder and the horror (*deinos*) of living. To feel the body of the disaster requires, I would add, that there be other bodies around us.

EROS STRONG AS DEATH

Because Levinas puts so much distance between me and other bodies, the experience of infinity risks flirting with death. One sees this flirtation not just in Levinas' idealization of what Freud (1924) calls moral masochism, the glorification of guilt and subjugation for the purpose of erasing the self, but in the way in which the desire for goodness beyond being comes so close to death. If I reach out to caress the voluptuous other, but am really seeking to touch infinity, then why not just cut out the middleman, or woman (T&I, pp. 257–8)? Seen from this perspective, Levinas' masochism is actually a moral principle, the only way in which participation in autistic-contiguous satisfaction may be ethically experienced: as another's hostage. Hostage-being provides some of the satisfactions of participation, while keeping me chained to this world—and in this life—through my duties and responsibilities to others. There are worse ways to live, and probably better ones too.

"Eros, strong as death" says Levinas. Though he does not tell us so, he is quoting from the Song of Songs (8:6).[20] Levinas means that love, like death, seeks infinity. Because the other is so other, to love another is like death (T&O, p. 76). But this is not the meaning of the phrase in the Song of Songs. There "love, strong as death" refers to the way in which passion makes us feel so real and alive that sometimes it seems as if our love could conquer death, even though we know it cannot. In the Song of Songs, love is opposed to death. Not in Levinas. In fact, Levinas is not just quoting from the Song of Songs. He is quoting from *The Star of Redemption*, where Rosenzweig (1985, p. 156) makes much of this passage. But Rosenzweig's point is similar to my own. Love feels so real and powerful that it "knows solely the present," and in that sense feels stronger than death—that is, love allows us to feel that the present will exist forever. It is Levinas, not Rosenzweig, who turns love toward death.

About the love of death in Levinas, Jeffrey Bloechl (2000, p. 149) concludes that "ethics ... has as much to do with *limiting* a desire beyond being as it does with keeping that desire in view." One limits this desire, one limits any desire, by giving it a frame and form, precisely what autistic-contiguous experience as transcendence does. The form is the human form, the body in all its guises, whose sheer immediacy is as close as we shall get to infinity in this life. In his phenomenology of the nude woman, Levinas seems to know this. But like so many, like Plato, he wants more from eros than it can give. It may be the great delusion of Western thought that intense experiences of living point to a reality beyond themselves.

If eros cannot carry us everywhere we want to go, it may be able to transport us to more places than we can imagine, places that have the transitional quality that Winnicott writes of. Consider Luce Irigaray's (1991) essay "Questions to Emmanuel Levinas: On the Divinity of Love." Levinas, she says:

> knows nothing of communion in pleasure ... For Levinas, the dis-
> tance is always maintained with the other in the experience of
> love ... This autistic, egological, solitary love does not correspond to

the shared outpouring, to the loss of boundaries which take place for both lovers when they cross the boundary of the skin into the mucous membranes of the body, leaving the circle which encloses my solitude to meet in a shared space, a shared breath, abandoning the relatively dry and precise outlines of each body's solid exterior to enter a fluid universe where the perception of being two persons (*de la dualité*) becomes indistinct. (ibid., pp. 110–11)

Irigaray wonders if it is because Levinas is a man that he cannot conceive of the joys of fluidity, "of pleasures neither mine nor thine" (ibid., p. 111). For Levinas, the pleasures of fluidity and mixing come only when a son is born, a being both father and not father at the same time. Or at least that is what Levinas says. "My child is a stranger (Isaiah 49), but a stranger who is not only mine, for he *is* me" (T&I, p. 267). It is actually the criticism of some feminists, such as Irigaray and Chalier (1991), that comes closest to my own.

While we see the mingling to which Irigaray refers most dramatically in sexual intercourse between man and woman, it is everywhere humans have intercourse. Mingling comes close to the experience that Ogden calls autistic-contiguous. It is the experience that Irigaray calls communion. Sublimated, attenuated, and moderated, this experience is the ground of ethics. Only of course it is no ground at all. That's exactly the wrong metaphor. It is the fluid, flowing, non-ground of the human experience of each other in love and hate. Otherwise expressed, the experience of communion is the source of "love thy neighbor," and probably "hate thy neighbor" too, as others come to represent the bad and disowned parts of ourselves. Splitting and even the purification of boundaries are necessary, lest others be experienced as extensions of ourselves. Here Levinas has made a great contribution. Ethics is as much or more about separation and difference as it is connection. Above all, ethics is about the delicate dance of both. Because he distrusts attunement and rhythm, Levinas does not dance.

THE PRACTICE OF LEVINASSIAN ANALYSIS

What would a psychotherapy inspired by Levinas look like? Fortunately, we do not have to guess. Separated by over two decades, a pair of Levinassians has developed the implications of Levinas' theory for therapy (Halling, 1975; Kunz, 1998).[21] Both reflect an early moment in the reception of Levinas, when he was still considered a phenomenologist, busy reconstituting the character of intentionality so as to leave room for the experience of the other. As the date of Kunz's book reveals, this early moment in Levinas studies is still very much alive (even as it has become insupportable since Derrida's intervention), in good measure because it paints a picture of Levinas as one who has combined humanism with respect for the otherness of the other human. It's a fine ideal. It's just not Levinas.

I admire the *naïveté* of Halling and Kunz. A *naïve* reinterpretation of Levinas is my aim too. But, there is no virtue in *naïveté* for its own sake. We must become subtle and sophisticated in order to be truly *naïf*.

Interpolating interpretations of Levinas with brief case studies of therapeutic encounters, Halling (1975) writes as if Levinas were advising us to appreciate the otherness of particular others.

"His [Levinas'] writing can be characterized as presenting a philosophy of intersubjectivity and of ethics directed to our encounters with concrete others in our daily world." (ibid., pp. 206–7)
"It is only when I respond to the other as an integral person that I am face-to-face with him." (ibid., p. 210)
"I believe he [Levinas] is here referring to human separateness and independence." (ibid., p. 211)
"It is as I am secure in my identity that I can genuinely move towards the Other in what Levinas calls desire." (ibid., p. 211)
"What Levinas wants to emphasize is that ethics is a relationship with someone exterior to me, in other words, ethics arises in a genuine relationship." (ibid., p. 216)
"The therapy situation may be one place where we can hope for genuine discourse to take place." (ibid., p. 221)
"As I understand him, Levinas is not saying that in the face of the Other, the Same becomes meek, tame, or subdued. These three adjectives are still within the notion of a power relationship where the Other controls and dominates." (ibid., p. 215)

Halling has transformed the other into a full partner in the therapeutic dialogue, transforming an ego-shattering experience of the infinite into a mutually rewarding encounter between independent, autonomous individuals, each secure in him or her self. Halling gets Levinas quite wrong, of course. Against any attempt to talk of the face as though it were a real human face, Levinas says simply "the face is signification, and signification without context" (E&I, p. 86). The face of the other is not an invitation to a relationship based upon deep appreciation of the unique otherness of the particular other. The face is a synonym for the shattering experience of infinity.

Demonstrating that Halling gets Levinas wrong is easy. The tough question is whether Halling's is a useful mistake. Could the abstract face about which Levinas writes inspire our relationship with real others, as it inspires Halling? Yes, but it is hard to imagine that this inspired relationship with real others would look very different from the relationships characterized by Halling, relationships deeply attuned to the particularity of others. If so, then what does Levinas add? Doesn't he really subtract, turning us away from the appreciation of particular others to an idea of the other?

The next chapter considers this possibility, turning first to Murdoch's invocation of "just love," a love of the particular reality of the other person, and then to Adorno's metaphysics of particularity, if that is not an oxymoron. Here let us consider the improbable proposition that it is the obscure and prophetic style of Levinas that may be his greatest gift to therapy. Designed, evidently, to prevent the saying from immediately congealing into the said, Levinas' style intentionally keeps the reader off balance. If we have to think about what Levinas is saying, if he puzzles and disturbs us, then a breach arises between the saying and the said, allowing the saying to linger for a moment before becoming the word. In this breach I may come to doubt all that I believe is true, above all that I exist as a free and independent being. That doubt would be real progress.

A Levinassian analyst might try to achieve a similar result with a comparable but less turgid style. Think here of the style of Winnicott rather than Freud, of playfulness rather than interpretation. Or think of the Zen master who tells his pupil "don't cling ... and don't cling to not clinging." Some of the therapeutic encounters described by Mark Epstein (1995) in *Thoughts Without a Thinker: Psychotherapy from a Buddhist Perspective* come close to this ideal. Don't interpret, don't intrude, and resist being intruded upon. Resist merger, but don't make a fetish of it either. Listen carefully; be abundantly present and totally vulnerable. Relentlessly persecute your own narcissism, your own will to know, your will to make sense of the other's experience. Resist even your desire (how do you know it is not your will?) to make the other better. Wilfred Bion's (1984, pp. 143–6) suggestion to approach the analytic hour without memory or desire captures something of this perspective.

From the perspective of Levinas, the therapeutic goal is not to refound or reground or integrate the self. The goal is to find productive—that is, involved with other humans—ways to give oneself away. One lives most vividly and freely by serving the other: above all other people, but also the other in me, for example a gift for music or art, which is often first encountered as an alien presence.[22] About the vitality that stems from giving oneself to others, Kunz's (1998) reinterpretation of Levinas' teaching as popular psychology in *The Paradox of Power and Weakness: Levinas and an Alternative Paradigm for Psychology* is just right, and a great contribution, more valuable than a hundred dense academic tracts. Where Kunz and other followers of Levinas have faltered is only in failing to understand how close Levinas' cure comes to death.

But even Levinas' flirtation with death looks a little different from the perspective of therapy, that is a living relationship. From the perspective of therapy, the self-sacrifice that Levinas endorses may be read as a prescription for the analyst, even the philosophical analyst, the one who would try to know reality in all its guises. The task of the analyst is to subdue his or her will. The persecution of the narcissism of the I, as Levinas puts it, means to abandon one's will: the will to power, the will to meet totalization with totalization, including the will to show how much one knows, how great one's insight is. Instead, one is passive, resisting destruction while not retaliating.

If psychoanalysis were politics, this strategy would be called passive resistance. If this saying of the analyst could be transformed into the said, it would read something like this. "Behold, I am here for you, naked and alone. You may do to me (in fantasy and in words) anything you wish, but in the end you will learn that it does not satisfy. But I will not teach you this with words or interpretations, only by my remaining other, a mystery to you, as you are to me." In putting these words into the mouth of my imaginary Levinassian analyst, I am borrowing them from Winnicott, imagining what he would say to one who seemed to believe he had to destroy the analyst in order to know him as a separate being.

People are always complaining, says Levinas, that they cannot get close to other people. "The themes of solitude and the breakdown in human communication are viewed by modern literature and thought as the fundamental obstacle to universal brotherhood" ("Other Proust," p. 164). Forget about trying to get close, Levinas responds. Try to get more distant! Get far enough away to feel awe at the sheer otherness of another person. Then maybe you will feel the wonder of a world filled with others. It's good advice, as long as we understand it in human terms.

What do I mean by "human terms?" Especially since I argue that

Halling understands Levinas in all too human terms. Consider Thomas Wall's (1999, pp. 32–3) characterization of the encounter with the other in terms of a relationship older than the relationship to the self, with one who has already sunk into the self, prior to any memory or repression, a relationship with one who makes the self possible. To think in these terms is fruitful, not just about one's parents, who were there first, but about everyone we meet. People slip inside before we know them outside, and one of the marks of maturity is that we come to some awareness of this, responding as best we can to others' reality, not our fantasy. This is what Murdoch means by just love.

It is not what Wall means, as he goes on to argue that the essence of the encounter with the other is an encounter with nothingness. The fact that the other is in me before I am means that I am nothing (Wall, 1999, pp. 43–4). No, the fact that the other is in me before I am aware of myself means that I am a mix, an unstable compound, each part of me twinned with another part that is more another than myself, at least at first. The self is complex, a house of many mansions, and that's my point. Inspired by Levinas, but perhaps not reading Levinas in all his complexity, Wall would grossly simplify the self: either it is all self or all other, and hence nothing. Not simplification, but separation, a gentle teasing apart of the unstable compounds that compose the self, is the goal.

My concept of the self as paired with its objects, as analysts call them, mainly aspects of other people, is inspired by Otto Kernberg's (1985, pp. 315–6) definition of the self. From this perspective, the self is composed of countless pairs of affect-filled representations of the self in interaction with others: real others, imaginary others, but always aspects of others, never their complex reality. The goal of self-development is not to sever these pairs, but to loosen the bonds that bind the twins. Not Zeus' cleaver, but Penelope's scrupulous unraveling, would become the metaphor for psychoanalysis.

For Levinas, the leading metaphor for psychoanalysis is the saying of the mother, a motto that comes a little closer to Zeus than Penelope, but just a little. Jacques Lacan (1977, p. 66) writes about the "law of the father," by which he refers to the Oedipal father, who enforces limits and boundaries. Under the "law of the father," saying becomes the said, the relationship of prohibition put into words and limits. "Thou shalt not. . . ." It's an important role, but it is not the leading role in Levinassian analysis.

For Levinas the saying of the mother is the starring role. It is the encounter with the (m)other, who is there for me and at the same time infinitely other that throws my ego into chaos. I cannot totalize her, and I cannot abandon her either. Somehow I must come to terms with an other who is not me, and in the process I become both less and more than myself.

We need both mothers and fathers, of course, and the dialectic of saying and said is the provision of maternity and paternity. What would be mistaken is to imagine that the analyst mother is somehow less other than the more distant analyst father. They are equally other, otherness in different dimensions. In some ways, the otherness of the saying of the mother is actually more striking. We expect the father, the book, and the law to be other. We do not expect it of the saying of the mother, which is why it is so striking, an intimacy without closeness. Isn't this just the right language to describe the therapeutic relationship? For Levinas, it is the right language to describe every relationship.

3

Murdoch, Adorno, and Levinas

A book comparing Adorno and Levinas was published several years ago. For both authors, enlightened reason is a recipe for totalization and in this regard their comparison seems apt, if not obvious. The same cannot be said of Levinas and Murdoch. What an unlikely comparison, the reader may be saying to him or herself. In fact, I compare Levinas and Murdoch for the same reason and along the same lines as Levinas and Adorno. Murdoch too is a critic of totality. Not reason, but narcissism and convention, are the source of totalization in Murdoch's account. In other words, she is a more practical critic of totality, but that does not make her criticism any less profound. Only in intellectual style is she more removed from Levinas than Adorno.

"What breaks the drive of consciousness to totality is not an appeal to an abstract social or linguistic whole, but an encounter with the concrete other person." Levinas did not say this, nor did Iris Murdoch. Maria Antonaccio (2000, pp. 181, 223) says it in a book about Murdoch, in which she compares Murdoch's views to those of Levinas. What they share, says Antonaccio, is this critique of totality, even if "Murdoch would reject the language of command, lordship and accusation that pervade Levinas' account. . . "

Certainly Levinas' language of persecution is one of the most striking aspects of his account, and I do not ignore it. But it is not the most important thing that distinguishes him from Murdoch. One might argue that it is the "concrete other person" that distinguishes Levinas from Murdoch, for in many respects the other is an abstraction for Levinas. This distinction comes closer to capturing the difference between them. My goal is to better understand Levinas by comparing him with Murdoch. This requires that Murdoch's philosophy be seriously considered, though perhaps not as seriously as that of Levinas. Murdoch is the other, Levinas the subject. Possibly we will end up understanding the other better than the subject. Especially when the other takes pains to be transparent.

Murdoch's focus on the sheer reality of the other person reveals her to be no object relations theorist. On the other hand, we should not make too much of object relations' neglect of reality for fantasy. The first object relations theorist, Melanie Klein (1975a), argued that the depressive position begins with the recognition that the mother we would destroy in our fantasies is a real person who cares for us. To know this reality is to know the most important thing, the thing that might make us moral. Winnicott makes a similar point regarding the use of the object. It would be quite mistaken to imagine that psychoanalysis in general, or object relations theory in particular, values fantasy over reality. On the contrary, it is the contribution of object relations theory to show how hard it is to enter into and remain in contact with reality. Reality is depressing (in Klein's sense of emotional integration) which is why we should stay there.

It is difficult, says Murdoch (1970b, p. 72), when doing philosophy to know if one is saying something public and objective, or whether one is merely erecting a barrier against one's own fears. "It is always a significant question to ask about any philosopher: what is he afraid of?" For Levinas, the answer is "there is." Murdoch makes a good point, but the question seems a little more complicated. Not what is the philosopher afraid of, but how do the philosopher's fears resonate with those of his or her readers? A public and objective philosophy is not one without fears, but one that shares the fears of the public. Fortunately, both Levinas and Murdoch are quite up-front about their fears. On the surface they look similar: fears of vanity and narcissism, the self trapped in its own little world. Not the fear, but the defense, if I may call it that, is what separates them. I prefer Murdoch's defense, not because it is more effective in reducing the anxiety of Murdoch and her readers, but because it fosters a richer and more humane existence. Levinas is, of course, not interested in a richer and more humane existence, but a more meaningful one, dedicated to eternity. That is not my choice, but it is one that I admire. Not the superiority of Murdoch's choice, but what the difference between them reveals about Levinas is my concern.

IRIS MURDOCH: LOVE'S KNOWLEDGE

For Murdoch, the leading moral problem is the tendency of the ego to erase the reality of others. Her solution is love. "Love is the perception of individuals. Love is the extremely difficult realisation that something other than oneself is real" (Murdoch, 1999a, p. 215). Already we see evidence of how similar, and how different, Murdoch is from Levinas. The problem is the same, the problem that both define in terms of the "drive of consciousness to totality." But Murdoch's solution comes close to a solution Levinas rejects, knowledge of the real world of others.[1]

"The central concept of morality," says Murdoch, "is 'the individual' thought of as knowable by love" (1970b, p. 30). The goal is to see the other person justly, honestly, and compassionately. Doing so means moving away from universality and principles, and toward increasing depth, privacy, and particularity. Murdoch illustrates her argument with a story about a mother reflecting on her son's choice of a wife. The mother feels hostile toward her daughter-in-law, whom she finds common and unpolished, lacking in dignity and refinement. Her son, she is sure, has married beneath himself. The mother, always correct, nonetheless behaves beautifully toward her daughter-in-law. Time passes, and mother decides it is time to reevaluate her position. Her daughter-in-law, she discovers, is not really vulgar, but refreshingly simple, not undignified, but spontaneous. The mother's conduct never changed; she was always and continues to be perfectly correct. But the mother has gone on a moral journey, a pilgrimage of the soul (Murdoch, 1970b, pp. 17–23).

The question of whether mother's new vision of her daughter-in-law is in fact more accurate does not arise for Murdoch. Not the correspondence of the mother's vision with some objective reality, but the ability of the mother-in-law to overcome narcissism and convention, and thus see the other more clearly is at stake. Instead of the term narcissism, Murdoch uses the term "neurosis," but she means the same thing. Neurosis refers to "fantasies that inflate the importance of the self and obscure the reality of others." Convention refers to the tendency of the individual to become "sunk in a social whole which we allow uncritically to determine our reactions, or because we see each other exclusively as so determined" (1999a, p. 216). Both narcissism and convention acted as barriers to the mother-in-law's perception of her daughter, though in what mix is impossible to tell.

Narcissism and convention are barriers to loving knowledge. "The enemies of art and of morals, that is the enemies of love, are the same: social convention and neurosis" (ibid.). Both obscure our vision of the particular other, what Murdoch calls "attention," a term she draws from Simone Weil "to express the idea of a just and loving gaze directed upon an individual reality" (Murdoch, 1970b, p. 34).

Compare this simple story with Levinas' story about answering the doorbell. The most obvious difference is that for Murdoch the particular other is important. The goal of morality is to know the unique other person. Murdoch does not say serve the other, but since this knowledge is impossible absent a love of the particular other, one can hardly imagine that it could be used to exploit the other, at least not intentionally. This, of course, is the problem. Must any contact with the real other exploit the other? If our answer is yes, then what sort of human relationships shall we have in this world?

For Murdoch, the closer I get to the separate reality of the other person, the harder it becomes to treat the other as thing. Of course, getting close to the separate reality of the other person requires a type of stepping back as well: from myself, my vanity, and my needs, as well as from a certain type of dense attachment to the other. What is needed is "just love," in the double sense of the term: a loving attention to the other person that is not so in thrall to the other that it cannot see clearly.

What Murdoch means by "just love" comes close to what Martha Nussbaum means by "love's knowledge." Imagine, says Nussbaum (1990, p. 41), that Peter is the most important person in the world for Joan. You know this because she has told you this many times over lunch. Suddenly Peter dies, and Joan just goes on with her life, hardly pausing to go to the funeral. You would have to say (unless you think Joan was lying) that Joan does not yet really "know" that Peter has died, and that it will take a while for the knowledge to sink in. When it does she will be devastated. Certain types of knowledge, it appears, are inseparable from love. As Plato points out in the *Symposium* and *Phaedrus*, one must love well to know wisely, and vice versa.

"The highest love is in some sense impersonal," continues Murdoch. Not in the Kantian sense, which prefers good will to attachment. Love remains "the general name for the quality of attachment" (Murdoch, 1970b, pp. 75, 103). What is wanted is a quality of attachment which sees the imperfections of self and other clearly and still loves. She finds the epitome of this love in great art. "The realism of a great artist is not a photographic realism, it is essentially both pity and justice" (ibid., p. 87). Pity and justice not just for the subject, she might have added, but for the human race.

Is not Murdoch talking about something vague and imprecise? Yes, as vague and imprecise as human relations in all their complexity, as vague and imprecise as just love. But, if just love is difficult to define, it is not difficult to tell stories about. Murdoch's 26 novels are just that, stories about how hard it is to just love, how easy it is to miss the mark as Rupert does in *A Fairly Honourable Defeat*. "Rupert didn't love goodness. He loved a big imposing good-Rupert image" (1970a, p. 428).[2] For Murdoch the leading virtue is humility, by which she does not mean speaking softly and shrinking into the corner, but a selfless respect for reality, "one of the most difficult and central of all virtues" (Murdoch, 1970b, p. 95). Murdoch is about as vague and imprecise as Aristotle. Both are concerned with cultivating virtue, something that cannot be readily defined, even as it is fairly easy to identify the extremes. The difference, of course, is what the virtues look like. For Murdoch (1970b, p. 87), *arete* is seeing clearly and responding justly. That requires putting myself, my vanity, and my consoling fantasies into the background.

Murdoch writes as Levinas might if Levinas were interested only in overcoming totality, not in cultivating infinity. More precisely put, she writes as Levinas might write if he thought one could do the former in the absence of the latter, as if overcoming totality were a strictly mundane task. Does this make Murdoch and Levinas similar or worlds apart? Could they be both at once? They come closest in Murdoch's reinterpretation of Kant's account of the sublime, but only before going off in different directions.

For Kant, beauty results from a harmony between imagination and understanding, whereas sublimity results from a conflict between imagination and reason. The sublime shatters human categories, which is why Kant thought the experience was most likely to occur in our encounters with nature. Like Levinas, Murdoch is not impressed with natural beauty, except as it distracts us from our egos. The true experience of the sublime, says Murdoch, is "not of physical nature, but of our surroundings as consisting of other individual men." What ruptures our preshrunk categories is not the Grand Canyon at sunset, but "the spectacle of human life" in all its manifold and amazing diversity and particularity (Murdoch, 1999b, p. 282). The sublime is close at hand, if only we would but look. Close at hand, but never within our grasp, the sublime is most fully experienced in the disturbing recognition that "others are, to an extent we never cease discovering, different from ourselves" (1999a, p. 216).

More than one student of Levinas has seen the connection between Kant's account of the sublime as that experience that ruptures human categories and Levinas' account of the experience of the other (Dalton). Like Murdoch, Levinas transforms the experience of the sublime into an experience of other people. There they diverge, Levinas far less interested in the concrete reality of the other person, whose fleshy reality can only get in the way of transcendence. Murdoch, who does not seek transcendence, is vitally interested in the reality of the other as it may be known through what she calls "love: the non-violent apprehension of difference" (1999a, p. 218). It would be good to know if transcendence and particularity are antithetical.

Transcend comes from the Latin, meaning to climb over or go beyond the limits of something. Like Levinas, Murdoch's goal is to go beyond the limits of the self. One enters the realm of the reality of other beings through "techniques of unselfing" as Murdoch calls them. "This is the non-metaphysical meaning of the idea of transcendence ... the attempt to pierce the veil of selfish consciousness and join the world as it really is. It is an empirical fact about human nature that this attempt cannot be entirely successful" (Murdoch, 1970b, p. 93). And how is this world? It is the world of the unself, filled with particular others, far more different from us than we ever imagined.

By techniques of unselfing, Murdoch means nothing esoteric. She refers instead to mundane experiences of nature and art, intellectual studies, such as learning a language, and paying attention to other people. Imagine, says Murdoch, the experience of looking out the window in an anxious and resentful state, brooding on some damage to my prestige:

Then suddenly I observe a hovering kestrel. In a moment everything is altered. The brooding self with its hurt vanity has disappeared. There is nothing now but kestrel. And when I return to thinking of the other matter it seems less important. (1970b, p. 84)

In a similar way, intellectual studies (a category Murdoch thinks about in terms of Plato's *techne*), such as learning a language, confront one with

an authoritative structure which commands my respect ... My work is a progressive revelation of something which exists independently of me. Attention is rewarded by a knowledge of reality. Love of Russian leads me away from myself towards something alien to me, something which my consciousness cannot take over, swallow up, deny or make unreal. (ibid., p. 89)

Especially when she is talking about overcoming tendencies toward totalization, Murdoch sounds so much like Levinas one wants to cheat and call them soulmates. Yet they are talking about something quite different. For Murdoch, "the self, the place where we live, is a place of illusion." Levinas would never call the self an illusion. The self is remarkably real, a tangible greedy thing that threatens to become a prison made of being. For this reason, knowledge of the reality of others will not overcome it. A transcendent experience is necessary, one that does not bring me closer to my deliverer, but on the contrary emphasizes the infinite distance between us. Only this can open me up—not to reality, but to infinity.

I've compared Levinas' vision to that of Socrates in Plato's *Symposium*. Murdoch would create a symposium (her novels have this quality) whose participants climb the ladder of love only high enough to be free of their vanity and egoism, but never so high as to leave the world behind. Her Socrates is James Taper Pace, a spiritually charismatic but limited character in her novel *The Bell*, who says:

> The chief requirement of the good life ... is to live without any image of oneself ... We were told at school ... to have ideals. This, it seems to me, is rot. Ideals are dreams. They come between us and reality—when what we need most is just precisely to see reality. And that is something outside us. Where perfection is, reality is. (1962, p. 131)[3]

Where perfection is, reality is. The good is to know it, which means to see as clearly as possible. The less ego, the more we know, and the less we are led to totalize, which means to put ego in place of other.

Murdoch leaves room for tragedy. Our capacity to know others through love does not lead to harmony. We may know them as justly and truly as we can, and still not be able to get along with them (1999a, p. 216). Love's knowledge is not love's concord. Which suggests a point insufficiently appreciated by both Murdoch and Levinas. Both assume that the problem is the ego: the narcissism of the pre-doorbell state of "living from" as Levinas calls it, "neurosis," as Murdoch calls it. In fact, much of the misery in life comes from what might be called dependent attachment, something Murdoch writes about repeatedly in her novels, only occasionally in her philosophy. Charles Arrowby, protagonist of *The Sea, The Sea*, holds his long-lost girlfriend, Hartley, a prisoner in his country house. One might argue that this represents the power of totalizing egoism, but it seems more a sign of his utter dependence upon her to keep from going insane.

In her novels, but not in her philosophy, Murdoch recognizes the power of our need for others. Not the vanity but the insufficiency of the ego, its terrible need to find its other half, spoils relationships, turning them into tyrannies.[4] Murdoch knows this in her novels; Levinas knows this in his philosophy. Need of the other is the enemy of respect for otherness. Murdoch would have us know the reality of the other person. That requires we stand back a little. Levinas would have us experience the shock of otherness. That requires that we stand back as far as infinity.

There's no tragedy in Levinas, for the same reason there is none in Plato. There never is for those who believe in exit. Infinity is incompatible with tragedy. One might argue that infinity produces its own tragedy in Levinas. The needs of others are infinite, and so is my responsibility to them. But my capacity to meet the needs of others is finite, no matter how I suffer. Is this not a type of tragedy? No. Guilty man is not tragic man. Levinas' favorite quotation (he quotes it a dozen times throughout his works) is from *The Brothers Karamazov*. "Every one of us is guilty before all, for everyone and everything, and I more than others." The triumphant idealization of guilt is incompatible with tragedy.

In Chapter 5, I suggest that the absence of a tragic vision in Levinas is his greatest failing, reflecting an inability to find even temporary residence between totalization and exit, between the lives of Odysseus and Abraham as Levinas puts it. That place would be this world, our home away from home, except that there is no other. Though Murdoch plays no role in my argument in Chapter 5, her vision of tragedy informs my own. It is, she says, "the role of tragedy ... to show us suffering without a thrill and death without a consolation ... Masochism is the artist's greatest and most subtle enemy" (1970b, p. 87). By masochism she means glorification of suffering.

Masochism is often seen as a type of fusion, in which I passively abandon myself to the other. "Moral masochism" Freud called it, in which the subject "destroys his own real existence" (1924, p. 170). Though much of what Levinas writes about could be read in these terms, as Kantor (1999) does, I would put it differently. Substitution, hostage-being, suffering for your sins, the persecution of the narcissism of the I: all serve as modulators of attachment, barriers to ordinary human relatedness, enabling a relation without relation, as Levinas puts it. To be a hostage is to participate in a relationship, but hardly a fully human one. But that is the point. Hostage-being keeps me in the place I want to be, involved in the world but disconnected from the other and from my ego, perpetually prepared for exit, or rather in a condition of perpetual exit. In a sense, at least, Freud is correct about moral masochism. In order to be available for exit, I destroy my own real existence. For Levinas this is good.

While there is no tragedy in Levinas, there is a passion quite missing in Murdoch, the author who writes of love.[5] One is tempted to refer to the passion of Jesus Christ, and many Christians have read Levinas this way, and for good reason, as when Levinas says "I am responsible for the persecutions that I undergo" (E&I, p. 99). Levinas means, of course, not that I am the cause of my own persecution, but that even the persecuted one remains responsible for all the others in the world. But passion is not just guilt and suffering in Levinas. A barely contained passion for otherness, exit, and transcendence runs through Levinas, a thrill that in his early works is expressed in the experience of the voluptuous nude body. Levinas distances the other not simply to maintain the other's power to provoke transcendence, but to protect the other from the power of passion. For all her knowledge of love, passion's power is oddly missing in Murdoch.

Passion's power was not missing in Murdoch's own life, if Peter Conradi's (1986) recent biography is to be believed, and there seems no reason to doubt it. A more passionate private life is hard to imagine. Still, there is something about Murdoch's authorial presence that lacks ardor, as though her characters were marionettes pulled by the strings of desires somehow alien to their creator. One is reminded of Plato here, whose own life hardly lacked passion, if his seventh letter is to be believed. Levinas, on the contrary, does not remind one of either Plato or Murdoch. Not an author of submerged desire, Levinas' desires are all on the surface.

ADORNO

Levinas is frequently compared with the deconstructionists, above all, Jacques Derrida. How can one respect an unknowable otherness in a text that by its very nature as text must say something about the other? This is the challenge posed by Derrida. Much has been written about this encounter, including a few words of my own in the first chapter, so I am going to write about another encounter. Or rather, I am going to create an encounter that never took place, but would have been fascinating: between Levinas and the Frankfurt School of Critical Theory, especially Theodor Adorno and Max Horkheimer.

Since the parallels between Adorno's work and the deconstructionists have been frequently noted, one could see mine as an argument by transitivity, so to speak: Levinas is to the deconstructionists as Adorno is to the deconstructionists, so the Levinas and Adorno must be similar. Both investigate those "heterogeneous fragments that slip through the conceptual net, rejecting all philosophy of identity" (Eagleton, 1981, p. 141). Or do they? This is how Adorno proceeds in the fight against identity thinking, the reduction of the other to the same. It is not Levinas' way.

The strategy of transitivity turns out to be misleading. It will be better to imagine what Levinas and Adorno might have said to each other. Better still might be to imagine their mutual incomprehension.

I know of only a passing reference by Levinas to Adorno, in a late (1988) interview, where Levinas says "I learned quite recently that the philosopher Adorno has already denounced the jargon of authenticity" ("Other, Utopia & Justice," p. 226). In *Theologie im Pianissimo: Die Aktualität der Denkfiguren Adornos and Levinas*, Hent de Vries takes up their relationship. Though I too am fascinated by their apparent similarity, de Vries works too hard to make them complementary, downplaying what is so different and disturbing about Levinas.

For Levinas, Western philosophy is an egology, "the reduction of the other to the same." It begins with Plato and the doctrine of anamnesis, according to which I already know everything I might learn. Much of Levinas' work, at least until *Otherwise than Being*, was an account of this egology, by which Levinas means not a selfish teaching, but one which after many twists and turns eventually discovers that what appears alien, different and mysterious was really an alienated part of me. Like the Frankfurt School, Levinas takes Homer's *Odyssey* as the *leitmotif* of Western thought, the aim always to return from where one started.

Consider Husserl, who according to Levinas began by turning to the things themselves, only to conclude that the other is knowable only in so far as he is like me. Or consider Heidegger, who while surely concerned with the presence of others in my world (*Mitsein*), experiences them only as though they were always already there, part of the furniture of my life, not an intrusion of shattering otherness. Or consider Kant, for whom the basic categories I think that I discover in nature (the synthetic a priori) are really projections of human reason, the way the world must be, given humans as they are. About Hegel, the less said the better according to Levinas. More important is to see how the process of incorporating history into reason (the other into the same) that is so dramatic in Hegel's work is present in all enlightened thought. For each of these authors, indeed for Western thought, "knowledge is always an adequation between thought and what it thinks." The Frankfurt School said almost exactly the same thing (Adorno, 1973, p. 5). Neither the Frankfurters nor Levinas meant it as a compliment.

One can debate the accuracy of Levinas' analysis of Western thought, which is only somewhat less glib than my summary of it. But of course one could say the same thing of the Frankfurt School. There is something in itself totalistic about sweeping summaries of Western thought, as though each thinker was not more complex than his system, as though Western thought were defined by a dozen thinkers. However tendentious Levinas' interpretation, in this he is matched by the Frankfurt School.

"Nothing at all may remain outside, because the mere idea of out-sideness is the very source of fear." That is the mark of Western thought, say Horkheimer and Adorno (1972, p. 16). The source of the fear is the same as that identified by Levinas, that the world is alien and other. Adorno (1973, p. 22) writes of "idealism as rage" at a world too alien to be dominated. Idealism is rage against the sheer otherness of the natural world, which refuses to be devoured by the sovereign mind of man. If not rage, then nausea at the sheer swooning abundance of the natural world, like that felt by Sartre's narrator Roquentin: this is what the mind of Western man can hardly stand.

Idealism is not confined to philosophy, according to *Dialectic of Enlightenment*, legend of the Frankfurt School. Science is as idealistic as philosophy. Science too subjects the world to an idea, the idea of nature as meaningless, fungible units to be broken apart and calculated according to whatever theory predicts them. Under this broad definition, idealism is at work wherever concepts rule, wherever the goal of thought is to name and categorize, so that nothing is left over, and nothing is left outside. It began with Genesis, man naming the animals, as though to name them was to own them.

Not only do Levinas and the Frankfurt School share a similar analysis of totalistic thinking, but they share the guilt of it. For Levinas, the pri-mordial experience of consciousness is the guilt of having taken away the other's possibilities of existence. One does that every time one fails to acknowledge the otherness of the other, instead assuming that the other is like me, an instance of my categories. In a similar fashion, Adorno (1973, p. 47) writes of making apologies to the object for having sought to sub-sume it under this or that concept, which must always distort the manifold reality of the object. If this sounds extreme, as though one must apologize every time one places someone else in a category, such as man or woman, the reader might find Edward Said's *Orientalism* (1979) helpful. Even such a seemingly benign and objective category as "the Orient" serves the interests of Western dominion. The Orient does not exist, says Said.

Their analyses of the disease of Western thought are so similar, both in tone and content, including the tone that is their guilt at the self-assertion necessary to exist in this world, that it comes as a surprise that in many respects Levinas and the Frankfurt School are talking about different things. Both are concerned with the tendency toward totalization, best defined as the reduction of the other to the same, the elimination of difference. Both, for example, see Heidegger's ontology as one more instance of the will to grasp the whole (Adorno, 1973, pp. 61–5). The moment one looks at their solutions, however, it becomes apparent that they mean something quite different by totality and same. Against totality Adorno sets the particular; Levinas sets infinity. The difference could not be any more fundamental than that, or so it seems.

In analyzing the difference, I will focus on the work of Adorno, and to a lesser extent his collaborator Horkheimer, as representative of the Frankfurt School, contrasting both with Levinas. Only occasionally shall I turn to Herbert Marcuse. Not because I find less to admire in Marcuse, but because aspects of Marcuse's work come too close to that criticized by Levinas, the discovery of the other as an instance of the same. Finding in nature an eros akin to human eros, Marcuse sometimes writes as if reconciliation with nature meant humanity discovering its true erotic self in nature (Alford, 1985, pp. 37–68). Adorno's manner and style come closer to Levinas, but not too close. If it were similarity that I was looking for, then Walter Benjamin, friend and student of Gershom Scholem, would be the Frankfurt School theorist closest to Levinas. Even then, the similarity would be misleading. Levinas is not looking for redemption, not even in fragments.

More than other members of the Frankfurt School, Adorno was suspicious of reconciliation between subject and object, imagining how readily reconciliation might be extorted from vulnerable object or needy subject. More than other members of the Frankfurt School, Adorno feared eros, except perhaps in the smallest doses, what he calls velleity. More similar in tone than teaching, Adorno invites comparison with Levinas.

SUBJECT AND OBJECT

Reversing Kantian subjectivity, Adorno would let the object take the lead in defining itself. Yield to the object; do justice to its qualities; refrain from definition. Let the object be, approach it with utmost velleity, help it to become what it is (Adorno, 1973, p. 43). These are the watchwords of Adorno's approach, whose utopian goal is, as Martin Jay (1984, p. 68) puts it, "the restoration of difference and non-identity to their proper place in the non-hierarchical constellation of subjective and objective forces he called peace."

What would this beautiful but obscure idea mean in practice, helping the object to become what it is? Perhaps the simplest way to put it is that the object needs the subject to get it wrong. If, that is, the subject is willing to know he or she is wrong. Trying to grasp the object with this or that concept, the subject discovers that the object keeps slipping away. The shadow of the concept never completely covers the object. The object escapes, more multi-faceted than the subject can ever know. Humane subjects are pleased to learn this, and we are reminded of Winnicott's discussion of the "use of an object," in which we know the separateness of the other only after we have tried and failed to destroy it, in this case with our concepts. That too can be a kind of obliteration.

Levinas would not allow the subject to get close enough to get it wrong. Indeed, the very concept of "getting it wrong" does not make sense under Levinassian categories, in so far as "getting it wrong" implies that one might occasionally get it right, or at least less wrong. For Levinas, that would already be too close. One does not get the infinitely other right or wrong: one lets oneself be shattered by it.

In fact, the other about whom Levinas writes is not an object. The other is closer to an anti-object: an otherness so complete it explodes every human category, including object and being. To be sure, the other may be said to have qualities, but the subject misses the point when he or she notices them. Once I notice the qualities of the other, I have already gotten too close, entered into a social relationship and so invariably drawn the other into my needs, my project, or so Levinas argues (E&I, p. 85). What can rightly be said about the philosophy of both Murdoch and Adorno cannot be said about Levinas. "What breaks the drive of consciousness to totality is … an encounter with a concrete other person" (Antonaccio, 2000, pp. 181, 223).

Adorno writes about "beautiful otherness" (*schönen Fremde*), a term that implies a relationship of protected nearness to the distant and different.[6] Levinas would never put it this way; the experience of the other is too shattering to be close. The experience of the other for Levinas is more akin to the sublime, an experience of awe and terror because it shatters human categories, including the beautiful, which Adorno insists takes humans to appreciate it. For Adorno, the subject and object remain in a tender relationship, almost like the parent waiting patiently for his child to finish her long story without interrupting. Distant nearness, Jürgen Habermas has called it, a useful term as long as we remember to emphasize distance at least as much as nearness. For Adorno, beautiful otherness is principally an aesthetic experience, one that requires closeness, but not intimacy.

Adorno writes about non-being and infinity in terms that seem to resonate with Levinas. In fact, the different senses in which they use, or imply, the term "infinity" marks the difference between their projects. Levinas sees infinity in philosophical terms that demythologize an ancient religion. Infinity is a way of talking about a supreme non-being, an otherness so other that like Moses we cannot look upon its faceless face without being stricken. As close as we dare get is the face of the other. For Adorno, infinity means the way in which objects always overflow their concepts, the world more diverse than any concept can know. This sounds like the fourth sense of infinity listed in Chapter 1, except that Adorno's emphasis is not on the experience of the subject, but on the object, or rather objects. Infinity is the profusion of particulars. "To these objects, philosophy would truly give itself" (Adorno, 1973, p. 13).

Does this difference in infinities reflect some deeper divergence in their projects? I can find no deeper divergence, only different ways of expressing this same deviation. Not all refer to infinity, at least not directly. Most refer to the question of what is the opposite of totality? Is it particularity, or is it the other, a category neither universal nor particular?

NATURE AND ART

We must urgently defend man against this century's technology. Man will lose his identity and become a cog in a vast machine that chews up things and beings. In the future, *to exist* will mean *to exploit* nature: but in the vortex of this self-devouring enterprise there will be no fixed point. The solitary stroller in the country, who is certain of his belonging, will in fact be no more than the client of a hotel tourist chain, unknowingly manipulated by calculations, statistics, planning. No one will exist for himself.

The statement might have been written by Marcuse, even Adorno, particularly the next to last sentence, the theme not so much reconciliation with nature as what nature's rationalization does to man. In fact, the statement was written by Levinas for the purpose of rejecting it ("Heidegger & Us," p. 231). The eternal seduction of paganism, says Levinas, is the filtering of the sacred through the natural world. Only the other's hunger is sacred, by which Levinas means not just physical hunger, but the other's need. To see nature in any terms but as means to alleviate human suffering is to turn nature into an idol.

Levinas leaves little room for the dialectic of enlightenment. Technology demystifies nature, freeing us from pagan superstition. In this regard, technology is simply liberating. "Technology wrenches us out of the Heideggerian world and the superstitions surrounding Place" ("Heidegger & Us," pp. 232–3). Unlike the Frankfurt School, Levinas does not worry about remythification. Or rather, because he sees the danger of remythification everywhere, science is not unusual, or unusually dangerous in this regard, certainly less so than art.

Some, such as Llewelyn (1991), have wondered if Levinas' refusal to grant nature the status of a respected other, a third other, could be rectified within the framework of Levinas' thought. Perhaps it could within the formal structure of Levinas' thought, but not within its spirit. Nature for Levinas is characterized by its massivity, the only neologism I will employ in this chapter. By massivity I mean the opposite of passivity. In passivity I am open, receptive, and exposed to the other. In massivity I am enclosed in my dense, dark being. Levinas writes about nature as though it were marked by massivity. Not a hint of the sublime penetrates Levinas' writings on nature. One suspects this is because nature is too close to "there is," a thing that will just go on being forever. Even to come close risks being absorbed in its silent being. To admire the sublime in nature is to worship a pagan god.

Karl Jung favored rocks as icons because they have been around longer than any other being on the planet. Murdoch too favored rocks as icons, particularly those washed and rounded by the sea. Rocks all look so similar until you get close, when you discover that each one is different. For Murdoch, rocks symbolized individuality (Hampshire, 2001, p. 25). Levinas would be appalled. Not just that humans would be enchanted with a piece of non-human nature, but that one might admire something for its mere being: being there, being different, being so massive and real, being so utterly unconcerned with me. The whole point of the other is that it is otherwise than being. Anything but a strictly instrumental relationship to nature must, it seems, risk contaminating man with a reverence for being.

For Levinas, the other is a virtual God. If the other is infinitely other, then how much more other can God be? Were Levinas to regard nature as anything but mere being on hand for human purposes, he would be teaching pantheism, God everywhere that otherness is. The relegation of nature is a consequence of Levinas' assimilation of otherness, infinity, and God. Into this trinity nature cannot intrude without the risk of idolatry.

Art too is idolatry for Levinas. For Adorno and the Frankfurt School, art represents a way of knowing that avoids the dialectic of Enlightenment, in which both science and philosophy are snared. Art is non-conceptual.

Visual art is iconic, and so not an instance of identity thinking. Instead of subsuming the particular to the universal, art would represent the universal in the particular, all the while knowing, and showing by virtue of being art, of being semblance, that it cannot be done. This is particularly true of modern or "de-aestheticized" art, argued Adorno, but it is true of all art. The mimetic dimension of art, its implicit tribute to natural beauty, prevents it from coercing nature in the same way as theory does. Even at its most abstract, art copies nature, and thus lets nature take the lead. In this regard art represents an ideal relationship to nature, and to the other in general (Adorno, 1984, pp. 107–115).

Not for Levinas. For Levinas, art is the idol. We worship it, and so escape the world. "There is something wicked and egoist and cowardly in artistic enjoyment. There are times when one can be ashamed of it, as of feasting during a plague" ("Reality & Shadow," p. 142). As one moment of the dialectic, the Frankfurt School, especially Marcuse (1978), would recognize this statement. An aspect of art always lies, granting beautiful form to the most ugly realities, and so suggesting they are not really so terrible. But an aspect of art often tells the truth too, the "*promesse de bonheur*," the promise of happiness. It is in the play of these two aspects of art that one finds its emancipatory power. Adorno (1984, pp. 79–85) referred to this aspect as the "riddle-like" character of art, its status as uneasy mixture of mimetic and creative elements. Not for Levinas, who sees all art as though it were a statue, a thing frozen in time.

At first, Levinas' analysis of art seems strictly Platonic. Art is an illusion of an illusion, the "shadow of reality," Levinas calls it, a reality that is itself an illusion, shielding us with its sheltering sky from infinity. A second reading suggests a different perspective. Art is not an illusion of things. Art is frozen in thinghood. Art is trapped in itself, imprisoned in signs referring to signs, unable to get out, unable even to point to the larger world. Art points only to itself. Like participation, art is mock transcendence, directing us not toward the world, but back somewhere into our selves. While the scholar and philosopher refer "unequivocally" (*sans équivoque*) to the object, the poet, says Levinas referring to Proust,

> is concerned not to express but to create the object. Like images or symbols, reasoning is called on to produce a certain rhythm in which the reality that is sought will appear by magic. The truths or errors articulated are of no value in themselves. They are spells and incantations. ("Other Proust," p. 161)

Everything that Levinas says about participation and rhythm applies to art, all art, not just music ("Reality and Shadow"; Robbins, 1999, pp. 75–90). Rhythm is the language of the different parts of the soul calling to each other. As such, rhythm is as present in the literary as the musical arts, but in neither art form is it interesting. What does it matter what the different parts of my soul say to each other? All that matters is what the other says to me. Art for Levinas is always about things going out of control, Dionysus tempting us to turn from the other back to ourselves by persuading us that the boundaries it plays with are more than just the edges of our own minds. In this respect, art is really an instance of the "there is," tempting us toward the anonymity of mere being.

All this raises an interesting question. If art is so bad, then why does Levinas refer to literature so frequently, particularly when trying to explain "there is?" It can't be that art explains "there is" in a bad way, merely by exemplifying it. Artists from Blanchot to Rimbaud, Racine to Shakespeare, are drawn upon by Levinas to explain "there is" in the deepest and most subtle terms imaginable. Levinas quotes a phrase from Dostoevsky's *The Brothers Karamazov* more than a dozen times throughout his work, so much so that it becomes Levinas' motto: "Every one of us is guilty before all, for everyone and everything, and I more than others." Even Proust is revealed to be covertly concerned to depict Albertine as the other ("Other Proust," pp. 164–5). Doesn't Levinas' artistic practice deny his critique?

In response, Levinas says that good art interrupts itself ceaselessly (*Proper Names*, p. 41). By this he means that good art imitates a form of ethical discourse that like his own performs its own putting itself into question (Robbins, 1999, p. 145). The poet Paul Celan, for example, "interrupts the ludic order of the beautiful, of the play of concepts and of the play of the world" (*Proper Names*, p. 66). Maybe, though what Levinas seems to mean is that good art is art that is concerned with the themes he is concerned with, in roughly the same way he is concerned with them. Levinas' attempt to make this agreement a formal quality of art is not very persuasive, primarily because it does not allow us to distinguish, for example, Nietzsche from Dostoevsky. The former interrupts himself a lot more than the latter.

This raises the interesting question of form versus content, though of course to put it this way is misleading. The interpenetration of form and content would put it more accurately, as long as we remember that interpenetration is not identity. In *Theologie im Pianissimo: Die Aktualität der Denkfiguren Adornos and Levinas*, de Vries finds an affinity between

Adorno's negative dialectics and Levinas' "*alternierenden Reflexion*." At a high enough level of abstraction, what de Vries calls "formally considered," the comparison works. Levinas alternates between the "there is" (*il y a*), mere being, and the absolutely other, and one might even call this movement a negative dialectic in so far as there is no solution, no *Aufhebung*. In this regard Levinas' approach is similar to Adorno's negative dialectic, which also never achieves a conceptual synthesis between self and other, largely in order to protect the other. Similarly, Levinas' distinction between saying and the said resonates with Adorno's hesitance to name the other (de Vries, 1989, pp. 271, 277). If, that is, one wants to find a harmony between the authors. But, why work so hard to find a formal similarity? The only reason I can imagine is to render what is so strange and unusual about Levinas more familiar, by translating him into a more familiar dialectic—that is, dialogue.

It does not work very well, and the reason is because Adorno's object, the non-identical, has little to do with Levinas' other, which is not just other than me, but other than being. That's a big difference, one that makes their methodological similarities pale in comparison. Frequently referring to the metaphor of the trace (*Spur*) in Adorno and Levinas, de Vries downplays that it is a trace of something quite different for each. For Adorno, like Marcuse, for whom it is a favorite phrase, the "*ganz Anders*" is a world turned upside down, relationships among man, woman and nature seen from the standpoint of redemption. What exactly that would look like remains obscure, but the basic idea is clear, a world of peace and contentment, where the lion lays down with the lamb. For Levinas, the trace of the "ganz Anderen, d.h. des göttlichen Unendlichen," as De Vries puts it, is not just a revelation, but the redefinition of human concerns in the light of infinity (de Vries, 1989, p. 321).[7] One might argue that redemption and redefinition in light of infinity have something in common, as they certainly do. Nevertheless, the redemption that the Frankfurt School has in mind is spelled out strictly in human terms, the pacification of existence. One cannot say the same for Levinas.

If Levinas never develops a sufficiently dialectical interpretation of art (or rather, if his use of art remains more subtle and dialectical than he ever explains), the same cannot be said of his account of humanity and nature. An aspect of Levinas' work comes—for just a moment—close to the Frankfurt School's critique of instrumental reason. One sees this aspect most clearly in several articles on current events that Levinas wrote for *Esprit*, the voice of "progressive, avant-garde Catholicism," as Levinas put it (Caygill, 2000, p. 7).[8] In "Reflections on the Philosophy of Hitlerism," originally published in 1934, Levinas writes of the return of paganism, the forces of race and nature, what he calls the forces of fatality. In a 1956 essay, "Sur l'esprit de Genève," referring to a summit conference that for a brief moment promised relief from the Cold War, Levinas writes of forces without faces, by which he means nuclear weapons. In both essays the guiding idea is the same—that humans are no longer in charge of their history. We have given ourselves over to the forces of a reified nature, the forces of fatality, be they race or atomic energy.

> The inhuman, which in those centuries was prodigious, came to us still through the human. The human relations that made up the social order and the forces that guided that order exceeded in power, efficacy and in being those of the forces of nature ... [Now] for the first time social problems and struggles between humans do not reveal the ultimate meaning of the real. The end of the world will lack the last judgement. The elements exceed the states that until now contained them ... For politics is substituted a cosmo-politics that is a physics. ("Sur Genève," p. 164)

So many echoes are here. "There is" appears not as a psychological and ontological experience, but as a critique of mass society and the modern world, in which things rule. "There is" is the reification of human history. In this assessment Levinas shares much with the Frankfurt School's critique of the dialectic of Enlightenment. Both see reason and progress as leading to a return of the primitive, as the natural world is invested with new powers to reign over man. That too is paganism for Levinas. These forces also constitute a third, an alienated, inhuman other that threatens to make human politics obsolete.

It's not just Levinas' arguments that fascinate, however. Fascinating are the echoes of concepts such as "there is," transformed into a social theory that sees mass society as the real danger, a society of individuals without faces. Seen from this perspective, the face takes on a new importance, last remnant of the human in an increasingly inhuman world. From the perspective of Hitlerism and the Cold War, even Levinas' charge of paganism looks a little different. No longer a way of removing the sublime from the experience of nature, pagan refers to the remythification of nature by the categories of science and pseudo-science. For a moment, paganism sounds like instrumental reason.

Paganism sounds even more like what de Tocqueville (2000, pp. 425–6) called "pantheism," to which he thought men in democratic eras particularly susceptible. By pantheism de Tocqueville meant not so much nature worship as the desire of men and women to see themselves as one more piece of nature, and so share in its anonymous power. Man "seeks his identity in the very universal, mass forces to which he regards himself as subject" (de Tocqueville, 2000, p. lxv, editor's introduction). One does not think first of Levinas as critic of the loss of individuality in mass democracy, but that too is one of his themes.

While the *Esprit* articles are fascinating, an obtuseness that sounds like essentialism, but is more likely a fixation on the particular, occasionally emerges. Consider Levinas' discussion of the West as possessing an essential national and cultural identity that must be protected from the East, above all the Chinese. The context is an article written in 1960 on the Sino-Soviet rapprochement:

> In abandoning the West, does Russia not fear to drown itself in an Asiatic civilization ... The yellow peril! It is not racial, it is spiritual. It does not involve inferior values; it involves a radical strangeness, a stranger to the weight of its past, from which there does not filter any familiar voice or inflection, a lunar or Martian past. ("Débat Russo-Chinois," pp. 171–2)

Is the history of the East really the history of another planet?[9] Without much conviction, Caygill tries to get Levinas off the hook of his prejudice, arguing that "it is almost as if Levinas was undertaking the experiment of mounting a particularist argument against the universal claims of Hegelian-Marxist philosophy" (2000, p. 11). Considering the influence of Marxism in France during this era, Caygill is probably on the right track. Context is even more important in evaluating short works than long. Nevertheless, it is no accident that Levinas is as clumsy with particularism as with the "essence of the West." For Levinas the particular is not just unique and different. It is alien, coming terrifyingly close to "there is," a haunting presence. Conversely, much of Levinas' project can be read as an attempt to apportion the world into self, other, abstract third, and infinity. The result is little room left over for the particular.

What if you didn't like universals, but weren't especially fond of particulars either? Universals threaten to devour the world, and particulars become totems, threatening to imprison us in a world of being. Then, like Levinas, your theory would not be dialectical. Like Levinas, you would not concentrate on the delicate dance between self and other, universal and particular. You would not say things like "the material object needed the rational subject in order to release the truth it contains," as Adorno might (Buck-Morss, 1977, p. 81). Such statements presume both parties need each other. Instead, you would look for a world with neither universals nor particulars. That is the real meaning of infinity for Levinas.

Fortunately, Levinas does more than apportion the world. He tells stories about it, and so draws us back into a particular world, giving narrative frame and form to the desire for exit. In so doing, Levinas gives dread meaning. Let's look at a couple of these stories. Because he is so abstruse, one does not immediately think of Levinas as a great story teller, but he is.

ODYSSEUS AND ABRAHAM

Even if it is sometimes misleading, as I argued regarding de Vries' comparison, one can understand and appreciate the great temptation to bring Levinas and Adorno together on the same page. For both Adorno and Levinas, the *Odyssey* epitomizes the dubious legacy of the Enlightenment. For Horkheimer and Adorno, the myth explains why Enlightenment returns as myth. For all his cunning, Odysseus must deny his own nature to outwit the regressive forces of nature, such as Circe, and the Sirens. In the end, Odysseus' cunning is deployed against himself, as when he has himself tied to the mast, so that he cannot hear the Sirens' call. Like the good bourgeoisie, he can hear the deadly beauty of the song, but he is paralyzed, unable to respond. Their ears stuffed with wax, his men, like laborers everywhere, are deaf to the deadly beauty, which represents the desire for peace and satisfaction, an end to the labor of conquest, whose ultimate object is oneself. The result of repression is rage (idealism as rage) against a nature that requires such terrible harshness against oneself, rage at what one must do to oneself in order to survive. One sees the rage in the casual way in which Odysseus has hung the dozen servant women who consorted with Penelope's suitors (*Odyssey*, 22: 445–97). The cunning of instrumental reason finds its origins in the will to survive not just nature's dangers, but her temptations. Eventually cunning erupts in rage, using the instruments of science in the service of what are essentially mythic goals, such as the purification of *Blut und Boden* (blood and earth, a Nazi ideal). The dialectic of Enlightenment is not just an explanation of the Holocaust, but it is that too.

For Levinas, the *Odyssey* is metaphor for totalization, the reduction of the other to the same. As Odysseus struggles to return home, so Western philosophy struggles to reduce the other to the same, demonstrating that what appears distant and different is really an instance of human reason, finally come home to itself. Not Odysseus, but Penelope, is the true hero of this tale, forever unraveling what she started.

If Penelope is Levinas' hero of the *Odyssey*, it is Abraham who is Levinas' true hero, the one who leaves home and never looks back (Levinas, *Découvrant*, pp. 188–91). Nor does Abraham allow his son Isaac to return. While a number of critics have commented on the contrast between Odysseus and Abraham, none, to my knowledge, has looked closely at the story of Abraham (Genesis 12–25). If Abraham is an exile, he is no ordinary one, for Abraham goes with God's blessing. Leave your home, and I promise you a greater one, above all nations. That is God's command, and promise. This Abraham does, and eventually the prosperous and powerful Abraham and his wife are buried together in land he purchases from the Hittites. Isaac, together with his wife, Rebecca, fetched from home by Abraham's servant, live nearby, populating the land with descendants as numerous as the stars. But is it really leaving home when you send your servant back instead, with orders to fetch a native wife for your son? Is it really leaving home when your father (even if He is in heaven) promises to give you a new and better one?

It will not do to be too crass, or too literal, about stories. Nothing in Levinas' philosophy or theology suggests a conventional view of God as a supreme being. On the contrary, Levinas' God is a supreme non-being. What I want to suggest is that the distinction between homecoming and exile, and with it openness to infinity, is not always so clear. It makes all the difference how one returns home. As Agamemnon does (to mix metaphors, or at least stories), in bloody triumph after wasting the lives of his men, as well as that of his lovely daughter. Or as one who tries to remember what home was really like, free of the grasping, clinging desire to regain it, trying to know it on its own terms, even if it was hell?

But, perhaps this is not quite right either. If home is where we start from, then we never really return home. We just keep going farther away. Eventually we cross the threshold of infinity. That is to say, we die. Along the way, some people are able to establish a home away from home, a temporary place of human shelter and comfort. This is, I will argue in Chapter 5, how the Athenian polis should be understood. Not the real polis, but the polis idealized in Greek tragedy, a place somewhere between home and infinity. It is this category of being (or should I say the temporary absence of non-being?) that is missing in Levinas. To be sure, this category is acknowledged in Levinas' political theory, but it finds little place in his metaphysics.

One reason this category is missing in Levinas is because of his neglect of particularity. The particular is powerful because it is real, here, now, realized neither by return nor exit, but by just being there. "Don't get up close," the priest warns a young man in a short story by F. Scott Fitzgerald (1989, p. 271), "because if you do you'll only feel the heat and the sweat and the life." The priest is cautioning against going to an amusement park, but it applies to life, to every human body. Getting up close may absorb us in being, but this very absorption is the way through which we distinguish among beings, between my being and yours, and so avoid totalization. Absorption in particularity makes otherness. Absorption in particularity does not automatically make *respect* for otherness, however. I may be fascinated with your blue eyes and blond hair, but admire them in almost fetish fashion, as though they were you. It is this that Levinas is legitimately concerned with.

Think back on when you first (or last) encountered another hot, sweaty human body filled with life. To encounter this body is already to know the difference, in part because of the awe such encounters provoke, an awe that gains its power not from another's closeness to infinity, but from the other's terrible reality. In his studies of eros Levinas tries to leverage this experience, much as Plato would, turning it into a gateway to infinity. Consider the possibility that this is precisely how the world does *not* work. Once we try to leverage experiences like this we have already lost the point, and much of the power. We have lost the power of the particular to show us the otherness of the real.

Can we not, asks Levinas, arrive at an "indifference to essence" (OB, p. 178)? Yes, and there are two ways to do it. One is to seek infinity, a realm beyond being. The other is to cultivate particularity. Horkheimer and Adorno knew the power of the particular. This is how they understood reconciliation with nature, as an encounter that remembers nature's awesome otherness even as it would assimilate this otherness into myths of return. In other words, reconciliation with nature knows that it is totality that is the real myth. Jay (1984, p. 68) calls it the "reverential recollection of an object always prior to the remembering subject." It is only by trying to return home that one knows for certain that one has already left. It is only through the construction of myths of totality that we know they are myths. If, that is, we allow our myths, our selves, to be overwhelmed by the power of the particular. The result is increased insight into sep–

arateness. Not the separateness that is infinity, just the terrible, wonderful everyday separation of self and others, self and world. Isn't that enough?

Here is a topic, distinctions between self, other, and world, that begs for a light paradoxical touch, not a categorical one. Here are distinctions that deserve to be woven, not set in concrete, as Plato's Stranger almost puts it. Does Levinas not avoid totalization by turning inward, away from the world to the realm of self-reference, the project of *Otherwise than Being*?[10]

Let's play with the story of Odysseus a little more. Imagine that it is Levinas tied to the mast. What does the mast represent? No, not that! For Horkheimer and Adorno, the mast represents the restraints of reason that prevent Odysseus from abandoning himself to the Sirens' promise of joy that comes too close to death, the pleasure of self-abandonment as self-obliteration, the loss of boundary and limit.

Why would Levinas need to be tied up? This is especially important because Levinas, like Adorno, stresses the virtues of passivity. For Adorno, passivity means mimesis, the method of negative dialectics, in which the subject responds to the object as it is, imagining that it might be different in only the slightest degree. About this method of exact fantasy, as it is also called, Adorno says it "abides strictly within the material which the sciences present to it, and reaches beyond them only in the smallest aspects of their arrangement: aspects, granted, which fantasy itself must originally generate."[11] For Adorno, passivity is the opposite of both instrumental reason and idealism.

For Levinas, passivity is not simply the opposite of activity. Passivity is opposed to spontaneity, the spontaneity of my ego and free will. Passivity is being open to possession by the other. Passivity makes me suffer by urging me to detach myself from my endless "desire to return to myself as ravenous center of the universe, avidly utilitarian, artistic, and practical" (Peperzak, 1997, p. 185).

From this perspective, the Sirens represent not the call of self-abandonment, but the false claims of the ego, evidently the opposite. It is this false reality that forever leads me around in circles trying to fulfill myself, trying to get back to the beginning, trying to find myself in everything and everyone I encounter. In tying himself to the mast, Levinas would tie himself to the other, becoming hostage-being, and so curtailing his spontaneity. Not reason but the binding claim of the other is what having himself tied to the mast represents for Levinas.

Adorno sees the ego as a too stern taskmaster, "O lastly over-strong against thy self."[12] Under pressure, the ego returns to its first principle, ritual sacrifice: first of nature, then others deemed closer to nature (servant girls, natives, Jews), and finally itself. "Though its irrationality makes the principle of sacrifice transient, it persists by virtue of its rationality" (Horkheimer and Adorno, 1972, pp. 53–4). Levinas sees the ego as more akin to Plato's leaky jar (*Gorgias*, 493b–d). The ego is caught in mythic time because it can never escape its desires, which lead it in circles. The only escape is in passivity, in which I abandon my ego for the other. For Adorno, there is no escape, only an exit from mythic time, in which I abandon not myself, but my quest for mastery over the world, and so come to enter the world as it is: me and a zillion other beings, in no particular order, and certainly no hierarchy. For a moment Adorno sounds like Murdoch.

A follower of Levinas might argue that while I abandon my ego to the other, I regain something more valuable, the other in me. "The psyche in the soul is the Other in me, a malady of identity" (Levinas, OB, p. 69). How much we should value this illness depends upon whether this other is just some other person, or the trace of infinity. It also depends upon whether the trace of infinity is itself a Siren call, a release from the burden of being. Is being-for-another valuable because it represents an escape from being-for-myself, or because it represents an escape from just being?

AN APARTMENT IN THE GRAND HOTEL ABYSS

If I presume to put Levinas in Adorno's story, shouldn't I put Adorno in his? I will, but I will have to do it a little differently, telling a story about an exile who never left home, a category that fits Adorno well.

Adorno criticizes Kierkegaard for confusing the existential condition of humanity under capitalism with the existential condition of humanity *per se*. One sees this, says Adorno, in the way Kierkegaard used the image of the bourgeois intérieur, the bourgeois apartment. Nothing gets in, and nothing goes out. Consider, for example, Kierkegaard's story of a father and son walking back and forth in the apartment, pretending they are strolling past exciting places in the outside world.

Or consider Kierkegaard's use of the image of the mirror, employed not just to see one's own reflection, but positioned in bourgeois apartments of the nineteenth century "to reflect the endless street lines of such rental apartments into the secluded bourgeois living space."[13] Called "spies," (a term Kierkegaard uses to describe himself), these mirrors were familiar furniture in the bourgeois apartment of the era. In them the external world is experienced from a space deep within the bourgeois interior, as the world is defined and bounded by this flat perspective, held in the image of a mirror. In reality, Kierkegaard was a *rentier*. That this economic exchange might be a more fundamental reality never enters his mind.

Adorno criticizes not just Kierkegaard, but Heidegger, who uses a similar example—the objects in his study. In attempting to define being, Heidegger writes of "equipment" (*Zeuge*), owned and manipulated by the bourgeois subject, as Adorno calls him, valuable only in terms of how they serve the interests of this man, never as they are for themselves. Unlike Kierkegaard's apartment, Heidegger's room lacks even spies, mirrors that reflect the outside world.

One may think about Kierkegaard's apartment, or Heidegger's study, as versions of Plato's cave. The difference with Plato, of course, has to do with what's outside. For Plato, outside the cave is true reality. For Adorno, outside is the concrete reality of everyday life as it is lived under capitalism, where nothing is rent free unless you own it, and the things in the professor's study are generally made by men and women who have no time to study, and no place to retreat.

This suggests what Adorno might say to Levinas, a man who wants an exit from this world and its burden of being. "Do you despise being, or a particular way of being, which drives you deep into the interior of yourself in order to find any lasting satisfaction?" "Do you dread 'there is,' or 'there is no meaning and satisfaction in my life?'" How would we begin to answer these questions if we could not compare ways of being, as well as non-being? The problem is not that Levinas does not answer these questions, but he does not allow us to ask them, treating all being as though it were one. Isn't that totalizing too? Once one begins to write in terms of being and the other, one has already made questions like these impossible to ask, questions that to be answered must refer to particular beings and others in all their historical specificity. One must, in other words, notice the color of the other person's eyes.

What might Levinas say of Adorno? Here we must be a little more imaginative, for Levinas does not write critique in the same style as Adorno. Levinas might say that Adorno never gets out of his apartment either. Negative dialectics is so turned inward, so afraid of "extorted reconciliation," as Adorno put it when writing about Lukács, so dedicated to not going along (*nicht mitmachen*), that Adorno's work becomes turned in on itself, a castle defending against the least misunderstanding which might be exploited by the powers that be.[14] Certainly that criticism has been made before. Adorno "never took a trip out of the simple desire to see," says an acquaintance. Adorno took up residence in the Grand Hotel Abyss, says another.[15]

Adorno (1974, p. 87) writes of the writer who sets up house in his text. "For a man who no longer has a homeland, writing becomes a place to live." What a house, filled with sentences and paragraphs so obscure and paradoxical they can only be described as ramparts, or a warren of tunnels like that created by the Ceaulşescus of Romania to evade their pursuers. Of course, the hermetic text describes not just Adorno's home, but that of many postmoderns as well, as though obscurity could create security for those who live there. One could say the same thing about Levinas, except that for all his obscurity, he desperately wants out.

It would be misleading to suggest that the intérieur quality of Adorno's works stems from linguistic style alone. The interior quality stems from the method of negative dialectics itself (ultimately inseparable from his style), which breaks apart and rejoins the elements Adorno writes about in order to reveal the "sociocultural reality" they constitute. But if Adorno's work becomes turned in on itself, this is more practice than theory. There remains a messianic moment in Adorno's project, albeit one experienced strictly by contrast.

Perspectives must be fashioned that displace and estrange the world, reveal it to be, with its rifts and crevices, as indigent and distorted as it will appear one day in the messianic light. To gain such perspectives without velleity (*ohne Willkür*) or violence, entirely from felt contact with its objects—this alone is the task of thought. (Adorno, 1974, p. 247)

Adorno would open the apartment door barely a crack, letting in a sliver of light, just enough to reveal how broken and distorted the world really is.

EXIT AND VERSE

Levinas would rip the apartment door off its hinges. There's nothing quite like it in Adorno, for whom the messianic light is pale. For Levinas the brilliance of infinity shatters my ego to pieces, releasing me from the prison of my apartment, and my being. But what if we thought about Levinas' experience in terms of Adorno's comment that:

it is not the purpose of critical thought to place the object on the

orphaned royal throne once occupied by the subject. On that throne
the object would be nothing but an idol. The purpose of critical
thought is to abolish the hierarchy. (Adorno, 1973, p. 181)

To be sure, Adorno's object is not Levinas' other, but one still needs to ask
if the other does not risk becoming an idol in Levinas' thought.

The answer is almost certainly no. The other is not so much a being to
be worshiped as one who shatters the complacency of my being, as though
my ego was worth something. Far from being an idol, the other shatters
the idol that is my ego and its projects. The question is whether my ego
and its projects were merely an idol in the first place.

Are the pleasures I feel in my own existence, as well with my attachments to others, merely the pleasures of a contented cow? And what's
wrong in being a contented cow, unless one drinks up someone else's milk?
Is there not a certain contentment at living and being a Siren call that we
should give ourselves up to? While it is a Siren call that is readily confused
with the ravenous ego, it may be quite different, akin to the pleasure in
being that I might feel lying out in the warm sun after a cold winter.
Levinas would make of that contentment a strictly narcissistic pleasure,
but he does not distinguish between satisfactions that take from others
without knowing or acknowledging our debt, and satisfactions that come
to us merely by virtue of being separate beings. Are there not pleasures
that fall between gluttony and servitude? In asking these questions of
Levinas, I admit that I am thinking more of Marcuse than Adorno, and
that is perhaps the problem.

Adorno cannot get out of his apartment, and one reason is because he
has too little eros, too little love of the world as it is. He's trapped in
velleity, the weakest kind of desire, one that does not lead to the slightest
action. Anything more would consume the object in fear and lust, or so
Adorno seems to believe. Levinas comes closer to Plato's Socrates in *The
Symposium*, writing of a purified desire that is not based on lack and need,
and so moves from the love of beautiful bodies to the love of the infinite.
Unlike Adorno, Levinas never loses his passion. Instead, his passion loses
its object, attaching itself to nothing. But perhaps that was the object all
along.

One could read all this and conclude "What else is new?" Only that
Adorno is a *little* more of a materialist than is usually appreciated. Against
the idealist Levinas (idealists come in many stripes), one would expect that
Adorno would find the messianic light pale, whereas Levinas finds it

strong. Substitute Benjamin for Adorno, and one would have theorists with more in common.

True enough, but it is hardly the whole story. If the messianic light is pale in Adorno, the impulse to reconciliation is stronger than in Levinas. Reconciliation is really not a Levinassian category, just as relationship isn't, at least not with the other. One might as well argue that the messianic light is absent in Levinas. Infinity is no more light than darkness. What it is, is *exit*, a way out of the burden of being in this world, an opening to another worldless world. But exit is not redemption, at least not for Levinas. It creates a whole new series of obligations that tie us tightly to this world, more tightly than Odysseus was tied to the mast. But perhaps this was the point after all.

Let's play with the *Odyssey* one more time. In Horkheimer and Adorno's version, the mast to which Odysseus is tied represents rational self-control. In my version, the mast to which Levinas is tied represents hostage-being. But is it clear that the Sirens represent the spontaneous ego? Have the Sirens not always represented something more, the desire to give oneself over to a peace and satisfaction that comes frighteningly close to death? If so, then Levinas has himself tied so tightly to the mast of hostage-being so that the attraction of non-being does not become overpowering. Levinas flirts with death, and it is the reality of the other that saves him, but only because Levinas would become the other's hostage, tied to the other with infinite threads, each representing an obligation so great it can never be met. But, that's good. Trying to do the impossible keeps one in this world one's whole life long.

Can one live in the world another way, one that does not require that I bind myself? Can there be an eros that does not consume its object as though it were prey? How can I live with the reality of other human beings? Is there an ethic of the ruthlessness of existence, any existence? As argued in the last chapter, any existence uses others. The only ethically important question concerns the limits of use, so that use does not become exploitation. About these questions, which are really versions of the same question, neither Adorno nor Levinas give us much help.

Certainly there are no simple answers. There is, however, an interesting point at which Levinas comes close to what is best in Adorno, the Adorno (1973, p. 14) who says "philosophy is the most serious of things, but then again it is not all that serious." I refer to the most playful aspects of Adorno, those least trapped in the Grand Hotel Abyss, more willing to come outside and play. One finds this spirit of play, otherwise so lacking in Levinas, in a curious place, Levinas' discussion of biblical interpretation, the hermeneutics of sacred texts. This is evidently because Levinas believes these texts are illuminated from within by inspired thought, and so resistant to the reifying powers of man. "We begin with the idea that inspired thinking is a thought in which everything has been thought, even industrial society and modern technocracy" ("Messianic Texts," p. 68).

Fortunately this does not lead Levinas toward literalism. On the contrary, it frees his imagination. In talking about the interpretation of sacred texts, Levinas sounds most like Adorno on exact fantasy, the method of negative dialectics, in which a paratactic style disrupts the hierarchical subsumption of objects under concepts, loosening the bond between subject and object, interpreter and text. Or as Levinas puts it, "exegesis would come to free, in these signs, a bewitched significance that smoulders beneath the characters or coils up in all this literature of letters" (*Beyond Verse*, p. 109).

Levinas compares his approach with Ricoeur's fusion of horizons, under which the horizon of the text blends with and extends the reader's horizon (*Beyond Verse*, p. 109; Davis, 1996, p. 115). Conversely, the reader gives something of him or herself to the text, so that it is never the same text. "Hermeneutic nihilism," as Gadamer calls it, is always a risk, but it is minimized by the fact that serious interpreters work within a tradition. As Levinas puts it:

> A distinction is allowed to be made between the personal originality brought to the reading of the Book and the pure play of the fantasies of amateurs (or even of charlatans); this is made both by a necessary reference of the subjective to the historical continuity of reading, and by the tradition of commentaries that cannot be ignored under the pretext that inspirations come to you directly from the text. (*Beyond Verse*, p. 135)

You can play with the text, but not too much, and not too freely. A tradition restrains you, which means that it gives you fences within which to play, a playground. Still, for Levinas this is a great liberation.

What if we thought about the relationship to the other like the relationship to a sacred text? The relationship would be delicate, respectful, free to innovate and play, but only within limits. You would not be hostage to the other; you would serve the other in a way that comes close to the Frankfurt School's project of speaking for those who cannot speak for themselves, the spiritually wounded and the dead. You could bring something new to the other, but only with the utmost care, as a mother presents a new toy to baby. This, Winnicott tells us, allows the other to create the object for him or her self.

Here Adorno and Levinas converge, but only for a moment. What is surprising is how much work it takes to get them this close. The reason is the difference between object and other. For Levinas, I turn to sacred texts for inspiration, but I turn to the other for an exit from being. There is really nothing quite like this in Adorno. It is actually Marcuse who comes closest to Levinas in the closing chapters of *Eros and Civilization*, which play with the conjunction of eros and thanatos.[16] Only for Levinas it is not play. Not the conjunction of eros and thanatos, but the assimilation of thanatos to eros is Levinas' project, so that desire might seek infinity.

For Levinas, the love of infinity, non-being, sometimes sounds like love of death. Not the *Liebestod* of Marcuse, with its images of Orpheus and Narcissus, who love silence, peace, night, and death. For Levinas, the attraction of non-being has more to do with a release from the burden of being: not instrumental being, or egoistic being, or alienated being. Just being. "It is not a matter of escaping from solitude," says Levinas, "but rather of escaping from being" (E&I, p. 59). It is, I believe, the Frankfurt School's commitment to the values of peace and satisfaction in this world as goods in themselves (that is, the School's materialistic inheritance, impoverished as it sometimes seems) that sets this limit for both Adorno and Marcuse. The limit is lacking in Levinas. Obligation to the other sets the limit for Levinas.

Both Levinas and Adorno were Jews who wrote in the shadow of the Holocaust. Adorno was half-Jewish and escaped Germany. Levinas was interned in a prison camp for French officers and escaped with his life. Adorno was an exile. The same cannot quite be said of Levinas, though their situations were similar. Levinas left Lithuania to study in France at the age of 17, and remained there the rest of his life. His wife and children survived the Holocaust while hiding out in a French monastery. His family in Lithuania was all slain. Isn't this the most important thing about Adorno and Levinas, one might well ask? Both are witnesses to the remains of a world on which God seems to have turned His back, but not to protect us from His glory.

Just as too much can be made of their formal methodological similarities, one can make too much of their parallel lives. What divides them is Adorno's love of the world. To be sure, Adorno's is the most cautious and broken love around, terrified of falsity and extortion. Indeed, it takes a comparison with someone like Levinas to see Adorno's love of the world. One wants to say that a little love for the world, resistant and shrunken as it is in Adorno, is necessary for social theory. In other words, social theory requires that one be more attracted to being than non-being. Not because Levinas cares less for the denizens of this world. He doesn't. But because one must dwell in the details of this world in order to know it as a social theorist. While one wants to say this, it is not quite so simple. Levinas' social theory (or rather, his hints in that direction; Levinas is not and would not want to be considered a social theorist) is remarkably present in the world. The next chapter turns briefly to this topic.

4

Psychoanalysis, Politics, and "Freedom With"

Charles Taylor (1979), in "What's Wrong With Negative Liberty," and Patrick Gardiner (1979), in "Freedom as an Aesthetic Idea," both published in a *Festschrift* for the twentieth-century's most famous theorist of freedom, Isaiah Berlin, argue that we need a more subtle and sophisticated moral psychology to talk intelligently about freedom. "The moral psychology of these authors is too simple, or perhaps we should say too crude, for its purposes," says Taylor (1979, p. 176). He is referring not just to Thomas Hobbes and Jeremy Bentham, but to all who fail to recognize the ways in which fear and false-consciousness may stand in the way of freedom. In a similar fashion, Gardiner (1979, p. 30) states that Schiller's reservations about Kant stemmed from a "comprehensive view of the human subject which sought to do justice to its mixed nature, and his own conception of freedom as it finally emerged can only be understood in terms of this."

It is hard to disagree with Taylor and Gardiner, and I do not. What I call "freedom with" implies a subtle psychology of human attachment, one that knows how much humans need each other even—or should I say especially—in order to be free of others. The object relations tradition in psychoanalytic theory, concerned not with the inner-psyche, but the inter-person, the quality of our emotional relations with others, provides a rich resource with which to think about "freedom with." Wilfred Bion's (1970, pp. 88–94) discussion of the container that neither crushes nor drops, but lightly holds us, is another metaphor for "freedom with." Freedom is being lightly held. Winnicott says that all creativity stems from this transitional space, a view that accords with my interpretation of Hannah Arendt as almost but not quite a theorist of "freedom with."

Not only political theorists are troubled with freedom. Among those influenced by psychoanalysis, freedom is a terrible problem. Many want to believe in it but can't, often because they share Freud's commitment to psychic determinism, which seems to imply that free will and free choice are myths. The psychiatrist Robert Knight (1972, p. 143) was more afflicted by this predicament than most, writing that a patient who is relieved of his obsessions and compulsions "will then feel free, and, to some extent, will be 'free' ... to 'choose.'" Even about the lesser experience of feeling free to choose, Knight cannot do without the quotation marks, for he knows that in reality all is determined.

Here is no place to go into the old debate between free will and determinism, a debate that has waylaid so many attempts to explore freedom psychologically. About the determinism at stake in psychology, the simplest thing to say is that it is *psychic* determinism, and as such more about meaning than cause (Smith, 1978, p. 92). Another thing to say about determinism is that it is a metaphysical postulate about which no scientific evidence will ever decide. In that sense at least it is uninteresting, as Stuart Hampshire argues (1975, p. 11). About the free will at stake, I argue that free will (indeed, will of any kind) has little to do with freedom. Freedom is not about freeing my will. It is about finding a place, always temporary, between losing and fusing, the poles of borderline experience. This has more to do with letting go of my willfulness than it does exerting my will.

Levinas is more helpful in thinking through the problem of freedom than one might suppose. To be sure, many of the things Levinas says about freedom sound like the worst abuses of the term, exactly the sort of thing Isaiah Berlin (1969) warns us against in "Two Concepts of Liberty." For Levinas, I become free to the degree I become responsible for the other, including his or her sins. I become free to the degree I abandon my will for thy will. For Levinas, freedom is heteronomy, not autonomy. Isn't this a terrible abuse of the term "freedom?" In order to answer this question it will help to look at Berlin's account in more detail, followed by several psychoanalytical accounts of freedom. We will see that Levinas' concept of freedom is not as bizarre or abusive of common sense as one might imagine. That one may find freedom in passivity is an old insight, and one Levinas participates in. Plutarch says that before his death, Alcibiades dreamed that his mistress dressed him as a woman and put make-up on his face (*Lives*, 39). It was, I think, a dream of freedom—that is, of release from his agony, the perpetual struggle for excellence that was Alcibiades' life.

It is unnecessary to infer how Levinas understands the place of freedom in the experience of answering the doorbell. Levinas tells us, defining ethics as the calling into question of my freedom (T&I, p. 43). Does this mean that ethics is more important than freedom? No, it means that I find my freedom in serving the other. Freedom is heteronomy, not autonomy. Not because freedom is servitude, but because in serving the other I open myself to the infinite, the absolutely other. "But the calling into question of this wild and naïve freedom for itself [a reference to Sartre], sure of its refuge in itself, is not reducible to a negative moment. This calling into question of oneself is in fact the welcome of the absolutely other" (Levinas, "Meaning and Sense," p. 54). This welcome is my passage to freedom. Though I have been critical of Levinas, I believe that his understanding of freedom is helpful, an antidote to the idealization of the will that so dominates discussions of freedom.

What is missing in Levinas, as it was missing in Alcibiades, is a sense of shared freedom, a freedom that involves my participation with others, neither serving nor enslaving them, but living with them, acknowledging my dependence upon others, but not transforming this dependence into an idealized servitude. "Freedom with," it might be called. A concept of "freedom with" is equally missing in Berlin, and Erich Fromm (1969), who wrote *Escape from Freedom*. Indeed, "freedom with" is absent in most Western thought on the topic. Neither Plato nor Hegel nor Kant nor Nietzsche nor the Sartre of *Being and Nothingness*, nor Rousseau has any place for "freedom with." Nor does Levinas, but the way he turns the Western concept of freedom upside down allows us to see the absence of "freedom with" more clearly. Levinas shows us the other extreme, freedom as heteronomy. That makes it easier to find the middle. In fact, this middle is no real middle at all. Spatial metaphors are almost always misleading. "Freedom with" comes closest to what Winnicott calls transitional experience.

BERLIN AND BORDERLINES

We should not, says Isaiah Berlin (1969), confuse freedom with its material conditions, such as a decent income and life chances. Everything is what it is, and not something else. Freedom means lack of restraint. Berlin calls it "negative freedom." To know my freedom, I have but to ask how many doors are open to me, and how wide they are open. "The rest is extension of this sense, or else metaphor" (ibid., p. lvi).[1]

Against negative freedom Berlin sets "positive freedom," the freedom to realize one's deepest ambitions, to participate in one's own governance, to become who one truly is. Positive freedom is similar to what Erich Fromm (1969) calls "freedom to": the freedom to realize my full potential, to become all that I can be, which includes mastery of my lower self. The trouble with positive freedom is that it invites abuse, as restrictions on negative liberty are held to be necessary to realize its positive counterpart. Exemplary is Rousseau's (1964) infamous claim that under the general will a man may be forced to be free to realize his higher self. So too should we be suspicious of Kant's claim that a free man will wish to do only what is rational.

Calling Freud "the greatest healer and psychological theorist of our time," Berlin sees the father of psychoanalysis as a defender of negative freedom. At least this is the interpretation of Peter Gay (1979, pp. 57–9), who admits that Berlin's position is not crystal clear. Though Freud (1933, p. 80) did write that "where id was, there ego shall be," this is in no way a positivistic conception of freedom, as though man could become whomever he wanted to be, if only he could overcome his split self. On the contrary, Freud meant that through analysis and reflection it is possible to open up a few more doors, a few more choices previously closed by compulsion, neurosis, and anxiety. As Freud (1923, p. 50n) put it, analysis seeks "to give the patient's ego *freedom* to choose one way or the other." Freud did not put quotes around the term 'freedom' (*Freiheit*); instead he emphasized it. Not the freedom of self-realization, but the freedom that stems from having a few more doors to walk through if one wishes: that is the freedom gained by analysis.

Writing during Freud's lifetime, the influential analyst Robert Waelder (1936) located freedom in the superego, a surprising place given Freud's (1923, pp. 56–59) well-known remarks about the superego as a pure culture of the death instinct. But by freedom Waelder does not mean doing what I want. He means the transcendence of my immediate desires and surroundings, a transcendence enabled by universal principles and ideals. In this regard, Waelder's view of freedom resembles Kant's. For Kant (1981), human freedom is the power of will to act independently of desire or inclination. With the term "will," Kant means practical reason, what he calls *Wille*, as opposed to *Willkür*, which might be translated as free or arbitrary will. The result of this distinction is that I am free not when I am doing what I want to do. That would be *Willkür*. I am free when I (that is, my *Wille*) recognize that the natural laws that bind me are the same laws I would give myself were I completely rational.

Waelder (1936, p. 93) puts it this way. The more a man "is in the thick of it the more he is in the grip of instincts and affects, the less this freedom is his." Winnicott (1986, p. 214) agrees: "The enjoyment of freedom only applies at all simply to the periods between bodily excitements." The biggest threat to freedom is not the punitive, demanding superego, but "fixation," by which Waelder means an obsession with particular sources of satisfaction. Lifting me out of this world into another no longer dependent on needs and objects, the superego creates and reflects the abstract and symbolic universe of cultural values, a much roomier place to be.

Writing more than forty years later, Joseph Smith (1978) develops an aspect of Waelder's thought that comes closer to the view I argue for. Freedom is "freedom from the compelling pressure of peremptory need" that is "nevertheless shaped by such needs" (ibid., p. 96). Freedom isn't liberation from need, as in having all I want, or no longer wanting anything. Freedom is relief from the tension of tyrannical need that nonetheless remains under the press of that need. The play we call freedom "sustains a dramatic quality," as our needs hover in the wings (ibid.). In this regard, Smith adds complexity to Winnicott's statement that freedom applies "simply" to the periods between bodily excitement. There is nothing simple about it. Freedom performs on a stage in which the needs that excite us are just resting between acts. That experience gives freedom its edge.

What links Waelder to Smith is their shared sense (Smith cites Waelder) that attunement to and dependence on others and the external world, above all the world of symbols and values, actually liberates us from being enslaved by our desires (Smith, 1978, p. 97). Freedom is not the rejection of need. That view would come closer to Kant. Freedom is the liberation from need, which itself presumes its partial fulfillment. Freedom depends upon the good enough fulfillment of need. Because there was enough, one need not devour it all. Alluding to Fromm, Smith calls his ideal of freedom "freedom for." Freed from the peremptory moment, one is free for the experience of seeing the object in new ways, not just as an object of desire, but as an object of play and wonder. Freedom is freedom to play with the object, as one is not possessed by need of it.

The theorist who comes readily to mind here is Winnicott, and I shall turn to him shortly to characterize freedom from the peremptory moment in terms of transitional experience. But freedom is more than a transitional experience. Freedom is a solution to the problem of life, how to live between claustrophobia and agoraphobia. This helps to explain why people are always talking about their security and their desires in terms of freedom. It's not just American ideology talking. Freedom is how we make our way in the world, a path that passes between the poles of losing all we care about (agoraphobia), and fusing with it, and so losing ourselves (claustrophobia). In other words, freedom is a way of negotiating borderline experience.

What's borderline?

When I refer to borderline experience, I refer to two things. First, to the disorder recognized by the *Diagnostic and Statistical Manual of Mental Disorders* of the American Psychiatric Association (*DSM IV-TR*), marked by affective instability and so forth. Borderline personality disorder it is called.[2] More generally, borderline experience refers to the predominance of primitive defenses. Probably the single most well-known and respected theorist of borderline personality disorder, Otto Kernberg (1985) explains borderline experience in terms of the use of the ego's most primitive defense, splitting, which divides the world in two. This would account for the leading attribute of borderline experience, the tendency toward extremes of idealization and devaluation. Do not some of our culture's ideal images of freedom, such as living in a world without boundaries or limits, free of all entanglements and obligations, able to do anything one wants, reflect borderline symptomatology?

Thinking about borderline experience in clinical terms could be misleading, were it taken as suggesting that it is not a problem faced by us all: the problem of living between agoraphobia and claustrophobia, between anomie on the one hand, being crushed by tradition and practice on the other. We all live between losing and fusing, as Roger Lewin and Clarence Schulz (1992) put it, referring not just to the poles of borderline experience, but to the poles of human experience. It is somewhere between these poles that freedom is experienced, though that puts it too spatially. Freedom is a way of negotiating and living with the dangers of agoraphobia and claustrophobia. In borderline experience we see the poles more clearly because we confront a way of being that lacks what it takes to modulate the swings between them: the cultivation of illusion.

What makes for borderline experience? Here I ask not "where does it come from?" but what does it lack that gives it such a terrible affinity for the extremes? Above all borderline experience lacks the gift of illusion, the ability to use abstract transitional objects, such as fantasies, illusions, and art, to modulate the swings between losing and fusing. "The mother's adaptation to the infant's needs, when good enough, gives the infant the *illusion* that there is an external reality that corresponds to the infant's own capacity to create" (Winnicott, 1971, p. 12). Illusion is the medium of transitional experience. Key to illusion is the way in which it resides in a realm between me and not me, neither inner nor outer. "I create it because it exists without me, but I won't be able to sustain this illusion if you keep asking me about it." If the psycho–logic of transitional experience spoke in sentences, this would be one. Illusion connects and separates internal and external reality, reflecting a separation from reality that is also a fusion with it, what Winnicott calls transitional space. It is in this space that freedom is located.

Though Berlin does not think about it this way (for Berlin, negative freedom is simply good, though it is not all that is good), I suggest that negative and positive freedom reflect the poles of borderline experience, the poles of losing and fusing. Negative freedom risks becoming "me and my will are sovereign over the world," and so losing the human connections that make life worthwhile. Positive freedom risks becoming the fusion of my will with all that is powerful and good, be it my higher self, God, or the Party. Needed is a concept of freedom that sees negative and positive freedom not as competing definitions, but as the ends to which freedom may be pursued, and so lost. Freedom is neither a place nor a possession. Freedom is a delicate balancing act.

As the psychologically attuned reader may have noticed, aspects of Levinas' formulation, not just of freedom but of life, have the quality of borderline experience, the quality of all or nothing-at-all. Either I am for myself, a narcissist wrapped up in my own world, or I abandon myself to the other utterly. Either I impose myself and my frameworks on the other, what Levinas calls totality, or I open myself to infinity. Much of this manuscript has been concerned with formulating ways of taking Levinas' concerns seriously while modulating the swings between losing and fusing, the poles of borderline experience. Murdoch, Adorno, and Winnicott all do this, which is why I have drawn upon them.

At about this point the reader may be asking him or herself whether it really makes sense to characterize a cultural tendency in terms of a psychiatric disorder, especially one as severe as borderline personality disorder. The answer, I think, is that it makes as much sense as Christopher Lasch's (1979) well-known characterization of American culture as a culture of narcissism. In fact, the connection is more than methodological or epistemological; it is substantive. What American psychiatrists and psychoanalysts call "narcissism," British object relations theorists often call "schizoid."

The term "narcissism" tends to be employed diagnostically by those proclaiming loyalty to the drive model (Kernberg) ... "Schizoid" tends to be employed diagnostically by adherents of relational models (Fairbairn, Guntrip), who are interested in articulating their break with drive theory ... These two differing diagnoses and accompanying formulations are applied to patients who are essentially similar, by theorists who start with very different conceptual premises and ideological affiliations. (Greenberg and Mitchell, 1983, p. 385)

Since borderline personality disorder is one of the most extreme forms of schizoid personality disorders, defined in terms of the predominance of primitive splitting defenses, it makes conceptual sense to say that there is a connection between the way of thinking about freedom that I am calling borderline and what Lasch called a culture of narcissism.

For Lasch, the culture of narcissism is a culture of control, achieved by shrinking one's world until it is compact enough to be mastered. That's what makes it narcissistic, the reduction of one's world to a size subject to total control. For most of us, that is a tiny world indeed. Though one hesitates to characterize the Great Tradition in philosophical thinking about freedom as narcissistic or borderline, that is exactly what it is according to Levinas. That is what "totalizing" means, reducing the world to an experience of me. That Levinas' own philosophy has a borderline quality only makes his observation ironic, not false.

ILLUSIONS OF FREEDOM

Freedom is an illusion, and development is marked by progressive disillusionment. Does this mean that development is in the direction of less freedom? No. It means that development requires the loss of the illusion that equates sovereign will with freedom. Surprisingly, many well-known accounts of freedom do not achieve this developmental stage. Instead, they are organized as defenses against the loss of illusion.

About disillusionment, a student of Winnicott puts it this way:

After initial experience of need gratification from a good enough mother, when additional needs arise, the infant develops the illusion that he "created" his object of fulfillment ... With the inevitable gradual disillusionment which occurs, transitional objects and phenomena appear as substitute satisfactions. They are created by the child's adaptation of a part of the external world to conform to the configurations of his needs. Since our needs are never completely satisfied, we are everlastingly preoccupied with attempts to adapt outer reality to inner need and express this in such "intermediate" forms of adult activity as artistic creativity. (Greenbaum, 1978, p. 195)

From this perspective, freedom comes awfully close to art. Freedom is the art of not always asking whether it is I who am conforming to the world, or the world that is conforming to me. Freedom is the paradox of needing and using others in order not to depend on them. This is as true when the other is mother as when the other is one's fellow citizens. "By flight to split-off intellectual functioning it is possible to resolve the paradox, but the price of this is the loss of the value of the paradox itself" (Winnicott, 1971, p. xii). The value of the paradox is freedom.

Most of the perversions of freedom, generally associated with what Berlin calls positive freedom, are the result of insufficient disillusion, in which the individual is unable to give up the original experience of omnipotence, as the narcissistic wound is unbearable. Most of the perversions of freedom attempt to solve the paradox, generally the worst thing we can do. Levinas generates a powerful critique of attempts to preserve the illusion of omnipotence. What Levinas calls totality is this illusion.

Freedom of the will, or meant to do that

When I was a toddler, just learning to walk, I would often stumble and fall. My coordination was not yet adequate to my will to walk. When I fell I would yell out "meant to do that, meant to do that," or so my parents tell me. I would, in other words, try to take control of my limits by turning them into an intention. This is not quite how Levinas interprets the history of Western thought, but it comes close, and Sartre is at the center. Says Sartre, "thus in a certain sense I *choose* being born" (1999, p. 67, author's emphasis). This, says Levinas, is the flaw at the core of Western thought. "We still reason as though the ego had been present at the creation of the world, as though the world, henceforth in its charge, had issued from the act of free will" ("Substitution," p. 54).

We reason, says Levinas, as though I (each of us, one by one) was there first, that I made the world, and so can be at home in it. As though being at home were the goal. As though I can be at home only in what I have made. As though I gave birth to myself. As though being at home and freedom had anything to do with each other. But that is how freedom has come to be conceptualized in the West. Being at home in the world comes to mean regarding the world as though I had made it, or would have made it this way if I could. It is this that unites a disparate group of authors. I am going to run through them terribly quickly, Western thinking on freedom reduced to a few paragraphs. My defense is that Levinas does the same in *Totality and Infinity*, and it is Levinas' vision I am after, even as I agree with his critique.

For Kant, human freedom is the freedom to accept objective reality, such as the laws of nature, or the categorical imperative. "The will (*der Wille*) is a kind of causality belonging to living beings insofar as they are rational; freedom would be the property of this causality that makes it effective independent of any determination by alien causes" (Kant, 1981, p. 49). Kant says this because he believes these laws are given their content by our own minds, so that to accept these laws is to accept what we have ourselves willed. He is not so different from Sartre in this regard.

For Hegel freedom is being at home in the world through full possession of it (*zu Hause sein in der Welt*). To be free is to know that one would have made the world as it is, as one can deduce its present structure from principles. The dualism, or conflict, between individual morality and social institutions is only apparent. Modern institutions such as family, civil society, and the state, do not require duties in conflict with my individual ends. Rather, these institutions are the realization of individual free will, a doctrine known as compatibilism. If one had known the course of history, and if one had the power to change it, one would have made it the way it is. "What is rational is actual and what is actual is rational" (Hegel, 1967, p. 10). Is that not the world-historical version of "meant to do that?"

For Nietzsche (1968a, p. 221), freedom is the will to power. Only we get Nietzsche wrong if we think the will to power has much to do with imposing my will on others. That's Nietzsche pop, the Nietzsche of my undergraduates who confuse him with Ayn Rand. When Nietzsche writes of the will to power he is generally writing about the will to power over myself, the will to conquer all that is weak and base in me, and so have the strength to will what is. *Amor fati* Nietzsche called it, the will to love one's fate, the will to wish it would never end. Ignominious adaptation to one's prison is what Theodor Adorno (1974, pp. 97–8) called *amor fati*, and he is just right. One must accept one's fate, but why must one love it? Is that not the core of self-deception? *Amor fati* is the philosophical version of "meant to do that."

For Rousseau, freedom means liberation from the knowledge of one's terrible dependence on others. It is this that unites *The Second Discourse*, *Emile*, and *The Social Contract*. The general will restores the freedom of the noble savage by making it as if I give myself up to all I give myself up to none. "Which means nothing else than that he shall be forced to be free; for such is the condition which, uniting every citizen in his Homeland, guarantees him from all personal dependence" (Rousseau, 1964, para. 54 [bk 1, c7]). For Rousseau, freedom means freedom from narcissistic humiliation, that knowledge that one is weak and needy of others.[3]

Jean Starobinski (1988, pp. xxii–xxiii) says that freedom for Rousseau is "defined essentially as freedom from difference or otherness." If it is "only" the reality of others that reminds us of our constraints, eliminate otherness and we shall all be free as the day we were born. That is, as ignorant as a baby of its dependence. Rousseau's freedom is identical with the pre-doorbell state, what Levinas calls "living from." Rousseau's freedom differs, however, from what Levinas calls "narcissism" (*narcissisme*). For Levinas, narcissism suggests an anxiety that one might be trapped in oneself, unable to escape (OB, p. 81). This is, of course, the dread of "there is."

In surprisingly similar ways, these authors transform freedom into the will that makes itself at home in the world by making the world as I would wish it to be, or at least as my higher self would wish it to be. At least in retrospect, at least in my imagination. Often, it is an imagination little different from "meant to do that."

While Levinas uses the language of ontology to describe this phenomenon, "the reduction of the Other to the Same," I have focused on the self-deception of the will. The reason is my topic, the close alliance, at least historically, between freedom and the will. In fact, says Berlin, and on this point he is echoed by Hannah Arendt (2000), it is this close alliance that has so often led to the self-deceptions of freedom. If my will that sits inside my head is sovereign, then politics must forever be the war of all against all, even if it is a war conducted with ballots instead of bullets. How could it be otherwise, for politics is where wills collide.

Positive freedom misunderstands freedom as an inner experience built upon a political model, a model of *arche*, or rule: higher over the lower, better over the worse. Plato was the first, *The Republic* built upon the correspondence between the proper (hierarchically) organized state and the proper (hierarchically) organized self. Of course, different theorists conceptualize the relationship between inner and outer freedom differently, but Berlin (1969, pp. 135–6) is not mistaken to see the connection: as the higher self finds its tally in higher laws, so obeying these laws is tantamount to obeying my higher self. And so it goes with Kant, Hegel, Rousseau, Nietzsche, and Sartre.

Almost all of the perversions of positive freedom that Berlin identifies are attempts to turn the loss of sovereign will into a species of freedom. Similarly, almost all of the self-deception that marks Western thinking about freedom stems from the attempt to render an unfree sovereign will really free. Though I have not mentioned Plato, surely Plato's Socrates belongs to this story too, a man who could never be made unhappy by things that happened to him, things that were beyond his control, what the Greeks called *tuche*. Socrates is free because neither his happiness nor his goodness depend on anything outside himself. It is only in Greek tragedy that one finds not suspicion about freedom but incredulity: of course man is not free. Look at what happens to him. Would anyone choose that? Are you crazy?[4]

A friend describes freedom as the freedom to lose herself in a book or play for a little while. She feels transported, given a glimpse of a larger world. What she fears most is to be trapped in her own little world, as though she were a prisoner in Plato's cave whose walls are her own bag of skin, as Lacan puts it. All who equate freedom with freedom of the will ignore this dimension of freedom, the freedom *not* to experience the world as my home (or my workshop), but as a place of strange wonder. Seen from this perspective, the moral masochism of Levinas is not intrinsic to his vision of freedom. Freedom as the freedom to be released from one's little self, in order to open oneself up to the awesome otherness of the world, may not be the whole of freedom, but it is a part, perhaps the most human part. Murdoch's view is similar. Levinas' vision of freedom is an escape from the freedom of the will, but it is not an escape from freedom.

A recent movie, *Being John Malkovich* imagines for one insane moment what it would be like if everyone looked and acted just like me. The answer is hell. Bill Gates writes about the wonders of modern technology, imagining that in a few years I will be able to watch a version of *Gone With the Wind* in which it is my face, not that of Rhett Butler or Scarlett O'Hara, that is the face of the hero or heroine. One does not need to be familiar with Levinas' evocation of the face of the other as a source of awe and wonder to see in Gates' imaginings a vision of the future as narcissistic hell.

There is, it seems, something about technological progress that magnifies and distorts the classic Western ideal of freedom of the will. Narcissistic fantasy becomes reality, as it becomes thinkable that I might really be the center of the world. This is *not* Kant or Hegel. In their accounts reason and history mediate between my will and my world. Drop out reason and history, and you've got Bill Gates.

Levinas offers a valid vision of freedom, and a grand critique of the Western way of thinking about freedom. In one way or another, so much of the Western tradition is about pretending that I have made (or would have made, had I the power and the knowledge) the world that limits my freedom. The Western idea of freedom is a defense against narcissistic humiliation. Levinas sees this because for him narcissism is no comfort but a trap, the prison that turns my being into a deadness that closes off the world, the horror of the "there is." To have seen this is a brilliant insight.

Like many brilliant insights, Levinas' vision is too dependent on the vision it opposes. Like many brilliant insights, it turns the vision it opposes upside down (inside out would be a better image in this case, my insides exposed to the universe). Against freedom of the will in all its guises, Levinas posits freedom of the abandonment of the will, an openness to the world. But it is an openness to the world that lacks rhythm, an attunement to other people, including the other people in oneself. This is not, I think, a humane vision of freedom, not even for the sake of the other human.

Nevertheless, there is much to learn from Levinas, above all the virtues of passivity and self-abandonment. Because this is a powerful but vague and frightening idea, I have tried to give it mundane content, talking about a friend who likes to lose herself in a book or play. Others like to lose themselves in romantic love, a phenomenon that Levinas obsesses over (for Levinas, obsession is good) because it comes so close to what he is talking about, and at the same time is so different, so bound to bodies (T&I, pp. 254–80). Where it gets truly frightening is when freedom is expressed as the desire to lose oneself to a political or social movement. But that is no longer Levinas. For Levinas, the other is never a group, and never an ideology.

Political theory of freedom

On the contrary, Levinas remains an individualist. I may in a certain sense, but only in a certain sense, give myself over to the other, but never to the group. I must always keep part of myself for myself, so that I possess the psychological resources to serve the other. Some *one* must be there to see the tears of the other. "The I alone can perceive the 'secret tears' of the Other, which are caused by the functioning–albeit reasonable–of the hierarchy" ("Transcendence and Height," p. 23). By "the hierarchy," Levinas means the social order. We require social order to live together as humans, but ethics requires that humans not give themselves over to that order. We must retain our individuality, so that we might give ourselves over to the other. This is the best part of Levinas.

All the others in the world make up what Levinas calls the third (*le tiers*), the other to the Other. "The Other and the third party, my neighbors, contemporaries of one another, put distance between me and the other and the third party" (OB, p. 157). The world is filled with others, each as obligating as the first. I may owe the other everything, but when there are many others I must distribute my obligations among them. "To the extravagant generosity of the for-the-other is superimposed a reasonable order ... of justice through knowledge," is how Levinas puts it in "Peace and Proximity," his most sustained treatment of ethics and politics (ibid., p. 169).

Questions of justice take on a new meaning with the introduction of the third. Indeed, questions of distributive justice first become possible, for there was never any question of how much I owed the other *vis-à-vis* myself: everything. Now I must consider how to distribute my responsibilities. While my responsibilities may be infinite, my resources, including time and attention, are not. The considerations involved are little different from ordinary procedures of distributive justice. "Comparison is superimposed onto my relationship with the unique and the incomparable, and, in view of equity and equality, a weighing, a thinking, a calculation" ("Peace and Proximity," p. 168).

Calling distributive justice a superimposition might be read as suggesting that it is not implied by the original encounter with the other. This though does not seem correct, as Levinas suggests that others were present all along, flanking, so to speak, my original encounter with the face of the other, "where in his turn the Other appears in solidarity with all the others" (T&I, p. 280). If so, then we must conclude that the imperative to care for all the others is itself part of the original encounter with the other. *How* we do so is the subject of justice.

Justice remains what it always was, from Aristotle to Rawls, a fair distribution. What changes is what is being distributed: neither rights nor resources, but infinite responsibility. The decisive question, says Levinas, is whether we see justice as the rationalization of violence (the war of all against all, including the violence that is the economic order), or as the rationalization of responsibility for the other. If we do not remember that it is the later, then justice all too readily becomes the war of all against all with a good conscience. Levinas would surely include John Rawls' *A Theory of Justice* here.

One seldom turns to politics with such a deep sense of relief. Not just because the tone of Levinas' politics lacks the hyperbole of his ethics, but because politics, the introduction of the third, saves us from being consumed by the infinite need of the other. The third party acts like the original third, the Oedipal father, who steps between the intimate, potentially incestuous relationship between mother and son to turn the son to the outside world. Concerned with how I distribute my obligations to many others, as well as the way others treat me as yet another other, the "law of the father" transforms an intimate, potentially suffocating ethical relationship into a relationship with a world of others. Saying becomes the said of law and institutions.

The double structure of community is how Simon Critchley (1999, p. 227) refers to this aspect of Levinas' thought. The community is a relationship among equals which is nonetheless based on the inegalitarian moment of the ethical relationship. In putting it this way, Critchley smooths over the tension between saying and said, the face-to-face and the community. To be sure, there is apparent evidence in Levinas for this interpretation. Critchley quotes Levinas as stating that justice is "an incessant correction of the asymmetry of proximity"—that is the asymmetry of the face to face relationship, in which I owe the other everything (OB, p. 158). But by this Levinas does not mean that through justice "I become the Other's equal," as Critchley (1999, p. 231) puts it. Levinas means quite the opposite: that we are all unequal before the other (Wingenbach, 1999, pp. 226–7).

Instead of creating a symmetrical relationship among equals, Levinas constructs an aporia, or perhaps it is just an impossibility theorem: that I be responsible for all the others as I was for the one other. As Jeffrey Bloechl (2000, p. 143) puts it, "it is not just this one other person who obsesses me, but all the Others too. This is more than an empirical complication: in the human face, I am commanded by all the Others at once." How can I do what cannot but must be done? This is the problem posed by Levinas for politics.

The introduction of the third, which appeared to be such a relief, turns out to be no such thing. While the third makes me an other to all the others, insuring that I too will not be sacrificed, the third adds another other (actually, an infinite number of others) whom I must serve. "The face is both the neighbor and the face of all faces," says Levinas (OB, p. 160). Rather than relieving me from obligation, Levinas' introduction of the third relieves political theory from having to justify what it can only serve. Politics need no longer fulfill the role it is incapable of fulfilling, that of founding philosophy. "The role assigned to philosophy is not to provide solutions, but to prevent the cynicism of political reason from silencing other dimensions of thought" (Davis, 1996, p. 144).

While the third provides only fugitive relief, another aspect of Levinas' politics provides more lasting appeal—its sheer quirkiness. Many of Levinas' political judgments seem to have liberated themselves from his philosophy. To be sure, this is not always good. Consider Levinas' tendency to essentialize about what he knows the least, such as the East, in his article on the Soviet–Chinese rapprochement ("Débat Russo-Chinois"). Consider his disingenuous claims, such as his reference to "my Muslim friend, my unhated enemy of the Six-Day War!" ("Space," p. 264). Is it better to kill an unhated enemy? Will that comfort his family? Are not such designations designed to comfort me instead, to persuade me of my goodness? Is Levinas immune to tragedy?

If Levinas' political writings don't always get it right, they have the virtue of reality: the reality of contemporary events, the reality of politics, even the reality of emotions, which do not always track our philosophies. What is certainly wrong, as Caygill (2000, p. 6) points out in his essay on Levinas' *Esprit* articles, is to see Levinas' political theory in terms of "a numerical formalism that moves from the dyadic ethical to the triadic political relation, from an ethical relation to the 'other' to a legal-political relation to the 'third.'" Important is not the structure of his political theory, but the fact that Levinas would dare direct his philosophy of obligation of one soul to another toward politics in the first place. The result is disorientation, but not incoherence. Levinas sometimes writes as if he had all along intended to challenge political theory, as when he opens *Totality and Infinity* with reflections on war and violence.

Levinas' political theory retains key elements of liberalism, even as it is defiantly non-liberal. Individualism remains a value, but only because it takes an individual to see the tears of the other. It is in letting myself be guided by these tears that I realize my freedom. Tears glistening in the other's eyes are, it seems, the one particularity I am allowed to notice. Perhaps it is the most important.

Against "liberalism," Levinas opposes none of the usual categories, such as communitarianism, but "secrecy," a surprising choice. With the term "secrecy" he is not talking about privacy or isolation, but the "secrecy which holds to the responsibility for the other" (E&I, pp. 79–81). Responsibility is an intimate relationship. While it may be rationalized, even bureaucratized, Levinas suspects that in the end it is mass society, in all its guises, liberal and totalitarian, that is the great enemy of responsibility, for mass society compromises the privacy of the soul. But soul has not been a political category for some time now. We are not necessarily better for it.

Putting politics and soul together on the same page is the act of a prophet, not a philosopher, it might be argued. True enough. Above all, Levinas is a prophet. That, though, is a more complex designation than it might first appear to be. In *The Symbolism of Evil*, Paul Ricoeur (1967, pp. 54–62) writes of prophecy in terms of the tension between infinite demand and finite commandment. We think of the prophet as the one who utters a demand aimed at the sinful human heart. Consequently, it is a demand that can never be met. The result is to place God at an infinite distance from man, the One who accuses. But, that is not the whole story according to Ricoeur. For a long time, biblical critics "failed to recognize this rhythm of prophetism and legalism. They also displayed an excessive contempt for legalism ... This tension between the absolute, formless, demand and the finite law, which breaks the demand into crumbs, is essential." Consider Moses. At the moment when "Moses is supposed to promulgate the moral and cultural charter ... it is to the inner obedience of the heart that he appeals" (Deuteronomy 6, 11, 29, 30) (Ricoeur, 1967, pp. 59, 61).

Levinas is no law giver. Levinas is a prophet in precisely that sense explicated by Ricoeur, one whose infinite demand takes the form of an accusation: you have done less than you could for the other because you have not done everything for one and all the others too. Not only that, but one can read Levinas' concept of saying (*le Dire*), in which I wordlessly expose myself to the infinite otherness of the other, as a characterization of what it is to be a prophet. Levinas both practices prophecy and characterizes it. Still, the tension between prophecy and law is not absent in his work. "Both the hierarchy [law, state, and bureaucracy] taught by Athens and the *abstract* and slightly *anarchical* ethical individualism taught by Jerusalem are *simultaneously necessary* in order to suppress violence," says Levinas, referring not just to physical violence, but to every way of living that does not put the other first. But while hierarchy and ethical individualism are both necessary, Levinas concludes that in our era the "protest against hierarchy" must take precedence ("Transcendence & Height," p. 24, his emphasis). In our age, violence is more likely to be the result of the smoothly functioning system than its breakdown. Ethical revolution is today more important than building up the institutions of law and justice, even as there might come a day when this was not the case.

The tension between prophecy and justice, the claims of the other and the claims of all the others, abides. There is no solution, no answer, just "permanent tension and ambiguity," as Bloechl (2000, p. 144) puts it. Justice remains a dangerous business, as likely to subdue the particular as serve it. But what is the alternative? It seems too easy to conclude, as one commentator does, that for Levinas "philosophy serves justice by both thematizing difference and reducing the thematized to difference" (Critchley, 1999, p. 235). To be sure, it is Levinas himself who says this, always a good source for a sympathetic critic (OB, p. 65). But that doesn't automatically make it right. Levinas downplays the radicalism of his own teaching, making it more symmetrical than it is, contributing to the formalism to which Caygill refers. Not symmetry but impossibility is the mark of Levinas' political theory, in which philosophy serves justice by reminding us that its task is impossible—to treat each and every other as though he or she were my world. Levinas would teach us to live with this impossible task without telling us how.

In taking up this impossible task, I become free. Not to do what I want, but to put my very being into question, and so open myself to the encounter with the other, as though the other were a wedge inserted into my ego, freeing me from the narcissism of my own little existence. For Levinas, that is the true meaning of freedom, the investiture of freedom he calls it, as though I were a knight sent on a sacred quest to serve the other (T&I, pp. 302–4). In taking up this calling, I become free.

The reader who has followed me this far might respond along the following lines. "Isn't this what Levinas is always doing, reversing the usual meaning of terms, and so turning freedom into slavery?" Sympathetic as I am to a humane and straightforward reading of Levinas, with this reading I cannot agree. Levinas understands something important about freedom: that it has almost nothing to do with will. That is the topic of the next section.

"FREEDOM WITH"

Levinas' vision of freedom is not alien to "freedom with," though they are hardly identical. For Levinas, exit is not freedom. Escape (*l'évasion*), the topic of Chapter 2, is not freedom. Freedom for Levinas means self-abandonment, as it does for many authors, but not abandonment of this world. Freedom ties us to this world in an endless series of obligations, and so prevents us from floating off into infinity. In this regard, at least, Levinas' vision of freedom resembles what I will call "freedom with."

"Freedom with" views freedom as a transitional object or experience, as Winnicott would put it.

The political philosopher Hannah Arendt's vision comes even closer to "freedom with." Arendt begins "What is Freedom?" by emphasizing that freedom is always an experience with others. She concludes her essay by writing as though these others exist to serve as audience for my virtuosity, my performance.

> Under human conditions, which are determined by the fact that not man but men live on the earth, freedom and sovereignty are so little identical that they cannot even exist simultaneously. When men wish to be sovereign, as individuals or as organized groups, they must submit to the oppression of the will, be this the individual will with which I force myself, or by the "general will" of an organized group. If men wish to be free, it is precisely sovereignty they must renounce. (Arendt, 2000, p. 455)

Like Levinas, Arendt rejects the equation of freedom with will. Unlike Levinas, she defines freedom in terms of creativity, able to give the virtuoso performance, and so bring something new into the world. Freedom is natality, the ability to weave something new out of the remnants of existence. Creation is the miracle that keeps the world from running down, or becoming a giant automaton. Natality defeats entropy, close cousin of what Levinas calls "there is" (Arendt, 2000, pp. 458–60).

In "What is Freedom?" Arendt writes as though it were the role of others to serve as audience to my virtuoso performance. A dancer could not create if there was no one to watch, no one who even knew what dance was. Arendt's vision of freedom recognizes the importance of others, but not their contribution. They are the audience, and freedom among others means, it seems, each taking his or her place in the audience before stepping on stage.

What if we took Arendt's image of the virtuoso performance and made it a shared accomplishment? Jazz musicians talk about being "in the groove," a state of improvisation that involves not just me and my music, but others as well if I am playing in a group. Although individual skills and talent are involved, they do not create the groove. The groove is created by the space among the players, not too close and not too tight. As such, in the groove is a temporary creation, as transient as the performance. The negotiation of talents it has been called, each player in tune with himself, the music, and the other players—at least for a little while.

While "in the groove" involves most of the experiences that Levinas spurns, including participation, rhythm, and play, it is hardly an unbounded experience. Abandoning myself to the anonymity of the All will hardly find me "in the groove." "In the groove" expresses a spontaneity built on hundreds of hours of negotiation, learning to barter the assertion of others with one's own self-assertion. The negotiation of wills it might be called, except that it is not just will, but will merged with talent to create something new. Intersubjectively warranted will, it might be called.

This sounds a little like that experience of positive freedom that Berlin condemns, in which I internalize the constraint of others and call it my own freedom. Whether this is bad depends, it seems, on what one is internalizing, a distinction Berlin recognizes when he calls attention to the difference between internalizing a piece of music and internalizing a doctrine. The former I can make my own; the latter almost always remains an alien presence (Berlin, 1969, p. 41).

Though Arendt does not write about shared experiences of freedom in "What is Freedom?" she does in her writing on revolution, stating that members of the French Resistance were "visited for the first time in their lives by an apparition of freedom." Not because they fought the Nazis. Millions did this. But because the revolutionaries abandoned their private lives, working together every day to create and sustain "that public space between themselves where freedom could appear" (Arendt, 1977, p. 4). Does this not sound like being in the groove? Of course, we should think twice about the virtue of abandoning one's private life, a theme central to Arendt but not Levinas. For Levinas I must retain my private life, so I can witness the tears of the other. In this regard, Levinas knows something important that Arendt does not.

While there is little sense of "freedom with" in Levinas, the concept is not entirely lacking. One sees its trace in his discussion of fecundity, which overcomes the boredom of aging by bringing new life to the world. "Fecundity continues history without producing old age ... In fecundity the I transcends the world ... not to dissolve into the anonymity of the *there is*, but in order to go ... *elsewhere*" (T&I, p. 268, author's emphasis). By fecundity, Levinas means not just producing children, but creating something new, such as a work of philosophy. Here Levinas sounds like Plato, but that is nothing new either. New is that Levinas sounds like Arendt on natality. One overcomes the entropy of "there is" not by exit, but by creation. To be sure, Levinas fudges, suggesting that creation and exit are close cousins. (Is "elsewhere" not a synonym for exit?) In creation

I bring something to the world before I exit. That is not the same thing as bringing something new to the world through exit, even though they are related. The imminence of my death may intensify my creativity.

One sees the distinction between life and death more clearly when one sees natality as a group project. "Freedom with" has the quality of what I called attunement when discussing Winnicott. Donovan sings that he rarely thinks of freedom without thinking of the times he has been loved. The tone of "Colours" is reverie, his memories segueing from the blond hair of the girl he loved to the blue color of the sky to the green color of the corn. He is alone, but he's not, and in this in-between state of reverie he can feel his freedom, connected to the world but separate at the same time.

Donovan's freedom is not an oceanic feeling that Freud (1961, p. 11) writes of; nor is it an experience of merger. Nor is Donovan's freedom "just another word for nothing left to lose," to mix popular songs for a moment. Donovan's freedom exists in some in-between place and time, most akin perhaps to what Winnicott calls being alone with another. In this state we do not pretend the other does not exist, or that we have no need of others. That is not freedom; that is avoidant attachment. Nor do we cling to other people or ideas. But we don't work at not clinging either. Donovan's "freedom with" has the quality of being lightly held, so lightly one can imagine being alone in the universe all the while knowing one is not. "Freedom with" knows that the realm of freedom is not the inner-person but the inter-person, the quality of my relationships with others.

For Friedrich Schiller (1983; Gardiner, p. 1979), freedom is reconciliation between reason and feeling. Man or woman is free to the degree he or she heals the divided self, and this is best done through play. The so-called *Spieltrieb*, or play drive, mediates reason and sensibility, suspending practical needs and demands, releasing our powers from instrumental purposes into an activity that is its own end and purpose. "Freedom with" is much concerned with play. "In the groove" has the quality of play. But it is not Schiller's play, for "freedom with" takes reality more seriously. "Freedom with" is less concerned with mediating between my reason and sensibility, and more concerned with mediating between me and other people, those to whom I am attached in love, hate, citizenship, and friendship. Not the freedom of the inner-person, but the freedom of the inter-person, is the concern of "freedom with."

"Freedom with" is practiced among others, and with others. "Freedom with" acknowledges that all of our experiences of freedom are with others: real others, imaginary others, but always others. Others are neither obstacles nor adjuncts to my will, but the condition having a will in the first place. This may be bad, as in the case of false consciousness, but this does not mean that "true consciousness" is pure will. True consciousness, or rather (since true and false consciousness are idealizations) fortunate consciousness, is formed through the dialectic of wills, the mutual education and elaboration of wills. We are, if we are fortunate, born into this dialectic of will, mother responding to our will, but never perfectly (if she did, we would become will monsters, utter narcissists), and so in turn shaping our will as we shape hers. And so it goes with fathers, teachers, friends, and citizens.

How "freedom with" might be relevant to politics is apparent, even if I haven't spelled out the details. At its best, politics is the negotiation of talents, the dialectic of wills. Locating freedom in the space between you, me, and all the rest, "freedom with" has the quality of the public space formed by the table around which we are all sitting, the table that separates and connects us at the same time, a favorite image of Arendt's. The difference is that "freedom with" is more dynamic, almost as though we had to keep making the table around which we are sitting. The space of freedom is not secured by the boundaries around it, the walls of the polis. The space of freedom is the space that must be constantly created by the relationships that connect and separate us. Freedom is located in the space between you and me.

Levinas takes us halfway to that space, and from the direction opposite from that usually traveled (usually from me to you, for Levinas from you to me). For that reason he is useful in shattering the conjunction of freedom and will. What is lacking in Levinas is any sense that freedom might have to do with playful relatedness, attunement, what's called in the groove. Freedom, it appears, is not so much about doing what one wants as it is about being in the world in a certain way with others. Seen from this perspective, freedom is not an act of egoistic self-assertion that must make mincemeat of Levinas' project. But seen in this way freedom remains incompatible with Levinas' project, hewing too close to what Levinas, following Lévi-Bruhl, calls participation. Only now we see that participation is not just about abandoning oneself to anonymity. It is about sharing the world, and oneself, with others.

In his introduction to a fine collection of essays on freedom, David Miller (1991, p. 2) argues that anything we say about freedom must be recognizable by the Chinese students in Tiananmen Square in Peking in 1989 as what they were fighting for. It is hard to know how to take such blanket statements, but the idea behind Miller's suggestion seems sound. We should not allow ourselves to become too esoteric or inward-oriented about freedom in a world in which many lack even the basic political freedoms. I believe that the Chinese students would recognize "freedom with," more so perhaps than my American students. For the Chinese students, as Miller points out, there was as yet no tension between democracy and liberty. Freedom was not about being left alone to make money. It was not even about being left alone to try my own experiment in living. Freedom was about creating a common world.

Coming from a culture as traditional as it is modern, as socialist as it is capitalist, the Chinese students might understand better than we that freedom is not from others, but with others. They might even recognize that this is the freedom they were practicing for a few days in Tiananmen Square. About this I can only guess, of course.[5] But if the reader finds my guess plausible, then I will at least have demonstrated that "freedom with" is not an idealistic, esoteric concept, but a practical, everyday one, albeit a concept requiring a subtle appreciation of everyday relationships.

5

Love, Pity, and Humanity

Ethics for Levinas must be lifted out of nature because love cannot be relied upon. Love is always flirting with selfishness, as in "I love you because you make me feel so good." Love wants reciprocity. Attachment, affection, even pity and ordinary human decency: all have the quality of a "transfer of sentiment," more the mark of a market exchange than an ethical relationship ("Substitution," p. 91).

To be sure, Levinas takes pains to distinguish between eros and love, but it is not a distinction that carries much weight for him. For Levinas, all love is at risk of becoming sensuous, which is why it must be transformed into responsibility. In "Phenomenology of Eros," Levinas suggests on one page that all love is touched with eros; on another page occurs the phrase "*amour sans Eros*" (T&I, pp. 256–66; *Totalité*, pp. 286–99).

> The love without *eros* to which Levinas once refers—and which Rosenzweig champions (on p. 163), though in treating God's love for man—gets referred to henceforth as responsibility in order to mark its difference from ego-based desire and to mark that it is indeed a response. (Llewelyn, 1991, p. 240)

Llewelyn has the trajectory of Levinas' project just right, from a modest and ambivalent confidence in love in *Totality and Infinity* to deep suspicion in *Otherwise than Being*.[1] The result, as Llewelyn recognizes, is that Levinas asks of man and woman what Rosenzweig would attribute to God.

Can we imagine another way of thinking about love, one that does not sharply distinguish between eros and responsibility, one that does not draw the line so definitively between self and other out of fear that self-ishness might creep in somewhere in-between? What about the love commanded by Jesus Christ: to love your neighbor as yourself (Mark 12:31; Matthew 22:39; Luke 10:27; Romans 13:9; Galatians 5:14; James 2:8)? It is, as noted in Chapter 1, not a commandment restricted to the New Testament (Leviticus 19:18).

Levinas was asked this question, and he hesitates to answer (*Of God*, pp. 90–1). Martin Buber and Franz Rosenzweig did not find the translation straightforward, rendering the phrase "love your neighbor, he is like you." They translated it this way, says Levinas, because "love your neighbor as yourself" sounds too much like you love yourself most. Commenting on the commandment to "love your neighbor" in *The Star of Redemption*, Rosenzweig (1985, pp. 239–40) says that it means that "man is not to deny himself. Precisely here in the commandment to love one's neighbor, his self is definitely confirmed in its place." I remain I, and you remain you, an equality of difference. Rosenzweig's view is compatible with Levinas', but the tone is different. So different that even Buber and Rosenzweig's version is unacceptable to Levinas. Indeed, their translation raises the whole question of how one best translates a questionable phrase. (The Greek phrase in Matthew 22:39 is simply "*agapao ho plesion sou hos seautou.*") [2]

The answer, suggests Levinas, is to translate in light of the entirety of the book. And the entirety of the Bible implies only one thing: the other always comes first.

> This is what I have called, in Greek language, the dissymmetry of the interpersonal relationship. If there is not this dissymmetry, then no line of what I have written can hold. And this is vulnerability. Only a vulnerable I can love his neighbor.

The translation Levinas settles on is "Love your neighbor; all that is yourself; this work is yourself, this love is yourself" (*Of God*, p. 91). Since the Greek phrase contains only three operative words, *agapao plesion seautou* (love neighbor self), Levinas' translation is, of course, actually a gloss.

Levinas' idea is that your neighbor is already in you, more you than you. But if your neighbor is inside you, you are there too, and it remains unclear, no matter *where* the boundary is located (that is, inside or outside the self), why you and I must be separated by infinity (in the third sense of Chapter 1) if I am to treat you decently. Why can't we be intimate, even woven together, and still care? Levinas *does* sometimes sound like Kant (1959) on pathological love, a love that is so personal it distracts us from our universal obligations.

Levinas writes much about the maternal as a model for morality, but the maternal is as much about attachment as separation, as any mother knows. The maternal is best conceived as that transitional space Winnicott writes about, neither self nor other, not because they are confused, but because no one has to ask. Levinas is always asking, or rather telling: keep self and other distinct, lest selfishness (totalization) creep in. Instead of always returning to the razor's edge of infinity, let us dwell with transitional experience, that space between self and other that is so precious precisely because it is indistinct. It is transitional experience that is the undefined locus of morality. It is this transitional experience that makes sense of the command to "love your neighbor as yourself." I love my neighbor as myself because a part of me is identified with my neighbor, because my neighbor is in me, and I assume I am in him or her, and no one can ever sort it all out, but fortunately we often don't need to try. Levinas is always trying. For Levinas, morality is the product of sharp distinctions and infinite distances.

TRAGEDY, LOVE, AND PITY

Tragedy takes place in transitional space, that space between myth and poetry. Tragedy takes place in that transitional space between Abraham and Odysseus, the poles of Levinas' project. Abraham represents Jerusalem, land of faith and revelation. Odysseus does not, however, represent Athens. To be sure, Odysseus is not Achilles either; the *Odyssey* is not the *Iliad*. Not heroic values, but civilized ones prevail in the *Odyssey*. Nevertheless, the *Odyssey* is located in a deeply mythic and feudal world. Greek tragedy was, as Jean-Pierre Vernant and Pierre Vidal-Naquet (1988, p. 51) puts it, "born when myth began to be assessed from a citizen's point of view." They mean when myth began to be assessed by the standards of law and justice, but I would add by the standards of fellow-feeling for humanity (not just fellow Greeks, as Aeschylus' *Persians* reveals). Greek tragedy was born when citizens became able to see, and not just see but feel, the tears of their fellow citizens. Greek tragedy is participation (not just seeing, but participation) in another's sorrow.[3]

Permit me this digression. Follow me from the land of Levinas to another, the land of Greek tragedy. Not the Greek tragedy of the Oedipus complex, but the Greek tragedy that tells an even more subtle story about human relations. Melanie Klein (1975b) thought this Greek tragedy was the *Oresteia*, an account of Orestes' depressive guilt at killing his mother, and his cure at the hands of Athena, who pities his suffering humanity. I think the analytic theme is even grander than that, or rather an extension of this theme from gods to humans. The pity and compassion of others for ourselves, and ourselves for others, make human life worthwhile, creating some of the deepest, and deeply satisfying, connections between us. It is an autistic–contiguous satisfaction, one that hews close to dread, and (surprisingly) even closer to eros.

Greek tragedy may not be the real Athens; certainly it is not the land of her philosophers. A land of pity for one's fellow humans is the Athens idealized by her tragic poets. All along the problem with Levinas has been the dualisms: self or other; egoism or self-abandonment; "there is" or infinity. There is no shared us, no "freedom with," no humanism of the fellow human. Greek tragedy is a humanism of the fellow human. Greek tragedy is the example I had in mind when I answered my friend, in my reply to his letter quoted in Chapter 1, that a humanism of the fellow human is the mortal answer to infinity. Greek tragedy provides another way to talk about a participation (in Lévy-Bruhl's sense as interpreted by Levinas) that does not lead to abandonment of the self, but sharing in others.

The pity of Greek tragedy is not the same as love. To pity one's neighbor is not the same as loving him or her. But, I will argue, they are closely related. For the ancient Greek, pity had the quality of sensuousness, eros. Pity was the province of Dionysos, just a baby step from love. Since it is not Levinas' suspicion of love *per se* that I am concerned with, but his suspicion of ordinary human attachments, pity is a fine stand-in for love.

Most of the criticism of Levinas' anti-humanism, as I call it, has focused on his separation of eros and ethics. Feminists such as Irigaray have been especially critical in this regard. I agree, but have sought to extend this argument from eros to attachment, arguing that Levinas can find no real place for human attachment. Pity is an example of an attachment not generally experienced as erotic or sensuous in the modern West. That, though, seems to be a misunderstanding; the ancient Greeks knew better.

It is fitting to begin a discussion of Greek tragedy and Levinas with a quotation from Heidegger (1949, p. 393), but only because Heidegger gets it wrong in exactly the way Levinas says he does.[4] Heidegger concludes "What is Metaphysics?" this way.

> The last poem of the last poet of the dawn-period of Greece—
> Sophocles' "Oedipus in Colonus"—closes with words that hark back
> far beyond our ken to the hidden history of these people and marks
> their entry into the unknown truth of Being.
> > But cease now, and nevermore
> > Life up the lament.
> > For all this is determined.

Whatever the merits of his praise of the pre-Socratic philosophers, Heidegger gets *Oedipus at Colonus*, and the tragic poets in general, backwards. The tragic poets sought not to build a house for Being to appear. On the contrary, they wished to build a house, a polis, in which men and women might find some human comfort and companionship in the face of a capricious Being (to use Heidegger's terminology for a moment) that cares nothing for human happiness and fulfillment. But baldly, the poets sought, unsuccessfully, to build a house to keep inhuman being out.

To be sure, inhuman being is not the same as infinity. The pre-Socratics lacked a concept of infinity, writing instead about chaos, a howling, shapeless void. From this shapeless mass came all things, according to Hesiod (*Theogony*, 116). According to the Orphics, time came before Chaos and his brother Aether. Chaos symbolized the infinite, while Aether symbolized the finite. Still, it would miss the point to demonstrate the similarity of Greek concept of the infinite to one of the senses in which Levinas uses the term.

Not an abstraction like infinity, but a world filled with forces that care nothing for human happiness, except perhaps to thwart it. This was the cosmos of the tragic poets, a cosmos represented by the *Moirai*, the three Fates, who sing in unison with the Sirens. It is a cosmos represented by the Greek gods, so far from infinity that they are more like mortals. Or rather, like elephants among mice. Lacking the power to keep these forces out, all humans can do is weave a human web of comfort, a web the tragic poets called pity. In this one thing humans are greater than gods.

For Levinas, exposure to infinity is exposure to absolute otherness, an experience both terrifying and joyous, liberating me from my burden of being. Lacking such a concept of infinity, the Greeks saw absolute otherness as a howling void. Liberation meant creating a human shelter from the storm, a shelter called pity. Amphitryon, father of Heracles, says to Zeus. "I, mere man, am nobler [have more *arete*] than you, great god" (Euripides, *Heracles*, 342). Ordinarily such a statement would be hubristic. In this case it is not. It is mere fact. Amphitryon is nobler than Zeus in so far as he is capable of depths of pity and compassion that Zeus can hardly imagine.

The gods do not pity, nor can they share human pain (nor do they seem to share each other's pain), for they lack *suggnome*, the capacity to identify intuitively with another's experience, a term Nussbaum (1990, p. 375) translates as "fellow-thought-and-feeling." Levinas would call it a "transfer of sentiment," using just about the same tone Kant uses to refer to "pathological love."

Hyllus, son of Heracles, puts it this way in instructing the servants in how to handle his father, who has been horribly burned:

Take him up, servants, showing your great fellow-thought-and-feeling (*suggnomosune*) with men concerning these events, and knowing the great lack-of-thought-and-feeling (*agnomosune*) of the gods concerning the events that have taken place—they who, having engendered us and calling themselves our fathers have overseen these sufferings (Sophocles, *Women of Trachis*, 1265–70).

Hyllus is telling it like it is, in terms any Greek would recognize. Pausanias (1.17.1) states that there was an Altar of Pity at Athens, though it may have been Hellenistic.

It is interesting to compare the pity of Hyllus, and the chorus generally, with the pity of Theseus. Mythical king of Athens, Theseus is almost a god, virtually a male version of Athene, whose benevolence is similar detached. Theseus is benevolently human, *philanthropos*, but genuine pity remains the province of humans. Pity is, in other words, the one excellent thing humans can do better than the gods. What the Greeks called pity bears a family resemblance to what Melanie Klein called reparation.

It is on this excellence that the tragic poets would found a polis. A strange excellence it is, so unlike the heroic excellence of figures like Achilles, or even Plato, who would make justice (*dike*) the virtue of civilization. For pity is an excellence that can only be shared. Bennett Simon (1978, p. 136) says about Euripides' *Heracles*, "a new notion of heroism is defined in the *Heracles*, a heroism that incorporates rather than disowns the suffering and enduring that are the lot of the old, the child, and the woman." Or as Winnington-Ingram (1980, p. 328) puts it in *Sophocles: An Interpretation*, "pity inspires every work of his that has come down to us—pity and *suggnome*, the capacity to enter into the feelings of another which made possible every aspect of his dramatic creation."

In a typically Greek remark, Oedipus locates his greatness in his ability to bear enormous pain, more than any other mortal (*Oedipus Tyrannus*, 1415). This is not the poets' final teaching, however, but its precursor. Civilizing agony means measuring a man's greatness not just in terms of pain bearing, but pain sharing. Not Oedipus' ability to bear more pain than another, but his willingness to share the pain of the citizens of Thebes, granting it priority over his own, marks the true measure of his greatness (*Oedipus Tyrannus*, 59–64, 93–4).

If one looks at what the protagonists, including the chorus, of Greek tragedy do, we see that they spend a lot of time participating in others' suffering, mourning with them over their pain and so joining in it. As Neoptolemus says to Philoctetes, "I have been in pain for you. I have been in sorrow for your pain" (Sophocles, *Philoctetes*, 805). Often pain sharing is the task of the chorus. We see this nowhere more clearly than in Sophocles' *Electra* (135, passim), where the chorus of women of Mycenae seeks to become one with Electra's suffering. The chorus in Aeschylus' *Prometheus* (1065, passim) seeks to do the same, as do the choruses in *Philoctetes*, Euripides' *Trojan Women* (198–210, passim), and a number of other plays. The chorus represents not so much the ideal observer as the ideal pain sharer. In Sophocles' *Ajax*, the chorus of sailors demands to play the role. "How at the start did the catastrophe swoop down? Tell us: we share the pain of it" (282–3).

About *eleos* and *oiktos*, the Greek terms translated as pity, Stanford (1983, p. 24) says:

> [T]here is no question here of the pitier being separate from another's agony. You respond to it in the depths of your being, as a harp-string responds by sympathetic resonance to a note from another ... The same depth of physical feeling is expressed in the Greek versions of the Bible by a verb that indicates a sensation in one's entrails (*splanchnizo*), and in the phrase 1 John 3, 17, translated in the Authorized Version as "bowels of compassion."

Pity is an intense expression of attunement, as Winnicott might put it.

The psychoanalyst James Grotstein (1985, p. 202) writes in *Splitting and Projective Identification* that what humans want most is to be "relieved of the burden of unknown, unknowable feelings by being able to express them, literally as well as figuratively into the flesh," so that the other person may come to know and share them. He calls this the need to be shriven, to confess one's pain and so receive absolution. One way we receive absolution is by sharing these unbearable feelings with a community of pain sharers. Sometimes this community is as tiny as mother and child, or analyst and patient. Sometimes it is as large as the Athenian polis, at least as it was idealized in Greek tragedy.

Not merely a representation of suffering and absolution, tragedy is this shared suffering, suggests Peter Euben. "The *Oresteia* does not end suffering but collectivizes it through the medium of dramatic performance" (1990, p. 90). Greek tragedy celebrates the willingness and the ability of

the citizens to share each other's pain. Part of a civic celebration, Greek
tragedy did not so much reflect Athens' values as enact them.

Greek pity stems from an overwhelming experience of another's suffering, one that shatters boundaries just as Dionysus does. (Infinity, in the
fourth sense named in Chapter 1, is not the only shatterer of boundaries.)
Tragic pity has many of the qualities of eros, a sensuous connection to
humanity. If this is so, then one can see why pity need not be life denying.
Far from being a retreat from life, pity represents its most sensuous and
painful embrace, the embrace of Greek tragedy. "Under the charm of the
Dionysian ... the union between man and man is reaffirmed," says
Nietzsche (1968b, p. 37). Imagine that this reunion takes place, at least in
part, through pity.[5]

What if pity were the province of Dionysus? Then pity would reflect a
rhythmic participation in the suffering of others that comes close to art.
Greek tragedy would be that art, a form that helps connect us to others
and separates us from them at the same time, what form has always done.
Greek tragedy would itself have the quality of a transitional object.
Finally, Greek tragedy would represent all that Levinas most fears about
participation, even as—I believe—it shows these fears to be unwarranted.

Levinas devalues pity for much the same reason that de Tocqueville
(2000, p. 538) devalues compassion in democratic eras. Assuming everyone
is just like everyone else, when I feel pity for you it is little different from
self-pity. Compassion is self-indulgence:

> Each of them can judge the sensations of all the others in a moment:
> he casts a rapid glance at himself; this is enough for him. There is
> therefore no misery he does not conceive without trouble ... It
> makes no difference whether it is a question of strangers or of ene-
> mies: imagination immediately puts him in their place. It mixes
> something personal with his pity and makes him suffer himself when
> the body of someone like him is torn apart.

Greek tragedy too was a product of a democratic era, but it was nothing
like American democracy that de Tocqueville wrote about. Or was it? Do
we really want to devalue compassion and fellow feeling, what the Greeks
called *suggnome*, as a cheap sentiment because I imagine the same thing
happening to myself? This seems to be what Levinas means when he refers
disparagingly to "transfers of sentiment." But isn't it sentiments like these
that sensuously join us to a human world?

Pity is not the most pleasurable aspect of human sensuousness, but it is in some ways the most profound. Life is not just appropriation and conquest and assimilation. It is also creating and joining, the eros that is so central to life for so many, from Plato to Freud to Marcuse: the eros that creates three out of two. To be sure, pity is not generative as eros is. Instead of creating a third it connects two souls, keeping at least one from falling out of the world. Pain and suffering isolate us. It is the reason Philoctetes says to Neoptolemus "the sickness in me seeks to have you beside me" (Sophocles, *Philoctetes*, 675). When Neoptolemus responds "I have been in pain for you: I have been in sorrow for your pain," Philoctetes knows that he is once again connected to the human world. It is no accident that Philoctetes' terrible suffering takes place on a deserted island, a psychologically acute metaphor for the experience of suffering.

Located in pre-political space, unusual for a Greek tragedy, *Philoctetes* may be read as a founding myth, an account of how pity may found a society, as Edmund Wilson (1965) once suggested in "*Philoctetes: The Wound and the Bow*." Greek tragedy takes this relationship between two people and makes it social, based on the recognition that we are all proper subjects of pity: for what has happened to us, or what has not yet happened but surely must, given life as it is:

Take pity on me (*su m'eleeson*).
Look how men live, always precariously
balanced between good and bad fortune (*Philoctetes*, 501–3).

Imagine that this is the founding motto of the polis. Contrast it with how Levinas thinks about politics. In practice there is perhaps not so much difference, responsibility for the other and pity leading to similar results. In theory the difference is significant. For the tragic poets, *suggnome* was enough (and not just enough, but all there is) to sustain a human world.

Aristotle defined tragedy as the *katharsis* of pity and fear (*Poetics*, c6). With katharsis Aristotle did not mean purging. He meant the clarification of the role of pity and fear in all our lives. Humans being who they are, the circumstances that bring fear and suffering to me are likely to be similar to the ones that bring fear and suffering to you: the body being torn apart that de Tocqueville mentions, loss of a loved one, pain, isolation, loneliness and abandonment. To pity humans who have these things in common is not to devalue individuality. It is to share a human world. Not the "transfer of sentiment," but the evocation of sentiment, because I know that no matter how different you are from me, you are a fellow human. Katharsis is human attunement, what makes Winnicott's holding possible.[6]

The world in which the Greek poets lived was not lacking in awe. Awe of otherness combined with a dreadful appreciation of the destruction visited upon those who lack this awe, such as Creon in *Antigone*. Consider the famous ode to man in *Antigone*, where man himself is first rendered *deinos*, that is, awesome, but only to reveal that he too will be destroyed if he thinks this endorses his mastery of nature or man (lines 332–73). Not an absence of awe, but a refusal to accord human value to what is deemed awesome and other is the mark of the tragic poets. Pity is a sheltering sky that keeps inhuman otherness out, so humans might care for each other for a little while, before we too join infinity.

If otherness lacks human value, then the only exit from being is that exit spoken by the chorus in the virtual last lines of *Oedipus at Colonus*, not the lines referred to by Heidegger, but the lines that look longingly toward man's return to the infinite darkness of non-being (lines 1224–6). Non-being or pity: these are the choices open to man in this world, and they are not mutually exclusive, for pity is the human dirge that accompanies us all on our way to non-being. If, that is, we are fortunate enough to live in a community of pain sharers.

Levinas writes about the caress as though it were a bridge to infinity (T&I, p. 259). Though one generally imagines the caress to be an instance of eros, it may also be an instance of pity. I imagine the caress of pity not as a bridge to infinity, but as a bulwark against infinity, two people and then a community touching one another gently and so holding up a human mantle designed to keep the inhuman world at bay for just a little while longer before it casually deigns to destroy us.

Understanding pity as residing in the province of eros does not, of course, solve all problems. Eros is dangerous not just because it is often selfish, but because it is possessive, particularistic, and jealous. Pity may partake of these traits, as when I devote my pity to those just like me, or to my hungry little dog, while millions of strangers are starving. Levinas' concern that the other not be too particular, so concrete and real that I can't see all the others too, is valid, which is why the other really requires the third in order that both may come alive. In other words, Levinas' ethics makes the most sense as political theory, as I have argued. What is striking about the Greek tragic poets is not that they didn't see the problem, but that they didn't see it *as* a problem. Humans being who they are, creatures of attachment, they will naturally be filled with pity. There is no shortage of pity to go around. Pity is potentially everywhere humans meet.

In a recent book, *Upheavals of Thought*, Nussbaum (2001) worries that pity and compassion may be so infused with eros that they will be contaminated by the vices of eros. Pity and compassion must be purified of the sins of eros, albeit not too much, not nearly as much as Levinas imagines.[7] I would put it somewhat differently. Pity needs to be educated. It's easy to feel pity. What's difficult, and requires education, is to feel pity toward the right person to the right extent at the right time for the right reason in the right way. Not everyone can do this. Hence to do it well is a rare, laudable, and fine achievement. This sounds like Aristotle (*Nicomachean Ethics*, 1109a25–30) because the idea is similar: pity may be natural, but it requires education and proper guidance in order to become a human excellence. Greek tragedy was this guidance. Would that we had as much and as good. What guidance we do have is, as Nussbaum suggests, most likely to be found in literature. That, and in the lives of a few friends and neighbors who, while far from heroic in their selflessness, manage to care for others as though they were their own.

"BE HUMAN AMONG HUMANS"

To find a human place in the polis is to find another place between Odysseus and Abraham, the poles of Levinas' philosophy. To know one's mortal place is to find a home with others on this earth. Not because God has fled the world, but because pity and compassion are the most humane things that humans can do, and we see this most clearly when we are attuned to each other. This way of thinking about the world we make with others is not the same thing as discovering that man has made it, so it is really his own. It is more akin to anxiously walking into a room full of strangers, only to find smiles on the faces of a couple of friends who recognize you.[8]

In discussing Murdoch, Winnicott, and Adorno, I have written of those who would know and love particular individuals, avoiding totalization not by absence of contact, but by a light and sometimes playful touch. There are differences, of course. Not love but velleity is Adorno's leading category, and Murdoch is not especially playful, and only a little paradoxical. All, however, embrace the paradox of human relatedness: that it is only closeness to the reality of the particular other person that allows distance. Take away this reality, and the space gets filled up with fantasy, the raw material of totalization. Even infinity might not be a big enough space to prevent this.

One can put this same point in another way, one that I hope appreciates the greatness of Levinas' project while still holding it to be mistaken. Levinas would create a space for the sacred to appear in everyday life. "Saying," the space between my words, myself, and you, is one such space, but his project is all about spaces. The infinite distance between you and me is this space. The great virtue of this project is that it opens the door to a non-mythological experience of the sacred, a way of talking about and experiencing the holy that does not depend on grand narratives, as they are called, that are no longer compelling. What attracts so many post-moderns to Levinas is the possibility that the experience of the other qua other may itself be a moral experience, even a sacred one. Levinas reveals theorists of difference and distance to have all along been doing ethics, even if they did not know it.

Trouble is, this is a hard world in which to summon up the sacred, a disenchanted world Max Weber rendered in terms of an icy polar night. In order to evoke the appearance of the sacred in such a world, a world distrustful of ambitious stories, Levinas must put so much distance between people that ordinary human relationships are suspect, becoming mere transfers of sentiment. What Melanie Klein calls reparation, what the Greeks call pity, can have no place. Ethics becomes unnatural, and humans come to live in two parallel universes that barely touch, the natural and the ethical. As Levinas, project developed, as it moved from totality and infinity to otherwise than being, parallel universes that once occasionally had intercourse (in the phenomenology of the nude woman, for example) became more and more distant from each other.

I have called for a return to paradox not because it is so important in itself, not because I love the postmodern ideal of play, but because paradox is a way of talking about the complexity of human relatedness, the way self and other mix and mingle, the way the closest closeness may remind us of the greatest distance. This paradox is expressed most fully by Winnicott: the intimacy that is distance, the distance that allows intimacy. It is a complexity not even begun to be captured by abstract philosophical categories such as same and other.

To conclude that Levinas finds no place for paradox would, however, be mistaken. Consider the category of proximity, which connects sensuality with infinity (OB, pp. 61–98). Originating in my confinement in my body, sensuality opens me to the infinite by bringing me into contact with the otherness of others through an experience of enjoyment. Says Peperzak:

against all forms of anthropological dualism [the spirit in the flesh], Levinas' analyses show that human subjectivity exists as a sensible, affective, working, speaking and suffering body, whose skin is the possibility of contact, proximity, and vulnerability and whose respiration is the dynamism of a moral inspiration and the expiration of someone who lives for Others who may continue to live after one's death. (1997, p. 68)

The deep, almost erotic sensuality of Greek pity is present in some degree in Levinas. He would recognize it. But Wyschogrod (2000, pp. x–xi) comes closer to the mark in characterizing Levinas as excelling in "corporeal figurations of the psyche as vulnerability." He does not excel in figurations of relatedness.

In the end, Levinas cannot sustain the paradox, the tension, the body that is both spirit and flesh. As much as Plato would make eros the vehicle of transcendence, in the end eros is Plato's enemy, tying us to this fleshy world. This is as true of the *Symposium* as the *Republic*, as true of the *Gorgias* as the *Phaedrus*, where Plato has the ugly wanton horse of desire jerked to a halt so violently that its mouth and jaws drip with blood (253d–254e).[9] Similarly, Levinas is a theorist of exit, and the vital role played by the other, opening us to infinity (for this is a human task for Levinas), also risks trapping us in this fleshy world, your flesh no better than my own as far as exit is concerned.

In an important respect, Levinas' political theory is an improvement over that of the Greeks. Levinas preserves individuality by way of a unique argument: only the individual can see the other person's tears. For this reason the individual is uniquely valuable. The Greeks did not conceive of pity this way, emphasizing the connection over the individuals (and hence the value of individuality) involved. Levinas represents progress in civilization. Which is precisely why Levinas' emphasis on exit, an expression of the horror of "there is," spoils much of value in his project. A part of Levinas' subject is never there, always in readiness for exit. For Levinas, this is good. To be there, in that place, is not just to be subject to the horror of "there is," but it is also to be egoistic, natural, taking one's place in the sun, putting oneself first.

I have argued that this is not so. What Murdoch, Winnicott, and others call love, what the Greeks call pity, is a natural transfer of sentiment that is not based on an experience of infinity, except perhaps in the tragic sense of finding shelter from it. Not from death, from which there is no shelter, but from all that cares nothing for human happiness. Love's knowledge;

respect for the otherness of the other human being, so like me in some respects, so different in others; human pity in the face of infinity: none require the experience that Levinas writes of. None are reinforced by it.

Consider once again the horror of "there is." If it is a horror of total unrelatedness, to self as well as others, then not exit but relatedness is the solution. Is not the equation of the human other with the otherness of infinity the problem not the solution? Is not the reduction of all human relationships to the common denominator of death the final escape from the horror of being? Nor is Levinas successful in turning this awe of the infinite into an inspiration for a human relationship. It is an inspiration for an inhuman relationship, hostage-being.

This is the fundamental flaw in Levinas' project, and it is not met by distinctions between ethical and ontological arguments, as they are called, distinctions between the transcendental and mundane. This distinction is an academic conceit, one Levinas was passionate enough to avoid. Instead, Levinas brings transcendent and mundane together, the source of so much that is powerful and puzzling in his work. One sees this most dramatically in his treatment of eros, but also in such categories as the face, both of which evoke awe at human particularity and uniqueness that his elaboration of the experiences denies. It is this that renders Levinas' work so disorienting, reflected in the different senses of infinity, as though the other could be a passage to infinity and a particular fleshy human being at the same time. Perhaps this duality is even true, but to experience it we will have to accept a lot more mixing and weaving of flesh with eternity that Levinas seems prepared for.

To render the other person absolutely other, not an alter ego, is to do violence to humans. To move the locus of the infinite to my ego, shattered by the experience of the other, is another fascinating strategy of the late Levinas (the fourth sense of infinity named in Chapter 1). Something like this experience is true, coming close to the experience of the sublime. But why equate that with infinity? On the contrary, all it takes to shatter my ego is an experience of finitude: my terrible realness, aloneness and smallness in a world filled with a zillion other beings. One might even say an infinity of other beings. What one cannot say is that this experience of infinity opens the door to my participation in the infinite, except in the real and limited sense of knowing and appreciating the real otherness of the world. Against this background, I may know and participate in the lives of a few particular beings. One might even say that making our lives together against the background of infinity we make our lives holy. This is my answer to the letter from my friend quoted in Chapter 1.

In response it might be argued that one can participate in ordinary human attachments and be devoted to the eternal (the second sense of infinity) at the same time. Isn't this the richest relationship of all, in which our bonds with other human beings are enriched as we experience them as participating in eternity? This is how Nussbaum (1986, pp. 200–3) interprets the relationship between the lovers in Plato's *Phaedrus* (255b–257c). This is how Aristotle interprets the highest form of friendship (N. Ethics, 1156b5–10). This is the meaning of Jesus Christ's reinterpretation of the commandments, in which one loves one's neighbor as part of loving God (Mark 12:30–1; Matthew 22:37–40; Luke 10:27). This is the message of Leviticus 19:18, in which just before, and immediately after commanding us to love our neighbor, God says "I am the Lord," as though to say, "it is because I am Lord that you are to love our neighbor. This is how you shall know me." This is how Rosenzweig interprets the commandment to love thy neighbor. This is how my friend reinterprets Levinas in his letter quoted in Chapter 1. But it is not quite Levinas, and that is all I am arguing.

To be sure, Levinas understands that love of God and love of fellow humans go together, but for Levinas this requires that humans be abstracted from their ordinary human qualities, what Levinas means when he says the trick is not to notice the color of the other person's eyes. Rosenzweig (1985, p. 218) says this too in *The Star of Redemption*. It is probably where Levinas got the image (T&I, p. 28). But Rosenzweig does not mean the same thing. Rosenzweig means ignore the color of your neighbor's eyes because *that* particularity doesn't matter. The particularity that matters is his or her actual real presence close to you. For Rosenzweig, one abstracts from superficial particularities to get closer to the particular reality of the other person. For Levinas one abstracts from the reality of the other person, interposing infinity between you and me. That is the true meaning of the face in Levinas' work.

"Be human among humans" says Ismene to her sister Antigone, in a modern version of the play by Sophocles. Antigone is endlessly in love with death, unable to acknowledge that anyone in her family will survive her, which means unable to acknowledge her sister Ismene's real existence. To be sure, Ismene is a minor character, unable to assert herself against her uncle Creon's transposition of life and death. Creon buries the living, and refuses to bury the dead. Still, and perhaps for that reason, Ismene has good advice. "Be human among humans" means that Antigone should quell her fascination with death, live among humans who love her, and think mortal thoughts. It's not bad advice.

To listen to it requires a sense of the human tragedy, above all the sense of human waste: wasted lives, wasted potential, wasted possibilities for happiness. Think of Levinas, writing about "there is" while a prisoner in the stalag. Think of Levinas saying that his life was "dominated by the presentiment and the memory of the Nazi horror" ("Signature," p. 291). Think of Levinas dedicating *Otherwise than Being* to the victims of the Holocaust, who suffered from "the same hatred of the other man." These victims included his parents, his maternal and paternal grandparents, and his two younger brothers. Isn't Levinas looking for an exit from all this too? Trouble is, if we look too hard for an exit from the human, even the awfully human, all we find is death. To help us not make that mistake, we have tragedy.

Notes

1 SOMEONE RINGS YOUR DOORBELL

1. Whenever possible, I have used English translations of Levinas, checking problematic terms and phrases against French originals. My source for English translations of some of Levinas' more obscure works is the bibliography of works of Levinas in English by Joan Nordquist (1997), an invaluable source, though by now a little dated.

2. For Socrates, I begin climbing the ladder of love hand in hand with my beloved, only to leave the other somewhere along the way on my ladder to the stars, the "good existing beyond being" (*agathon epekenia tes ousias*). For Levinas the leaving begins the moment I encounter the face of the other at my door. I leave the other before I even meet him or her. In putting it this way I am mixing the ladder of love from Plato's *Symposium* (211c) with Plato's account of the form of the good as beyond being from the *Republic* (509b–c). Since Plato characterizes the absolute beauty sought in the *Symposium* as beauty *per se*, and since this is how Plato characterizes the forms (Ideas) in the *Republic*, but not the form of the good (which is beyond being), this comparison is not quite fair. It does not, however, seem misleading in the current context.

3. Levinas (T&O, p. 64) says he differs from Plato in valuing enjoyment (*jouissance*) for its own sake. How similar he is to Plato in other respects depends as much on how one interprets Plato as Levinas.

4. I define object relations theory as Greenberg and Mitchell (1983) do in *Object Relations in Psychoanalytic Theory*. Founded by Melanie Klein, for whom the concept of a drive "concerns not merely the reduction of bodily tensions, but rather a fuller, passionate relatedness to another person" (ibid., p. 141), object relations theory was developed by W. R. D. Fairbairn, Harry Guntrip, and D. W. Winnicott, among others.

5. The historian Edward Cheyney points out that humanism has meant many things.

   > It may be the reasonable balance of life that the early Humanists discovered in the Greeks; it may be merely the study of the humanities or polite letters; it may be the freedom from religiosity and the vivid interest in all sides of life of a Queen Elizabeth or a Benjamin Franklin; it may be the responsiveness to all the human passions of a Shakespeare or a Goethe; or it may be a philosophy of which man is the center and sanction. It is in the last sense, elusive as it is, that Humanism has had perhaps its greatest significance since the sixteenth century. (quoted in Lamont, 1982, p. 11)

   My humanism includes all but the last philosophy. Not "man is the center and sanction," but human experience is the measure of human experience, is how I would put it.

6. It would be a mistake to see the development of Levinas' thought as linear. Two early

works, *De l'évasion* (original 1935), and *Time and the Other* (original 1947) contain the kernel of all that Levinas will contribute.

7. Critchley does not misread Derrida (1988, p. 153), who comes so very close to the position Critchley attributes to him, saying that he has "always *hesitated*" to describe the "injunction that prescribes deconstruction" in Kantian terms. Derrida hesitates not because he does not think the Kantian description is fitting, but because hesitation is the way deconstructionists proceed.

8. This is my version of Levinas' example in "Enigma and Phenomenon." I have elaborated upon Levinas' example, and made it more concrete. The introduction of Death at the door is my own variation, though I believe it is true to Levinas' intent.

9. I explain and explore narcissism as the term is used by Levinas and psychoanalysts in the next chapter. Here I use the term to refer not to egoism, but to an inability or refusal to acknowledge our dependence on others. See my *Narcissism: Socrates, the Frankfurt School, and Psychoanalytic Theory* (1988).

10. Levinas began as a phenomenologist, and sometimes writes about possibility as a strictly human project. This is not the sense in which I use the term here. Rather, "possibility" refers to the shattering intrusion of otherness that disrupts my ego and opens me to eternity. "Possibility" is a category on the border of human experience, an encounter barely knowable as experience.

11. There are no subtle nuances of the French term, "*violence*," that are not implicit in the English "violence." From "*violence verbale*" to "*répondre à violence par la violence*," the semantic range of the French and English terms are nearly identical.

12. "Even the feminine presence which shares the home ... does not constitute a danger to the self's tranquil possession of the world. She is a *tu* rather than a *vous*, a familiar part of my world rather than an *Autrui* who might put it into question" (Davis, 1996, p. 44). Feminists, such as Luce Irigaray (1986, 1991), Catherine Chalier (1991), and Tina Chanter (1991) have been harshly sympathetic to Levinas, an oxymoron that makes perfect sense when one reads them closely. All criticize Levinas' essentialization (as it is called) of the feminine, while remaining sympathetic to his project of founding ethics in experiences not rules.

13. Levinas' view is in sharp contrast to Rosenzweig's (1985) in *The Star of Redemption*, who emphasizes speech-thinking (*Sprachdenken*), as he calls it, in which I participate with another in creating "my" thoughts, which are really "our" thoughts, product of the inter-person. There is hardly a hint of this in Levinas.

14. The Greek term translated as forms is *eidos*. Since the Stranger uses the term "*genos*," or types, almost interchangeably with eidos, one should not imagine that Plato's Stranger is talking about metaphysical experiences rather than empirical ones. Debate exists over whether this dialogue is best interpreted as poetry or philosophy. (Those who study Levinas would ask whether the dialogue is ontic or ontological.) How one comes down on this debate will influence whether one interprets "eidos" here as a technical term of Plato's referring to the forms, but that debate need not detain us here. The Greek term for discourse is *logos*. Again, scholars debate how technically to understand the term in this context. The Prologue to Rosen's *Plato's Sophist: The Drama of Original and Image* (1983, pp. 1–31) covers these issues well.

15. The internal quotes are from the analyst R. E. Money-Kyrle.

2 LEVINAS, WINNICOTT, AND "THERE IS"

1. Levinas writes even more about paternity, but the context is different. Paternity

expresses the tension between the father seeing himself in his son (for Levinas it is always a son), and seeing his son as an entirely different being. (T&O, p. 92; T&I, pp. 267–77). Maternity is less involved in the struggle with identification and difference, more concerned with caring for others.

2. Steen Halling's (1975) "The Implications of Emmanuel Levinas' *Totality and Infinity* for Therapy," is just that, a practical application of Levinas' early masterpiece. George Kunz's (1998) *The Paradox of Power and Weakness: Levinas and an Alternative Paradigm for Psychology*, applies Levinas to the theory and practice of psychology. Noreen O'Connor's (1991) "Who Suffers?" is one of the first essays to compare Levinas and Freud. Alon Kantor's (1999) "Levinas's Law" explores masochistic themes in Levinas from a psychoanalytic perspective. James Faulconer's "Levinas: The Unconscious and the Reason of Obligation" argues that the unconscious, conceived in Levinassian terms, might be the source of ethics. A half-dozen essays collected in *Levinas and Lacan: The Missed Encounter* (Harasym, 1998), struggle mightily to engage these two contemporaries (Lacan was born in 1901, Levinas in 1906) who never once referred to each other.

3. The reference in Paul's letter to the Galatians (5:14) refers not to Christ's teaching, but to God's commandment in Leviticus (19:18).

4. Llewelyn (1995, pp. 98–9) says that one can read Levinas as suggesting in an interview that he once thought (*Autrefois, je pensais*) that agape could be derived from eros because otherness begins in the feminine, and the feminine is the realm of eros. Now (1986) Levinas knows better. This would fit the trajectory of Levinas' project from *Totality and Infinity* to *Otherwise than Being*, a path I discuss shortly.

5. The lines are from Hasenclever's *Antigone*, produced in Germany in 1917. The translation is from George Steiner, *Antigones* (1986, p. 146).

6. Attunement is Daniel Stern's language (1985). Adam Phillips (1988) suggests the similarity between attunement and holding in his book on Winnicott.

7. It is not given that Plato understands "participation" as Levinas says he does, a sharing that maintains separation. The Greek terms translated as "participation," as in participation in the Ideas, include *suneinai*, the ordinary term for sexual relations, *mimeisthai*, or mimic, and *aphomoionsthai*, which is often translated as "assimilate" (*Symposium*, 212a2; *Republic* 500c–d). As has frequently been noted, Plato writes about humanity's relationship to the forms in the language of union.

8. "Transcendence and Height" was first presented in 1962, shortly after the publication of *Totality and Infinity*. In later work, especially *Otherwise than Being*, Levinas would employ the term "neighbor" frequently. This represents not so much a change in thinking as a change in perspective, from a focus on the other to a focus on the subject. From the perspective of the subject, the neighbor and other are one, an experience best characterized with the term "proximity," which implies both closeness and distance (OB, pp. 81–97). In no way does Levinas suggest the neighbor is closer or more intimate than the other. On the contrary, the neighbor is even more obscure.

9. Seven papers on the "use of an object" are collected in Winnicott (1989b), Chapter 34. Rather than cite each paper separately, I cite the page numbers to this source. The lead paper is "The Use of an Object and Relating through Identifications," which is reprinted in *Playing and Reality*.

10. The ruthless use of the object probably comes closest to the attitude Melanie Klein (1975c) characterizes as the scooping out of the breast. The difference is that Winnicott does not think this requires reparation.

11. Raum is generally rendered as "space" by Rilke's translators, but "infinity" is a not uncommon translation of the German term. For Rilke (1992), Raum is actually a place of fusion and flow, where "we are incessantly flowing over and over to those who

proceeded us, to our origins and to those who seemingly come after us." This does not seem to be Winnicott's sense of the term, and that is my concern here. But perhaps infinity and fusion are not so different as one usually imagines.

12. Richard Cohen (T&O, p. 71, fn 47) agrees. "The earliest published text containing what is perhaps the nascent kernel of Levinas' thought . . . is entitled *De l'évasion* . . . Its main theme is the escape of the self from its enchainment with itself."

13. Ethical agoraphobia is a play on words by Llewelyn, referring not just to an experience of exteriority, but also to the *agora*, the Greek market where everything is subject to the exchange principle. It is because exchange is not enough, not even the exchange of sentiments that might lead me to care for your suffering, that Levinas turns to infinity, trading one agoraphobia for another, so to speak. I mostly follow Llewelyn's translations from *De l'évasion*, with the exception that I translate "l'évasion" as escape, not evasion. This fits a common French use of the term to which Levinas refers, *littérature d'évasion*, which we call escapist literature.

14. This statement applies, of course, only to the early Sartre of *Being and Nothingness*, for whom the other was the sinkhole of my consciousness. By the time he wrote *Critique of Dialectical Reason* (1976), Sartre came to hold that the other was a social construction, a reification that social practice might make transparent. This, though, was not the last step in Sartre's intellectual journey. At the end of his life, in a series of interviews with Benny Lévy, Sartre said that "one must try to learn that one can only seek his being, his life, in living for others" (Anderson, 1993, p. 172). Though some have questioned whether Lévy was putting words in the mouth of an old man, it is fascinating to consider that Lévy was a friend of Levinas, and "frequently referred to Levinas in his conversations with Sartre" (Anderson, 1993, p. 193). Could Levinas have influenced Sartre both at the beginning (Levinas published *De l'évasion* three years before Sartre published *Nausea* in 1938) and the end of Sartre's long career?

15. Most of the time, "there is" sounds like a thing, mere being. Sometimes, however, Levinas writes about "there is" as though it were the sheer, anonymous life force, not a thing but an endless energy that has become meaningless because it is no longer connected to subjective experience. This latter sense of the term is most pronounced in *Otherwise than Being*, which begins and ends with a discussion of "there is." Richard Cohen notes that sometimes Levinas uses the term "elemental" (*élémental*) to talk about experiences that sound like "there is" (Levinas, T&O, p. 46, fn. 15). Perhaps this is the best way to reconcile these two slightly different senses of the term, even if it takes a little linguistic legerdemain to do so. "There is" is elemental in the sense both of being an elemental force, and an element, as in the periodic table of the elements, a pure and indivisible instance of a thing. Certainly there is nothing inherently contradictory in seeing the anonymous life force as itself a primal being.

16. Levinas says that Blanchot's novel, *Thomas the Obscure*, "opens with the description of the 'there is' . . . The presence of absence, the night, the dissolution of the subject in the night, the horror of being, the return of being to the heart of every negative movement, the reality of irreality, are admirably stated there." ("There is," p. 36) In another book (Alford, 2001), I employ Blanchot's study of how impossible experiences defy description (the disaster de-scribes, says Blanchot) in order to make sense of the experiences of whistleblowers, men and women who have had their lives turned upside down. I mention this to confess my propensity to treat philosophical concepts as if they were real lives.

17. I am making a distinction *within* the autistic-contiguous position between the autistic and contiguous poles (which roughly mirror the distinction between dread and transcendence within the autistic-contiguous position) that Ogden develops via the introduction of the paranoid-schizoid and the depressive positions. The latter two positions were developed by Melanie Klein (she calls them positions, rather than

stages, to suggest they are never outgrown). The autistic-contiguous position is, according to Ogden, the underbelly of the paranoid-schizoid position. Ogden develops the autistic-contiguous position in constant contrast with the paranoid-schizoid and depressive positions, and I describe it that way in another work (Alford, 1997, pp. 38–45). Doing so here would not, I believe, be as helpful.

18. Levinas puts it this way:

> Between a philosophy of transcendence that situates elsewhere the true life to which man, *escaping* from here, would gain access in the privileged movements of liturgical, mystical elevation, or in dying ... and a philosophy of immanence in which we would truly come into possession of being ... we propose to describe ... a relationship with the other that does not result in a divine or human totality, that is not the totalization of history, but the idea of infinity. (T&I, p. 52)

19. *Duineser Elegien*, first elegy, my translation.
20. Robbins (1999, p. 91) makes the fascinating point that Levinas frequently alludes to, rather than cites, literary works. The result is actually a lack of respect for the otherness of the text, as Levinas draws the work into his text, frequently reversing the original meaning as he does here, what Robbins (ibid., p. 111) calls reinscription. Levinas does not, in other words, always practice what he preaches. Who does?
21. I might have turned instead to Ignacio Matte-Blanco, a psychoanalyst who puts the unconscious experience of infinity at the heart of psychoanalysis. For Matte-Blanco, the unconscious naturally thinks in terms of infinity, taking limited experiences and making them infinite under the pressure of intense emotion. An example given by Matte-Blanco (1975, pp. 184–5) comes from Plato's *Symposium*, where Socrates moves from the love of beautiful boys to the love of beauty *per se* (that is, beauty that is infinite) under the pressure of eros. For Matte-Blanco, psychoanalysis aims at separating persons and things from their symbolic meaning, which tends to confuse the individual with the infinite class. From the perspective of Matte-Blanco, Levinas is practicing reverse psychoanalysis, reminding us of the origins of our experience of individual others in infinity. The advantage of this perspective is that it reveals once again how deeply in tune Levinas is with the power of the unconscious mind, precisely what makes his work so evocative.
22. Though I may experience parts of myself as though they were other, this does not, of course, accord these parts an equal ethical status with the other.

3 MURDOCH, ADORNO, AND LEVINAS

1. Though most of Murdoch's work is a defense of moral particularity, she devoted much attention to developing an ontological proof of the reality of the good, which roughly parallels the ontological argument for the existence of God. While hardly the stuff of everyday life, the proof remains concerned with establishing the reality of goodness in this world. In *Metaphysics as a Guide to Morals* (1992).
2. This statement is made by Julius, who is not good, and probably evil, so we must take it with a grain of salt. Novels require us to pay more attention to who is talking than works of philosophy, but here too there is something to be learned from reading novels for reading philosophy. Philosophers too have several voices.

3. Murdoch also has a real Socrates, the character called "Socrates" who appears in *Acastos: Two Platonic Dialogues* (1986) about art, eros, and religion.

4. Friendly critics of Murdoch's novels, such as Elizabeth Dipple (1982) and Peter Conradi (1986), recognize a tension in her fiction between the saint and the pagan, between "unselfing" and hedonism, as Antonaccio (2000, pp. 140–1) puts it. Surprisingly, the pagan and hedonist seem about as admirable as the saint in most of her stories, and often more interesting. None, however, including Antonaccio, address the tension between the vice of vanity in Murdoch's philosophy, and the perils of dependent attachment in her novels. Most critics refrain from comparing Murdoch's philosophy and novels, and it is easy to see why.

5. Passion, usually destructive, is often present in Murdoch's characters, such as Crimond and Jean in *The Book and the Brotherhood*. I am not referring to Murdoch's characters, but to the tone and tenor of her authorial presence in both novels and essays. Passion, Murdoch seems to believe, is a barrier to seeing clearly, an obstacle to just love.

6. The term is from Eichendorff.

7. This deceptively simple phrase might be rendered "the entirely other, i.e., the infinity of God."

8. Founded by Emmanuel Mounier, who said he was inspired by the apparent imminent collapse of capitalism in 1930, *Esprit* represented the "personalist" movement in Catholic social thought, which sought to combine the insights of Marx and Kierkegaard. Among politicians the movement counted as supporters are Aldo Moro (former Prime Minister of Italy murdered by the Red Brigades in 1978) "and to a certain extent the current Pope, Karol Wojtyla" (Caygill, 2000, p. 7). All translations from the French are from Caygill.

9. In "Being a Westerner," Levinas writes approvingly of Léon Brunschvicg's claim that the great contribution of the West, "the essence of the West," is to teach "that a spiritual life should be one devoid of egoism" (pp. 47–8). Is this not the teaching of Buddhism as well? One might argue that Buddhism is half Western, coming originally from India, but then what happens to the essence of the West ... or East?

10. "It is not a question of a difference that is due to the absence or presence of a common trait; it is a question of an initial difference that is entirely self-referential" ("Transcendence and Height," pp. 28–9).

11. In "Die Aktualität der Philosophie" (p. 341), quoted and translated in Buck-Morss (1977, p. 86). In *Adorno*, Jay (1984, pp. 155–8) discusses the complexity of mimesis, showing that it is constructive, not merely receptive.

12. John Milton, *Samson Agonistes* (in *Paradise Regained*, 1671).

13. I draw heavily on Buck-Morss' (1977) discussion of this example from Adorno's *Kierkegaard: Konstruktion des Aesthetischen* (1966), and her similar discussion of Heidegger, in *The Origin of Negative Dialectics* (1977, pp. 117–21). Quote from Adorno (1933, p. 78); Buck-Morss translation (1977, p. 117).

14. Adorno's fears were not groundless. "When I made my theoretical model, I could not have guessed that people would want to realize it with Molotov cocktails." Quoted in Jay (1984, p. 55) from a newspaper article in *Die Süddeutsche Zeitung*.

15. Hans Mayer, in Jay (1973, p. 187). Georg Lukács (1971, p. 22) is the source for the "Grand Hotel Abyss" remark. Quoted in Jay (1984, p. 18).

16. In his choice of Orpheus and Narcissus as the culture heroes of eros, Marcuse picks figures who in the end choose death over life. But this is hardly Marcuse's last word. Opposing these characters to the usual culture heroes, Odysseus and Prometheus, Marcuse is playing with the conjunction of life and death. It's a dangerous game, but Marcuse rarely slips. See Marcuse's *Eros and Civilization: A Philosophical Inquiry into Freud* (1966, pp. 159–71).

4 PSYCHOANALYSIS, POLITICS, AND "FREEDOM WITH"

1. Like Berlin, I use the terms freedom and liberty synonymously. Following Wittgenstein (1961, 653–7), I make no distinction between term and concept, as though the concept of freedom were more powerful than the term.
2. The *Diagnostic and Statistical Manual* of the American Psychiatric Association (2000, p. 654) defines borderline personality disorder as "a pervasive pattern of instability in interpersonal relationships, self-image, and affects, and marked impulsivity beginning by early adulthood and present in a variety of contexts."
3. I develop this argument about Rousseau in *The Self in Social Theory* (1991, pp. 156–70).
4. I develop this theme in *The Psychoanalytic Theory of Greek Tragedy* (1992), Chapter 5, "Responsibility without Freedom."
5. Though I have never done research in China, I (Alford, 1999) interviewed a number of student leaders of the democracy movement in Korea that lead to the overthrow of the reign of the dictators in 1987. I know that many of them thought about freedom this way, and remain deeply disappointed that they have not been able to recapture this shared freedom of building something new together.

5 LOVE, PITY, AND HUMANITY

1. Llewelyn has the trajectory right, even if (as was discussed in Chapter 1) it is possible to set the disappearance of eros even earlier, as Chanter (1991, p. 133) argues.
2. I simplify the Greek phrase slightly, using the infinitive of agape for example, in order to render it easier to recognize in transliteration.
3. I first made this argument in *The Psychoanalytic Theory of Greek Tragedy* (1992). My view has changed little since then, with one exception. Reading Levinas has led me to appreciate more fully how awe in the face of otherness may reinforce community among humans, a community expressed in pity.
4. Levinas understands Heidegger, his admired and hated teacher, as filling the world with a mystical, pagan Being.
5. Nietzsche (1968b, p. 128), the reader will not be surprised to learn, is not much concerned with pity in *Birth of Tragedy*. His single reference there assumes that pity is the province of Apollo, in which we stand at a distance from another, experiencing the beautiful emotion of pity, which reconnects us in a more sublime way.
6. Aristotelian katharsis, argues Martha Nussbaum (1986, pp. 388–91), is best seen as the use of our emotions to obtain *clarification* about reality. In pre-Platonic texts, katharsis and related terms (*kathairo, katharos*) frequently refer to water that is clear and open, free of mud or weeds. Or they refer to a cleared area, to winnowed grain free of chaff, or to speech that is not marked by obscurity or ambiguity. The medical use of the term, referring to purgation, is a secondary and derivative usage. By the time Aristotle wrote, says Nussbaum, katharsis was employed as an epistemological term, without need for metaphor. When, in his *Prior Analytics* (50a40), Aristotle writes of a need to "examine and indicate each of these things with clarity (katharos)," it is obvious that the reference has nothing to do with purification or purgation. One sees this too in Aristotle's theory of rhetoric, in which the term is applied to speech that is clear and free of obscurity (*Rhetoric*, 1356b26). When Aristotle defines tragedy in terms of the concept of katharsis, he is therefore not writing about emotional purgation, but about how experiencing pity and fear at an artistic performance allows

us insight into the nature of these emotions, an insight that is at the same time an attunement. Those few who think still that psychoanalysis works its effect through katharsis should keep Nussbaum's definition in mind.

7. Nussbaum (2001) worries that eros may be too selfish, particularistic, and jealous, but she is deeply critical of almost all who have constructed purifying "ladders of love," which take us from the love of individuals to the love of beauty, God, or whatever. Among those who have constructed such ladders she includes Plato, Augustine, and Dante. Behind such ascents she finds wounded narcissism (ibid., p. 373): an attempt, motivated by shame at human weakness, to escape the contingency of the world, similar to the strategy I called "meant to do that" in Chapter 4. Levinas is an interesting character in this regard. The charge of wounded narcissism doesn't fit (on the contrary, what Levinas calls "totalization" is similar to Nussbaum's wounded narcissism), but Levinas too would climb the ladder of love so high that the particularity of the other fades away, precisely what Nussbaum views as an escape. It is fortunate that all philosophers do not fit neatly into one of two categories.

8. The polis is not a physical place, but an idea, an internal object. The Athenians abandoned their physical polis in the face of the Persian invasion, living in boats and on the shores of the Peloponnese for months. The polis was the human relationships it contained, the polis container and contained at the same time. When the Athenians returned to their destroyed city they built a wall around it, but it remained open to the sea. For those who fear and detest place, as Levinas does, this way of thinking about the polis may come as a partial relief.

9. Here I must part company from Nussbaum (1986, pp. 200–3), whose interpretation of the *Phaedrus* (255b–257c) I embraced earlier in a different context. While Nussbaum may be correct that together lovers will come closer to eternity than either would alone, this requires in Plato's account a harsh repression of eros. To call it "sublimation" or some such would not capture the self-inflicted violence involved.

References

References to works by Levinas are given in the text by short title or abbreviation. Other authors are cited in the usual form. Classical authors are cited in the text in the form that is usual in classical studies, and are not repeated here.

WORKS BY LEVINAS, IN ALPHABETICAL ORDER

"Being a Westerner" (1990) "Being a Westerner." In *Difficult Freedom: Essays on Judaism.* Translated by Seán Hand. Baltimore, MD: Johns Hopkins University Press, pp. 46–9.

Beyond Verse (1994) *Beyond the Verse.* Translated by G. Mole. London: Athlone Press.

"Débat Russo-Chinois" (1994) "Le Débat Russo-Chinois et la dialéctique." In *Les imprévus de l'histoire.* Montpellier: Fata Morgana.

Découvrant (1974) *En découvrant l'existence avec Husserl et Heidegger.* Paris: Vrin.

"Dialogue on the Other" (1998) "Dialogue on Thinking-of-the-Other." In *Entre nous: On Thinking-of-the-Other.* Translated by Michael B. Smith and Barbara Harshav. New York: Columbia University Press, pp. 201–6.

"Dialogue with Levinas" (1986) "Dialogue with Emmanuel Levinas." In *Face to Face with Levinas.* Edited by Richard Cohen. Albany, NY: State University of New York Press, pp. 13–34.

E&I (1985) *Ethics and Infinity: Conversations with Philippe Nemo.* Translated by Richard Cohen. Pittsburgh: Duquesne University Press.

"Enigma" (1996) "Enigma and Phenomenon." In *Basic Philosophical Writings.* Edited by Adriaan Peperzak, Simon Critchley, and Robert Bernasconi. Bloomington, IN: Indiana University Press, pp. 65–78.

"Ethics & Politics" (1989) "Ethics and Politics." In *The Levinas Reader.* Edited by Seán Hand. Oxford: Blackwell Publishers, pp. 289–97.

"Ethics & Spirit" (1990) "Ethics and Spirit." *In Difficult Freedom: Essays on Judaism*. Translated by Seán Hand. Baltimore, MD: Johns Hopkins University Press, pp. 3–10.

Evasion (1982) *De l'évasion*. Montpellier: Fata Morgana.

"Hegel & Jews" (1990) "Hegel and the Jews." In *Difficult Freedom: Essays on Judaism*. Translated by Seán Hand. Baltimore, MD: Johns Hopkins University Press, pp. 235–8.

"Heidegger & Us" (1990) "Heidegger, Gagarin and Us." In *Difficult Freedom: Essays on Judaism*. Translated by Seán Hand. Baltimore, MD: Johns Hopkins University Press, pp. 231–4.

Humanisme (1976) *Humanisme de l'autre homme*. Montpellier: Fata Morgana.

"I & Totality" (1998) "The I and the Totality." In *Entre nous: On Thinking-of-the-Other*. Translated by Michael B. Smith and Barbara Harshav. New York: Columbia University Press, pp. 13–38.

"Meaning & Sense" (1996) "Meaning and Sense." In *Basic Philosophical Writings*. Edited by Adriaan Peperzak, Simon Critchley, and Robert Bernasconi. Bloomington, IN: Indiana University Press, pp. 33–64.

"Messianic Texts" (1990) "Messianic Texts." In *Difficult Freedom: Essays on Judaism*. Translated by Seán Hand. Baltimore, MD: Johns Hopkins University Press, pp. 59–96.

OB (1998) *Otherwise than Being: Or Beyond Essence*. Translated by Alphonso Lingis. Pittsburgh: Duquesne University Press. [The French original, *Autrement qu'être ou au-delà de l'essence* (Paris: Kluwer Academic, 1978), is cited in the text as *Autrement*.]

Of God (1998) *Of God Who Comes to Mind*. Translated by Bettina Bergo. Stanford, CA: Stanford University Press.

"Ontology Fundamental?" (1996) "Is Ontology Fundamental?" In *Basic Philosophical Writings*. Edited by Adriaan Peperzak, Simon Critchley, and Robert Bernasconi. Bloomington and Indianapolis: Indiana University Press, pp. 1–10.

"Other Proust" (1989) "The Other in Proust." In *The Levinas Reader*. Edited by Seán Hand. Oxford: Blackwell Publishers, pp. 160–5.

"Other, Utopia & Justice" (1998) "The Other, Utopia, and Justice." In *Entre nous: On Thinking-of-the-Other*. Translated by Michael B. Smith and Barbara Harshav. New York: Columbia University Press, pp. 223–33.

"Peace" (1996) "Peace and Proximity." In *Basic Philosophical Writings*. Edited by Adriaan Peperzak, Simon Critchley, and Robert Bernasconi. Bloomington, IN: Indiana University Press, pp. 161–9.

"Philosophy & the Infinite" (1993) "Philosophy and the Idea of the

Infinite." In *To the Other: An Introduction to the Philosophy of Emmanuel Levinas*, by Adriaan Peperzak. West Lafayette, Indiana: Purdue University Press, pp. 88–119.

"Philosophy, Justice & Love" (1998) "Philosophy, Justice, and Love." In *Entre nous: On Thinking-of-the-Other*. Translated by Michael B. Smith and Barbara Harshav. New York: Columbia University Press, pp. 103–21.

Proper Names (1996) *Proper Names*. Translated by Michael Smith. Stanford, CA: Stanford University Press.

"Reality & Shadow" (1989) "Reality and its Shadow." In *The Levinas Reader*. Edited by Seán Hand. Oxford: Blackwell Publishers, pp. 129–43.

"Reflections on Hitler" (1990) "Reflections on the Philosophy of Hitlerism." *Critical Inquiry* 17 (Autumn): 64–71. Translated by Seán Hand.

"Signature" (1990) "Signature." In *Difficult Freedom: Essays on Judaism*. Translated by Seán Hand. Baltimore, MD: Johns Hopkins University Press, pp. 291–5.

"Space" (1990) "Space is Not One-dimensional." In *Difficult Freedom: Essays on Judaism*. Translated by Seán Hand. Baltimore, MD: Johns Hopkins University Press, pp. 259–64.

"Substitution" (1996) "Substitution." In *Basic Philosophical Writings*. Edited by Adriaan Peperzak, Simon Critchley, and Robert Bernasconi. Bloomington, IN: Indiana University Press, pp. 79–96.

"Sur Genève" (1994) "Sur l'esprit de Genève." In *Les imprévus de l'histoire*. Montpellier: Fata Morgana.

T&I (1969) *Totality and Infinity: An Essay on Exteriority*. Translated by Alphonso Lingis. Pittsburgh: Duquesne University Press. [The French original, *Totalité et Infini* (Paris: Kluwer Academic/Livre de Poche, 1971) is cited in the text as *Totalité*]

T&O (1987) *Time and the Other*. Translated by Richard Cohen. Pittsburgh: Duquesne University Press.

"There is" (1987) "There is: Existence Without Existents." In *The Levinas Reader*. Edited by Seán Hand. Oxford: Blackwell Publishers, pp. 29–36.

"Trace" (1986) "The Trace of the Other." In *Deconstruction in Context*. Edited by M. Taylor, translated by Alphonso Lingis. Chicago: University of Chicago Press, pp. 345–59.

"Transcendence & Height" (1996) "Transcendence and Height." In *Basic Philosophical Writings*. Edited by Adriaan Peperzak, Simon Critchley, and Robert Bernasconi. Bloomington, IN: Indiana University Press, pp. 11–31.

"True Disclosure" (1996) "Truth of Disclosure and Truth of Testimony." In *Basic Philosophical Writings*. Edited by Adriaan Peperzak, Simon Critchley, and Robert Bernasconi. Bloomington, IN: Indiana University Press, pp. 97–107.

WORKS BY OTHER AUTHORS

Adorno, Theodor (1966) *Kierkegaard: Konstruktion des Aesthetischen*. Tübingen: Verlag J.C.B. Mohr. [reprint of 1933 original].

—— (1973) *Negative Dialectics*. Translated by E. B. Ashton. New York: Seabury Press.

—— (1974) *Minima Moralia: Reflections from Damaged Life*. Translated by E. F. N. Jephcott. London: NLB.

—— (1984) *Aesthetic Theory*. Translated by C. Lenhardt. London: Routledge and Kegan Paul.

Alford, C. Fred (1985) *Science and the Revenge of Nature: Marcuse and Habermas*. Gainesville, FL: University Presses of Florida.

—— (1988) *Narcissism: Socrates, the Frankfurt School, and Psychoanalytic Theory*. New Haven, CT, and London: Yale University Press.

—— (1989) *Melanie Klein and Critical Social Theory*. New Haven, CT, and London: Yale University Press.

—— (1991) *The Self in Social Theory: A Psychoanalytic Account of its Construction in Plato, Hobbes, Locke, Rawls, and Rousseau*. New Haven, CT, and London: Yale University Press.

—— (1992) *The Psychoanalytic Theory of Greek Tragedy*. New Haven, CT, and London: Yale University Press.

—— (1997) *What Evil Means to Us*. Ithaca; New York: Cornell University Press.

—— (1999) *Think No Evil: Korean Values in the Age of Globalization*. Ithaca, New York: Cornell University Press.

—— (2000) "Levinas and Winnicott: Motherhood and Responsibility." *American Imago*, vol. 57, no. 3: 235–60.

—— (2001) *Whistleblowers: Broken Lives and Organizational Power*. Ithaca, NY: Cornell University Press.

American Psychiatric Association (2000) *Diagnostic and Statistical Manual of Mental Disorders*, 4th edition, revised text. Washington, DC: APA.

Anderson, Thomas C. (1993) *Sartre's Two Ethics: From Authenticity to Integral Humanity*. Chicago: Open Courts.

Antonaccio, Maria (2000) *Picturing the Human: The Moral Thought of Iris Murdoch*. Oxford: Oxford University Press.

Arendt, Hannah (1958) *The Human Condition*. Chicago: University of Chicago Press.

—— (1977) *Between Past and Future*, enlarged edition. New York: Penguin Books.

—— (2000) "What is Freedom?" In *The Portable Hannah Arendt*. Edited by Peter Baehr. New York: Penguin Books, pp. 438–61.

Berlin, Isaiah (1969) "Two Concepts of Liberty." In *Four Essays on Liberty*. Oxford: Oxford University Press, pp. 118–72. [Includes Introduction, ix–lxiii.]

Bernasconi, Robert (2000) "The Alterity of the Stranger and the Experience of the Alien." In *The Face of the Other and The Trace of God: Essays on the Philosophy of Emmanuel Levinas*. Edited by Jeffrey Bloechl. New York: Fordham University Press, pp. 62–89.

Bernet, Rudolf (2000) "The Encounter with the Stranger: Two Interpretations of the Vulnerability of the Skin." In *The Face of the Other and the Trace of God: Essays on the Philosophy of Emmanuel Levinas*. Edited by Jeffrey Bloechl. New York: Fordham University Press, pp. 43–61.

Bion, Wilfred (1970) *Attention and Interpretation*. New York. Basic Books, pp. 88–94.

Bion, Wilfred (1984) *Second Thoughts: Selected Papers on Psychoanalysis*. New York: Jason Aronson.

Blanchot, Maurice (1995) *The Writing of the Disaster*, new edition. Translated by Ann Smock. Lincoln, NB: University of Nebraska Press.

Bloechl, Jeffrey (2000) "Ethics as First Philosophy and Religion." In *The Face of the Other and the Trace of God: Essays on the Philosophy of Emmanuel Levinas*. Edited by Jeffrey Bloechl. New York: Fordham University Press, pp. 130–51.

Boas, George (1967) "Love." In *Encyclopedia of Philosophy*. Edited by Paul Edwards, volume 5: 89–95. New York: Macmillan.

Brown, Norman O. (1966) *Love's Body*. New York: Vintage Books.

Buck-Morss, Susan (1977) *The Origin of Negative Dialectics: Theodor W. Adorno, Walter Benjamin, and the Frankfurt Institute*. New York: The Free Press.

Caygill, Howard (2000) "Levinas' Political Judgment: The *Esprit* Articles." *Radical Philosophy*, no. 104 (November/December): 6–15.

Chalier, Catherine (1991) "Ethics and the Feminine." In *Re-Reading Levinas*. Edited by Robert Bernasconi and Simon Critchley. Bloomington, IN: Indiana University Press, pp. 119–29.

Chanter, Tina (1991) "Antigone's Dilemma." In *Re-Reading Levinas*. Edited by Robert Bernasconi and Simon Critchley. Bloomington, IN: Indiana University Press, pp. 130–46.

—— (1998) "Reading Hegel as Mediating Master: Lacan and Levinas." In *Levinas and Lacan: The Missed Encounter*. Edited by Sarah Harasym. Albany, NY: State University of New York Press, pp. 1–21.

Chateaubriand, Francois-René (1827) *Voyages in Amérique et en Italie*, vol. 2. Paris: Ladvocat.

Conradi, Peter (1986) *Iris Murdoch: The Saint and the Artist*. New York: St. Martin's Press.

—— (2001) Iris Murdoch: A Life. New York: W.W. Norton.

Cornford, F. M. (1950) "The Doctrine of Eros in Plato's *Symposium*." In *The Unwritten Philosophy*. Edited by W. K. C. Guthrie. Cambridge: Cambridge University Press, pp. 68–80.

Critchley, Simon (1996) "Obituary for Emmanuel Levinas, 1906–1995." *Radical Philosophy*, no. 78 (July/August).

—— (1999) *The Ethics of Deconstruction: Derrida and Levinas*, 2nd edition. West Lafayette, IN: Purdue University Press.

Dalton, Stuart (2001) "Obligation to the Other in Levinas and the Sublime in Kant" http://uhavax.hartford.edu/~dalton/sublimeobligation.html>

Davis, Colin (1996) *Levinas: An Introduction*. Notre Dame, IN: University of Notre Dame Press.

Derrida, Jacques (1978) "Violence and Metaphysics." In *Writing and Difference*. Translated by Alan Bass. Chicago: University of Chicago Press, pp. 79–153.

—— (1988) *Limited Inc*. Translated by S. Weber. Evanston, IL: Northwestern University Press.

—— (1999) *Adieu to Emmanuel Levinas*. Translated by P-A. Brault and M. Naas. Stanford, CA: Stanford University Press.

Descartes, René (1988) *Meditations on First Philosophy*. In *The Philosophical Writings of Descartes*, vol. 2. Translated by John Cottingham. Cambridge: Cambridge University Press.

de Tocqueville, Alexis (2000) *Democracy in America*. Translated by Harvey Mansfield and Delba Winthrop. Chicago: University of Chicago Press.

de Vries, Hent (1989) *Theologie im Pianissimo und Zwischen Rationalität und Dekonstruktion: Die Aktualität der Denkfiguren Adornos and Levinas*. Kampen: J. H. Kok.

Dipple, Elizabeth (1982) *Iris Murdoch: Work for the Spirit*. Chicago: University of Chicago Press.

Eagleton, Terry (1981) *Walter Benjamin or Towards a Revolutionary Criticism*. London: Verso.

Elkin, Henry (1972) "On Selfhood and the Development of Ego Structures in Infancy." *The Psychoanalytic Review* 59: 389–416.

Epstein, Mark (1995) *Thoughts Without a Thinker: Psychotherapy from a Buddhist Perspective*. New York: Basic Books.

Euben, J. Peter (1990) *The Tragedy of Political Theory*. Princeton, NJ: Princeton University Press.

Faulconer, James "Levinas: The Unconscious and the Reason of Obligation.". <http://jamesfaulconer.byu.edu/levinas.html>

Fitzgerald, F. Scott (1989) "Absolution." In *The Short Stories of F. Scott Fitzgerald*. Edited by Matthew Bruccoli. New York: Scribners.

Freud, Sigmund (1914) "On Narcissism." In *The Standard Edition of the Complete Psychological Works of Sigmund Freud*. Edited by James Strachey, London: Hogarth Press 1953-74, vol. 14: 67–104.

—— (1915) "Papers on Metapsychology: Instincts and Their Vicissitudes." *The Standard Edition*, vol. 14: 117–40.

—— (1923) "The Ego and the Id." In *The Standard Edition*, vol. 19: 3–67.

—— (1924) "The Economic Problem of Masochism." In *The Standard Edition*, vol. 19: 157–72.

—— (1933) "New Introductory Lectures on Psycho-Analysis." In *The Standard Edition*, vol. 22: 3–184.

—— (1959) *Group Psychology and the Analysis of the Ego*. Translated by James Strachey. New York: W. W. Norton.

—— (1961) *Civilization and its Discontents*. Translated by James Strachey. New York: W. W. Norton.

—— (1962) *Three Essays on the Theory of Sexuality*. Translated by James Strachey. 4th edition. New York: Basic Books.

Fromm, Erich (1969) *Escape From Freedom*. New York: Henry Holt.

Gardiner, Patrick (1979) "Freedom as an Aesthetic Idea." in *The Idea of Freedom: Essays in Honour of Isaiah Berlin*. Edited by Alan Ryan. Oxford: Oxford University Press, pp. 27–40.

Gay, Peter (1979) "Freud and Freedom." In *The Idea of Freedom: Essays in Honour of Isaiah Berlin*. Edited by Alan Ryan. Oxford: Oxford University Press, pp. 41–59.

Glatzer, Nahum (1985) "Foreword," to *The Star of Redemption* by Franz Rosenzweig. Notre Dame, IN: University of Notre Dame Press.

—— (1999) "Introduction" to *Understanding the Sick and the Healthy*, by

Franz Rosenzweig. Cambridge, MA: Harvard University Press.

Greenbaum, T. (1978) "The 'Analyzing Instrument' and the 'Transitional Object.'" In *Between Reality and Fantasy*. Edited by S. Grolnick and I. Barkin. Northvale, NJ: Jason Aronson, pp. 191–203.

Greenberg, James and Mitchell, Stephen (1983) *Object Relations in Psychoanalytic Theory*. Cambridge, MA: Harvard University Press.

Grotstein, James (1985) *Splitting and Projective Identification*. Northvale, NJ: Jason Aronson.

Halling, Steen (1975) "The Implications of Emmanuel Levinas' *Totality and Infinity* for Therapy." In *Duquesne Studies in Phenomenological Psychology*, vol. 2. Edited by Amedeo Giorgi, Constance Fischer, and Edward. L. Murray. Pittsburgh: Duquesne University Press, pp. 206–23.

Hampshire, Stuart (1975) *Freedom of the Individual*. London: Chatto & Windus.

—— (2001) "The Pleasure of Iris Murdoch." *The New York Review of Books*, November 15, 2001: 24–26. [Review of Peter J. Conradi, *Iris Murdoch: A Life*.]

Handelman, Susan (1991) *Fragments of Redemption: Jewish Thought and Literary Theory in Benjamin, Scholem, and Levinas*. Bloomington, IN: Indiana University Press.

Harasym, Sarah (ed.) (1998) *Levinas and Lacan: The Missed Encounter*. Albany, NY: State University of New York Press.

Hegel, Georg Wilhelm Friedrich (1967) *Philosophy of Right*. Translated by T. M. Knox. London: Oxford University Press.

Heidegger, Martin (1949) "What is Metaphysics?" In *Existence and Being*. Translated by R.F.C. Hull and Alan Crick. Chicago: Regnery, pp. 353–93.

Horkheimer, Max and Adorno, Theodor (1972) *The Dialectic of Enlightenment*. Translated by John Cumming. New York: Herder and Herder.

Irigaray, Luce (1986) "The Fecundity of the Caress: A Reading of Levinas, *Totality and Infinity* section IV, B, 'The Phenomenology of Eros.'" In *Face to Face with Levinas*. Edited by Richard Cohen. Albany, NY: State University of New York Press, pp. 231–56.

—— (1991) "Questions to Emmanuel Levinas: On the Divinity of Love." In *Re-Reading Levinas*. Edited by Robert Bernasconi and Simon Critchley. Bloomington, IN: Indiana University Press, pp. 109–18.

Jacques, Francis (1991) *Difference and Subjectivity*. Translated by Andrew Rothwell. New Haven, CT: Yale University Press.

Jay, Martin (1973) *The Dialectical Imagination: A History of the Frankfurt*

School and the Institute for Social Research, 1923–1950. Boston: Little, Brown.

—— (1984) *Adorno.* Cambridge, MA: Harvard University Press.

Kant, Immanuel (1959) *Foundations of the Metaphysics of Morals.* Translated by Lewis W. Beck. Indianapolis: Bobbs-Merrill, Liberal Arts Press.

—— (1981) *Grounding for the Metaphysics of Morals.* Translated by J. Ellington. Indianapolis: Hackett.

Kantor, Alon (1999) "Levinas's Law." *American Imago* 56 (Winter): 357–85.

Keenan, Dennis King (1999) *Death and Responsibility: The "Work" of Levinas.* Albany, NY: State University of New York Press.

Kernberg, Otto (1985) *Borderline Conditions and Pathological Narcissism.* Northvale, NJ: Jason Aronson.

—— (1988) "Clinical Dimensions of Masochism." *Journal of the American Psychoanalytic Association* 36: 1005–29.

Kierkegaard, Søren (1957) *The Concept of Dread.* Translated by Walter Lowrie. Princeton, NJ: Princeton University Press.

Klein, Melanie (1964) "Love, Guilt and Reparation." In *Love, Hate and Reparation,* by Melanie Klein and Joan Riviere. New York: W. W. Norton.

—— (1975a) "A Contribution to the Psychogenesis of Manic-Depressive States." In *Love, Guilt and Reparation and Other Works.* Edited by R. E. Money-Kyrle. New York: The Free Press [vol. 1 of *The Writings of Melanie Klein*], pp. 262–89.

—— (1975b) "Some Reflections on the '*Oresteia*'." In *Envy and Gratitude and Other Works.* Edited by R. E. Money-Kyrle. New York: The Free Press, [vol. 3 of *The Writings of Melanie Klein*], pp. 275–99.

—— (1975c) "Some Theoretical Conclusions Regarding the Emotional Life of the Infant," In *Envy and Gratitude and Other Works.* Edited by R. E. Money-Kyrle. New York: The Free Press. [vol. 3 of *The Writings of Melanie Klein*], pp. 61–93.

Knight, Robert (1972) "Determinism, 'Freedom,' and Psychotherapy." In *Selected Papers of Robert P. Knight.* Edited by S. Miller. New York: Basic Books, pp. 131–48.

Kohut, Heinz (1977) *The Restoration of the Self.* New York: International Universities Press.

Kunz, George (1998) *The Paradox of Power and Weakness: Levinas and an Alternative Paradigm for Psychology.* Albany, NY: State University of New York Press.

Lacan, Jacques (1977) "The Function and Field of Speech and Language in Psychoanalysis." In *Écrits: A Selection*. Translated by Alan Sheridan. London: Tavistock Publications, pp. 30–113.

Lamont, Corliss (1982) *The Philosophy of Humanism*, 6th edition, revised and enlarged. New York: Frederick Ungar Publishing.

Lasch, Christopher (1979) *The Culture of Narcissism*. New York: Warner Books.

Lewin, Roger A. and Schulz, Clarence (1992) *Losing and Fusing: Borderline Transitional Object and Self Relations*. Northvale, NJ: Jason Aronson.

Llewelyn, John (1991) "Am I Obsessed by Bobby? (Humanism of the Other Animal)." In *Re-Reading Levinas*. Edited by Robert Bernasconi and Simon Critchley. Bloomington, IN: Indiana University Press, pp. 234–45.

—— (1995) *Emmanuel Levinas: The Genealogy of Ethics*. London: Routledge.

Lukács, Georg (1971) *The Theory of the Novel*. Translated by A. Bostock. Cambridge, MA: Harvard University Press.

Lyotard, Jean-François (1988) *The Differend: Phrases in Dispute*. Translated by Georges Van Den Abbeele. Minneapolis: University of Minnesota Press.

Marcuse, Herbert (1966) *Eros and Civilization: A Philosophical Inquiry into Freud*. Boston: Beacon Press.

—— (1978) *The Aesthetic Dimension: Toward a Critique of Marxist Aesthetics*. Boston: Beacon Press.

Matte-Blanco, Ignacio (1975) *The Unconscious as Infinite Sets*. London: Duckworth. [Also spelled Matte Blanco.]

Miller, David (1991) "Introduction." In *Liberty*. Edited by David Miller. Oxford: Oxford University Press, pp. 1–20.

Moore, Burness and Fines, Bernard (ed) (1990) *Psychoanalytic Terms and Concepts*. New Haven, CT: Yale University Press and the American Psychoanalytic Association.

Murdoch, Iris (1962) *The Bell*. New York: Penguin Books.

—— (1970a) *A Fairly Honourable Defeat*. London: Penguin Books.

—— (1970b) *The Sovereignty of Good*. London: Routledge.

—— (1973) *The Sandcastle*. New York: Warner Books.

—— (1986) *Acastos: Two Platonic Dialogues*. New York: Viking Penguin.

—— (1987) *The Book and the Brotherhood*. London: Penguin Books.

—— (1992) *Metaphysics as a Guide to Morals*. London: Penguin Books.

—— (1999a) "The Sublime and the Good." In *Existentialists and Mystics:*

Writings on Philosophy and Literature. Edited by Peter Conradi. New York: Penguin Books, pp. 205–20.

—— (1999b) "The Sublime and the Beautiful Revisited." In *Existentialists and Mystics: Writings on Philosophy and Literature*. Edited by Peter Conradi. New York: Penguin Books, pp. 261–86.

Newman, Michael (2000) "Sensibility, Trauma, and the Trace: Levinas from Phenomenology to the Immemorial." In *The Face of the Other and the Trace of God: Essays on the Philosophy of Emmanuel Levinas*. Edited by Jeffrey Bloechl. New York: Fordham University Press, pp. 90–129.

Nietzsche, Friedrich (1968a) "Beyond Good and Evil." In *Basic Writings of Nietzsche*. Translated and edited by Walter Kaufmann. New York: Modern Library, pp. 199–435.

—— (1968b) *The Birth of Tragedy Or: Hellenism and Pessimism*. In *Basic Writings of Nietzsche*. Translated and edited by Walter Kaufmann. New York: Modern Library, pp. 16–144.

Nordquist, Joan (1997) *Emmanuel Levinas: A Bibliography*. Santa Cruz, CA: Reference and Research Services [no. 45 in *Social Theory: A Bibliographic Series*.]

Nussbaum, Martha (1986) *The Fragility of Goodness: Luck and Ethics in Greek Tragedy and Philosophy*. Cambridge: Cambridge University Press.

—— (1990) *Love's Knowledge: Essays on Philosophy and Literature*. Oxford: Oxford University Press.

—— (2001) *Upheavals of Thought: The Intelligence of the Emotions*. Cambridge: Cambridge University Press.

O'Connor, Noreen (1991) "Who Suffers?" In *Re-Reading Levinas*. Edited by Robert Bernasconi and Simon Critchley. Bloomington, IN: Indiana University Press, pp. 229–33.

Ogden, Thomas (1989) *The Primitive Edge of Experience*. Northvale, NJ: Jason Aronson.

Peperzak, Adriaan (1993) *To the Other: An Introduction to the Philosophy of Emmanuel Levinas*. West Lafayette, IN: Purdue University Press.

—— (1997) *Beyond: The Philosophy of Emmanuel Levinas*. Evanston, IL: Northwestern University Press.

Phillips, Adam (1988) *Winnicott*. Cambridge, MA: Harvard University Press.

Porpora, Douglas (2001) *Landscapes of the Soul: The Loss of Moral Meaning in American Life*. Oxford: Oxford University Press.

Putnam, Hilary (1999) "New Introduction" to *Understanding the Sick and the Healthy*, by Franz Rosenzweig. Cambridge, MA: Harvard University Press.

Ricoeur, Paul (1967) *The Symbolism of Evil*. Translated by Emerson Buchanan. Boston: Beacon Press.

—— (1970) *Freud and Philosophy: An Essay on Interpretation*. Translated by D. Savage. New Haven: Yale University Press.

—— (1992) *Oneself as Another*. Translated by Kathleen Blamey. Chicago: University of Chicago Press.

Rilke, Rainer Maria (1923) *Duineser Elegien*. Leipzig: Insel-Verlag.

—— (1992) *Sonnets to Orpheus*. Translated by M. D. Herter Norton. New York: W. W. Norton.

Riviere, Joan (1952) "On the Genesis of Psychical Conflict in Early Infancy." In *Developments in Psycho-Analysis*, by Melanie Klein, Paula Heimann, Susan Isaacs, and Joan Riviere. London: Hogarth Press.

Robbins, Jill (1999) *Altered Reading: Levinas and Literature*. Chicago: University of Chicago Press.

Rosen, Stanley (1983) *Plato's Sophist: The Drama of Original and Image*. New Haven, CT: Yale University Press.

Rosenzweig, Franz (1985) *The Star of Redemption*. Translated by William Hallo. Notre Dame, IN: University of Notre Dame Press.

—— (1999) *Understanding the Sick and the Healthy: A View of World, Man, and God*. Cambridge, MA: Harvard University Press.

Rousseau, Jean-Jacques (1964) "Discourse on the Origin and Foundations of Inequality among Men" (Second Discourse). In *The First and Second Discourses*. Translated by Roger Masters and Judith Masters. New York: St. Martin's Press, pp. 77–228.

Said, Edward (1979) *Orientalism*. New York: Random House.

Sartre, Jean-Paul (1949) *Nausea*. Translated by Lloyd Alexander. New York: New Directions.

—— (1956) *Being and Nothingness*. Translated by Hazel Barnes. New York: Philosophical Library.

—— (1976) *Critique of Dialectical Reason*, vol. 1. Translated by Alan Sheridan-Smith. London: New Left Books.

—— (1999) *Essays in Existentialism*. Edited by Wade Baskin. Secaucus, NJ: Carol Publishing Group.

Schiller, Friedrich (1983) *On the Aesthetic Education of Man*. Edited by L. A. Willoughby. Oxford: Clarendon Press [English-German parallel text edition].

Simon, Bennett (1978) *Mind and Madness in Ancient Greece*. Ithaca, NY: Cornell University Press.

Smith, Joseph (1978) "The Psychoanalytic Study of Human Freedom." *Journal of the American Psychoanalytic Association*, vol. 26: 87–107.

Stanford, W. B (1983) *Greek Tragedy and the Emotions*. London: Routledge and Kegan Paul.

Starobinski, Jean (1988) *Jean-Jacques Rousseau: Transparency and Obstruction*. Translated by Arthur Goldhammer. Chicago: University of Chicago Press.

Steiner, George (1986) *Antigones*. Oxford: Clarendon Press.

Stern, Daniel (1985) *The Interpersonal World of the Infant: A View from Psychoanalysis and Developmental Psychology*. New York: Basic Books.

Taylor, Charles (1979) "What's Wrong with Negative Liberty," in *The Idea of Freedom: Essays in Honour of Isaiah Berlin*. Edited by Alan Ryan. Oxford: Oxford University Press, pp. 175–93.

Vernant, Jean-Pierre and Vidal-Naquet, Pierre (1988) *Myth and Tragedy in Ancient Greece*. Translated by Janet Lloyd. New York: Zone Books.

Waelder, Robert (1936) "The Problem of Freedom in Psycho-Analysis and the Problem of Reality Testing." *International Journal of Psycho-Analysis*, vol. 17: 89–108 [also spelled Wälder and Walder.]

Wall, Thomas Carl (1999) *Radical Passivity: Levinas, Blanchot, Agamben*. Albany, NY: State University of New York Press.

Wilson, Edmund (1965) "Philoctetes: The Wound and the Bow." In *The Wound and the Bow: Seven Studies in Literature*. New York: Oxford University Press, pp. 223–42.

Wingenbach, Ed (1999) "Refusing the Temptation of Innocence: Levinasian Ethics as Political Theory." In *Strategies*, vol. 12 (number 2): 219–38.

Winnicott, D. W. (1965a) "The Capacity to Be Alone." In *The Maturational Processes and the Facilitating Environment*. New York: International Universities Press, pp. 29–36.

—— (1965b) "Ego Distortion in Terms of True and False Self." In *The Maturational Processes and the Facilitating Environment*. New York: International Universities Press, pp. 140–2.

—— (1965c) "Group Influences and the Maladjusted Child: The School Aspect." In *The Family and Individual Development*. London: Tavistock, pp. 146–54.

—— (1971) *Playing and Reality*. London and New York: Routledge.

—— (1975a) "Anxiety Associated with Insecurity." In *Through Paediatrics to Psycho-Analysis*. London: Hogarth Press and the Institute of Psycho-Analysis, pp. 97–100.

—— (1975b) "Mind and Its Relation to the Psyche-Soma." In *Through Paediatrics to Psycho-Analysis*. London: Hogarth Press and the Institute of Psycho-Analysis, pp. 243–54.

—— (1984) "The Deprived Child and How He Can Be Compensated for Loss of Family Life." In *Deprivation and Delinquency*. Edited by C. Winnicott, R. Shepherd, and M. Davis. New York: Methuen, pp. 172–88.

—— (1986) *Holding and Interpretation: Fragment of an Analysis*. New York: Grove Press.

—— (1987) "Communication between Infant and Mother, and Mother and Infant, Compared and Contrasted." In *Babies and Their Mothers*. Edited by C. Winnicott, R. Shepherd, and M. Davis. London: Free Association Books, pp. 84–103.

—— (1989a) "Transitional Objects and Transitional Phenomena." In *Playing and Reality*, 1–25. New York: Routledge.

—— (1989b) "On 'The Use of an Object.'" In *Psycho-Analytic Explorations*. Edited by C. Winnicott, R. Shepherd, and M. Davis. Cambridge, MA: Harvard University Press, pp. 217–46.

Winnington-Ingram, D. W (1980) *Sophocles: An Interpretation*. Cambridge: Cambridge University Press.

Wittgenstein, Ludwig (1961) *Tractatus Logico-Philosophicus*. Translated by D. F. Davis and B. F. McGunness. New York: Cornell University Press.

Wollheim, Richard (1984) *The Thread of Life*. Cambridge, MA: Harvard University Press.

Wyschogrod, Edith (2000) *Emmanuel Levinas: The Problem of Ethical Metaphysics*. Second edition. New York: Fordham University Press.

Young, Iris Marion (1990) "The Ideal of Community and the Politics of Difference." In *Feminism/Postmodernism*. Edited by Linda J. Nicholson. New York and London: Routledge, pp. 300–23.

Index